Old Roots, New Routes

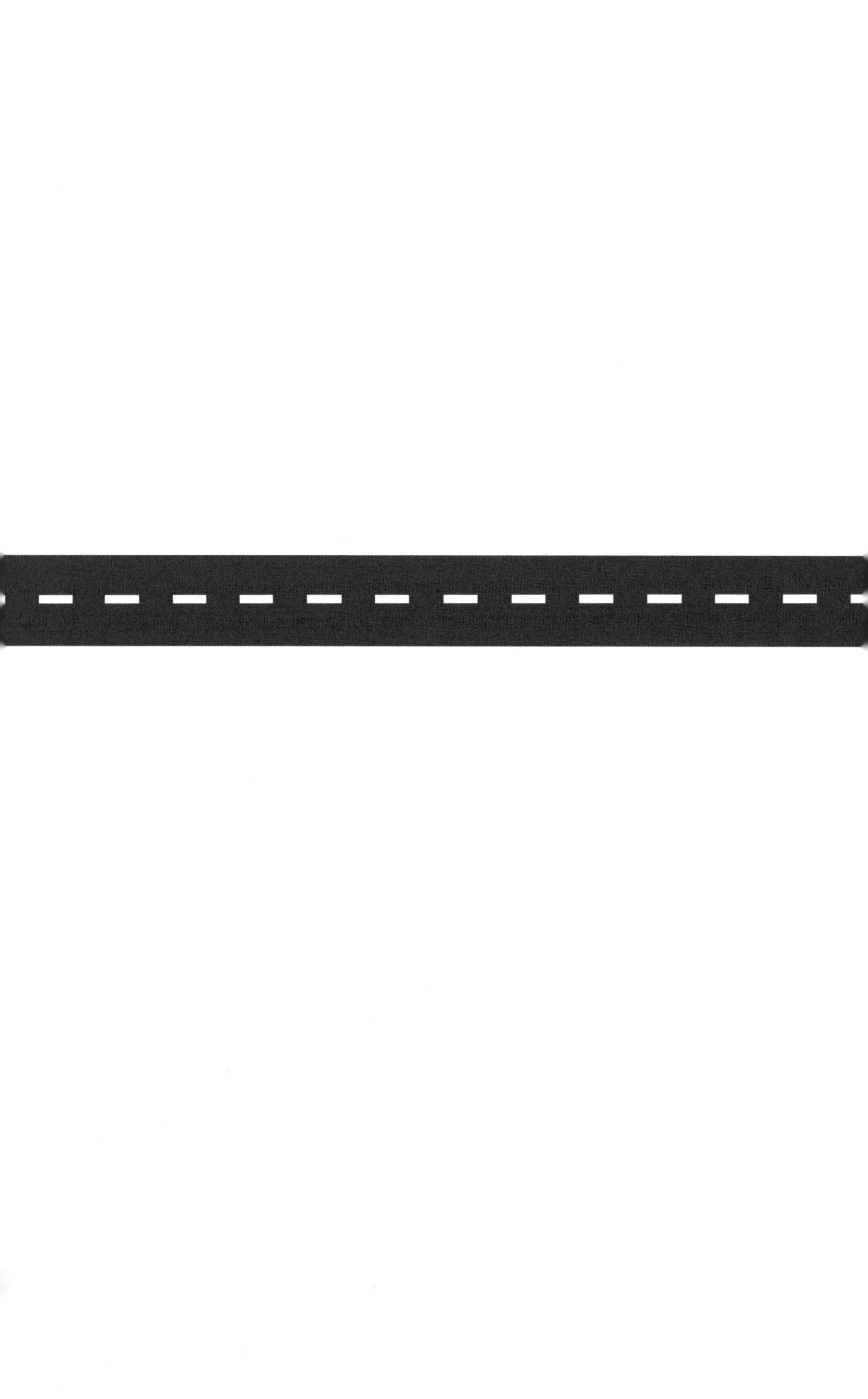

OLD ROOTS NEW ROUTES

THE CULTURAL POLITICS OF ALT.COUNTRY MUSIC

EDITED BY
Pamela Fox and Barbara Ching

THE UNIVERSITY OF MICHIGAN PRESS
ANN ARBOR

Published in the United States of America by
The University of Michigan Press
Manufactured in the United States of America
♾ Printed on acid-free paper

2011 2010 2009 2008 4 3 2 1

A CIP catalog record for this book is available from the British Library.

Library of Congress Cataloging-in-Publication Data

Old roots and new routes : the cultural politics of alt.country music /
edited by Pamela Fox and Barbara Ching.
p. cm.
Includes bibliographical references and index.
ISBN-13: 978-0-472-07053-4 (cloth : alk. paper)
ISBN-10: 0-472-07053-3 (cloth : alk. paper)
ISBN-13: 978-0-472-05053-6 (pbk. : alk. paper)
ISBN-10: 0-472-05053-2 (pbk. : alk. paper)
1. Alternative country music—United States—History and criticism. I. Fox, Pamela, 1958– II. Ching, Barbara, 1958–
ML3524.O64 2009
781.6420973—dc22 2008022956

Acknowledgments

This book, like the music it examines, is made from many voices. As the first scholarly study of alternative country music, that is the way it should be since popular music draws on so many ways we make meaning in our lives and no single traditional academic discipline addresses that tuneful complexity. In the time our contributors spent writing these essays, we were all able to engage in a sustained, multidisciplinary dialogue about what kind of alternatives this music imagines and about larger issues of alternative musics and cultures in the global marketplace. Now that the collection is in the hands of readers, we hope the dialogue and collaboration will continue.

Many of the people who shared their thoughts with us do not appear in these pages. Many thanks go to S. Renee Dechert for her early vision of such an anthology and for her initial work on this one. We are also indebted to Joli Jensen, James Kelly, Marian Leighton Levy, Michael Masterson, Richard A. Peterson, Betsy Phillips, John Rumble, Jessie Scott, Barry Shank, Timothy Taylor, and anonymous reviewers whose suggestions helped develop and improve each essay. To those who are anonymous due to our forgetfulness, we ask for forgiveness. We are especially grateful to our editor at the University of Michigan Press, Chris Hebert, for his enthusiastic support of the project, as well as his sharp critical eye, good humor, and efficiency.

We'd like to express our appreciation to the staff members and work study students at our respective universities who have assisted us in preparing the manuscript in its various stages: Donna Even-Kesef in the English Department at Georgetown University and Kelly Burchfield, Sarah Ellis, Verlinda Franklin, Crystal Hall, and Linda Sadler at the University of Memphis.

Pam would additionally like to thank Georgetown University colleagues and friends who provided valuable feedback on various draft versions of the introductory essay, including Leona Fisher, You-Me Park, Samantha Pinto, Matthew Tinkcom, Kelley Wickham-Crowley, and Christine Schiwietz; the Georgetown undergraduate and graduate students in her course "Class Fictions in the Contemporary United States" for helping her think about alt.country music more generally; friends who have expressed interest in this particular scholarly endeavor, including Holmes Brown, Barbara, Sam, and Ethan Dyer, Lori Merish, Michael Ragussis, Peter and Sheila Rowny, Peggy Shaker, Elizabeth Velez, and Steve Wurtzler; and her favorite people of all, those who have cheerfully lived with the music, writing, and time on task throughout her work on this volume: Mark and Ana Popovich. Many, many thanks for the support that materialized as child care and meals as well as overall enthusiasm! Finally, she'd like to express deep appreciation to Barbara Ching for being an inspiring, as well as reliable, partner in this collaboration.

Barbara owes a great debt to the Ching household—Michael, Lucy, and May—for unfailing support and encouragement. Colleagues David Evans and Jennifer Wagner-Lawlor gave important advice at various stages along the way, and many students over the past semesters have helped her see new perspectives and hear new sounds. She is especially grateful to Pamela Fox, who has been a model of perseverance, clarity, and generosity throughout this process.

As coeditors, we worked together on every aspect of this book and have alternated the order of our names in its various components to indicate our shared labor.

Contents

Old Roots, New Routes

BARBARA CHING AND PAMELA FOX

Introduction: The Importance of Being Ironic—Toward a Theory and Critique of Alt.Country Music

"I started this damn country band," sings Ryan Adams in Whiskeytown's "Faithless Street," "because punk rock was too hard to sing" (1996). That line, with all of its irony, is often cited to explain the genealogy of alternative country music, and even ten years later the *sounds* of the song convey much about the music. It opens, for example, with a nostalgic fiddle melody that evokes "The Tennessee Waltz," a huge pop and country crossover hit for Patti Page in 1950. Backed by plain acoustic strumming and brush percussion, the fiddle continues to remind you of dancing with a long lost sweetheart as a steel guitar heightens the sadness of this midtempo waltz. In the front of the mix, Adams' delivery of the lyrics touches on other familiar country music themes such as working class labor ("you work your whole life for someone else") and the despairing religiosity announced in the title. The invective conclusion—so I started this *damn* country band—gets special emphasis as the tempo slows and the fiddle stops each time the line comes around. It's this memorable line that overdetermines (so to speak) the experience of the song. It lets you know that country is the almost unwelcome answer to a question or the better-than-nothing solution to a problem. Rock (not just punk rock), with its hip oppositionality, was Whiskeytown's first resort, and country, which was there all along, came after rock disillusioned them.[1]

As an iconic alt.country text, "Faithless Street" initiates this genre's paradoxical cultural project. Metaphorically, the music promises to go where there's "no depression," a postmodern adjustment to art's Marcusian "promesse de Bonheur": the hope that aesthetic practices can restore a shared human dimension to lives increasingly ruled by economic interests.[2] But while the movement's purported origins and ongoing self-presentation foreground this hope, its practitioners continually cloud it in irony.[3] Our cover illustration from Bobby Bare Jr.'s *Young Criminals' Starvation League* (2002) offers a striking example of this conflicted stance in its photograph of a crossroads, showing one road sign pointing toward Nashville and the other toward Hope. Similarly, in this essay, we aim to provide a critical introduction to alt.country by first sketching out this particular tension or conflict and the myriad forms it takes in the music's promotional rhetoric and song texts. In Section I, we primarily survey how alt.country imagines and presents itself as the hopeful "alternative" to Nashville's contemporary country music. Section II more directly outlines our critique as we analyze the significance of alt.country's principal conflict, demonstrating how the clash between utopian and ironic impulses, related to the clash between free expression and commercial interests, produces a particular and troubling politics of taste in this increasingly influential music and fan culture. We believe our reading of alt.country's hip cultural agenda can be useful as well to critiquing the production and consumption of other, perhaps more familiar, modes of alternative music. In section III, we conclude with an overview of our contributors' essays to describe how the volume as a whole undertakes a much needed investigation of this late-twentieth- and early-twenty-first-century cultural phenomenon.

I. Meet the New Boss, Same as the Old Boss? Defining (and Interrogating) Alt.Country

The backstory is now well known to music industry insiders and practically sacrosanct to movement aficionados. In 1995, *No Depression,* alt.country's version of *Rolling Stone,* took its name from a three-strand braid formed by the Carter Family's "No Depression in Heaven," a characteristically solemn song promising a spiritual escape from the economic constraints of the 1930s; Uncle Tupelo's edgier, amplified 1990 version, which simultaneously conveyed a sense of escape from postmodern alienation and an irreligious angst; and the group of Uncle Tupelo fans who found each other through the

Internet and formed a discussion group.[4] At once ironic and constitutive, this blend of high technology and nostalgia allowed fans to identify themselves as a new audience for nonmainstream country music. While we will proceed to critique the obfuscations of such nostalgia, we open this essay collection by both acknowledging and attempting to understand alt.country's desire for the authenticity of a utopian community outside the marketplace, free from the depressing constraints of commodification. As we will discuss, many cultural critics question art's ability to break free of the mainstream, especially when mere opposition to it often constitutes the alternative mode.[5] Even alt.country musician Jon Langford cites the renowned theorist of co-optation on this question: "Herbert Marcuse said that whatever you throw at capitalism, it'll just sell it right back to you. And the music business is capitalism's right arm with a big fat catcher's mitt on the end."[6] However, alt.country culture and community have persevered as an alternative for more than a decade of overheated capitalism and globalization despite social critics such as Russell Jacoby, who can only pronounce, and lament, the contemporary failure of radicalism: "A new consensus has emerged: There are no alternatives. This is the wisdom of our times, an age of political exhaustion and retreat."[7] Rather than joining this "consensus," alt.country, with its blend of irony and optimism, keeps listening for a different drummer. In fact, when Jessie Scott, program director of XM satellite radio's alt.country station "X Country" (XM 12), was asked to name "quintessential" songs of the genre, she pointed to Robert Earl Keen's "The Road Goes on Forever" (2003), James McMurtry's "Choctaw Bingo" (2002), and Steve Earle's "Copperhead Road" (1988)—all first-person ballads of working-class *triumphs*.[8]

Nevertheless, in this volume, we pay particular attention to the increasing institutionalization of alt.country and its already powerful modes of reproducing itself at the same time that it continually publicizes the need for an alternative. While alt.country fans and journalists document their rankings and evaluations of songs and musicians, we use a variety of critical approaches, especially attuned to gender and class, to understand how "merit" is in fact constituted in alt.country discourse and how the artists who embody it make themselves audible and visible. In addition to focusing on the sounds and other expressive components of alternative country culture, we look at alt.country as a set of goods chosen by consumers with particular tastes: why else would Ryan Adams be cast in a Gap ad? We are especially interested in the ways alt.country itself promotes a commodified version of authenticity.

As musicologist Timothy D. Taylor notes, since the late twentieth century we have experienced an "ever-increasing commodification and marketization of virtually everything, accompanied by ideologies that construct everything as either a commodity or commodifiable. Everything is for sale; everything is appropriable in the name of making one's identity—or music."[9] As a music genre formed during this period of hyper-capitalism, alt.country clearly reflects *and* deflects such change. At the same time, by making country cool—by recasting it as a form of hipness attained through the fetishizing of country "tradition"—and thereby replicating the male-dominated taste-making practices prevalent in most high culture and popular music criticism, alt.country may participate in maintaining a tradition as selective and conservative as anything Matthew Arnold proposed.[10]

In the following pages, we will demonstrate that alt.country can be identified by an assortment of features, including a rhetoric of taste, ties to country tradition, and the cultivation of a contemporary, discerning community of liberal-minded fans distinct from the audience for mainstream country music. While many country songs self-consciously equate rustic suffering with the detritus of consumer culture, alt.country takes the opposite approach. We maintain that an *ironized* conflict between commodification and authenticity serves as its truly defining feature. Although fetishization constitutes commodities by hiding the human labor that created them in order to highlight the desirability of ownership, the converse—self-consciousness about good taste, craftsmanship, and artistry—can also mask the mediation of the marketplace.[11] Irony, so pervasive in contemporary culture, allows alt.country to persevere in looking for a way out of this market-bound impasse, offering a way to both recognize and refuse the dictates of advanced capitalism. As Linda Hutcheon has argued, irony can be utilized as a "tool for acknowledging complexity"; as such it involves "the attribution of an evaluative, even judgmental attitude" on the part of ironists and their audience.[12] In other words, it creates opportunities to recognize and possibly outwit the inevitable. Rounder Records cofounder Marian Leighton Levy similarly describes the success of her independent label's musicians as a sort of "escape artistry": "How do you [become] . . . successful enough to survive but not so successful that the sense of 'mystery' and being a 'cult discovery' is compromised? . . . There is something Houdini-esque about alternative musical cultures generally."[13] Unlike recent diagnosticians of contemporary irony such as Jedediah Purdy, then, we suggest that irony may at times be a necessary cavil, a sign of hope rather than despair.[14] In this respect, we believe a contemporary cultural materialist approach, including the work of humanists such as Herbert Marcuse and Raymond Williams and sociologists such as Pierre Bourdieu, can draw analytic attention to this music's rhetoric of contesting commodification and disputing taste. As we'll illustrate shortly, such an approach offers a useful perspective on a music genre self-consciously attuned to questions of aesthetic value and national politics yet apparently blind to its investments in dominant class and gender identity politics.

Until quite recently, this critique has been lacking. While alt.country has enjoyed widespread laudatory attention from mainstream media as well as the "alternative" press, it has, like the larger field of country music more generally, been relatively neglected by American studies and popular culture scholars, who prefer to concentrate on rock, pop, and hip-hop.[15] Country music scholarship overall, having had to fight for its very legitimacy in the academy, too often seems hesitant to venture beyond its own borders, safely focused inward and emphasizing documentation, cataloging, and traditional narrative history.[16] The result is twofold: journalistic coverage remains primarily descriptive or celebratory of alt.country's aims and achievements[17] while cultural studies academics seldom consider the role of this purportedly alternative culture in discussions of "popular" music in the late twentieth and early twenty-first centuries. The archive of academic work on alt.country is similarly scant, scattered, and preliminary.[18] Scholarly presses, for example, have yet to publish any sustained work on the topic but, evidently sensing the need, have instead issued collections of journalism such as *No Depression* editors Grant Alden and Peter Blackstock's anthology *The Best of No Depression: Writing about American Music;* photographer Steve Harris' collection of photographs and quotations *Texas Troubadours;* or *True to the Roots: Americana Music Revealed,* NASCAR journalist Monte Dutton's collection of artist profiles.[19] In 2008, *No Depression* moved to entirely online publication due to decreased advertising revenue and increased printing and mailing costs; at the same time, they began a partnership with University of Texas Press to publish a semiannual book/magazine hybrid.

This volume, then, deliberately functions as neither a history of alt.country nor an encyclopedia of alt.country musicians. Its scope likewise extends beyond a strictly musicological analysis since alt.country is a social and cultural phenomenon formed with music *and* its cultural meanings, only some of which are sonic. As both a critique of the alt.country movement and an example of broadly conceived popular music studies, *Old Roots, New Routes* offers an interdisciplinary approach to alt.country's evolving discourses, representations, and ideologies. Our contributors interrogate a variety of artists and events, but they all focus on the question of how this music proposes an alternative to mainstream country through the production of music, images, narratives, journalism, advertising, and a fan community. In particular, they stress that alt.country's very existence as a style and structure of feeling poses important questions about the possibility of alternatives, about the nature of "country" and related tropes, and about the making and reception of music in the global economy.

(Re)Defining "Alternative"

TASTE

Popular culture's inevitable commodification gives rise to many forms of music purporting to be "alternative," a phenomenon defined by Barry Shank as "an insistence upon personal integrity and a firm belief in the legitimacy of one's honestly held and boldly stated tastes."[20] Susan Sontag, writing specifically on the legitimacy of a taste for camp, broadly insists that "taste governs every free—as opposed to rote—human response."[21] Professing a taste for alternative music thus suggests that one's aesthetic preferences are genuine and independent—an expression of a desire to break with the ties that bind human expression and pleasure to the marketplace and an equation, however subconscious, of the cultural mainstream with an "illegitimate" empire over taste. Locating this desire in the *country* amplifies the sense of independence since, as Raymond Williams has demonstrated, *country* in this abstract sense often connotes an *un*industrialized territory free from the pressure to consume and inhabited by uncorrupted rustics whose time isn't money and whose labor produces food and folk art rather than exchange value. Indeed, some notion of taste, at once seemingly "natural" and an act of free choice, softens the paradox inherent in selling authenticity. But to profess a *taste* for music made in rural isolation, or at least in a simulacrum of such isolation, situates the consumer in a very different, more sophisticated world than the imagined source of the admired music. As Ching and Creed have demonstrated, while the number of people living in rural areas continues to diminish, and as the penetration of mass communication shrinks their isolation, the opposition between the country and the city, the urban and the rural, and the urbane and the rustic has become more elastic, making these terms all the more symbolically charged.[22]

Alternative country, then, can be usefully and skeptically imagined as a cultural form deliberately swimming out of the mainstream into a newly dug backwater. Its other common appellations, "Americana" and "roots rock," similarly convey a sense of rusticity.[23] Fittingly, in place of the globalized entertainment industry (called "Nashville"), alt.country highlights regional influences and collaborative communities. Formally, this characteristic has resulted in numerous compilation discs offering samples of a label's roster or a region's music. While Texas obsesses many fans, nearly every other part of the country gets some recognition. *A Town South of Bakersfield* (a countrified name for Los Angeles) was the name of a seminal early 1990s three-volume CD compilation of California-based acts. The cover of *Points West: New Horizons in Country Music* (1994) used a pinpointed map of the United States to show its variance from Nashville. From its earliest issues in 1995, *No Depression,* originally based in Seattle, has featured reviews of live shows in midwestern college towns and reports on local scenes. Twangfest, which Dale Watson calls "the future survival of country music . . . and a home for us survivalists," celebrated its eleventh anniversary in Saint Louis in the summer of 2007.[24] A recent article in the *Journal of Country Music* credited a 1970s Manhattan music scene with "spawn[ing] the stars of Americana."[25] In its cyber-manifesto (located at http://www.bloodshotrecords.com/manifesto), Bloodshot, founded in 1994, underscores its base in Chicago and hyperbolically dramatizes the struggle to stay afloat in its urban backwater: "[F]rom our shabby office complex on a bleak stretch of Irving Park Road on the Northwest Side of Chicago, we will, with your support, continue to forge ahead in an environment hostile to the little guy and keep making music that matters."

This anticorporate rhetoric accompanies old-fashioned notions of work that evoke the hope that country music can be *made,* in the original sense of that word (*poeisis*), by human minds, voices, and hands instead of by corporate management. As *No Depression* editors Alden and Blackstock put it, "to the mainstream music industry . . . [alt.country] became code for 'doesn't sell'; to fans, it came to describe a network of hardworking bands that fused punk rock's DIY [do-it-yourself] spirit to country music's working-class honesty."[26] Their word choices, connecting "hardworking" musicians with a working-class country music audience, subliminally clash with the recherché adjective *alt*, which simultaneously asserts an allegiance to the old ways even as its orthography, with the use of the period between *alt* and *country*, announces a comfortable immersion in the forward-looking rhetoric of digital literacy (although many journalists and bloggers drop the period in favor of the hyphen: *alt-country*). Of course, this concept of work complicates alt.country, too. Once you stop strumming a guitar on your back porch and begin seeking a record deal, an audience, a movement, and a magazine eager to put your photograph on the cover, you are also leaving your "home down on the rural route" (to quote Hank Williams) and deliberately entering a culture in which, as Raymond Williams notes, your tastes, no matter how boldly and honestly stated, are expressed by engaging in capitalist consumption.[27] You will, to go back to Hank's version of this dilemma, end up with a case of the "honky-tonk blues," wasting your money and talent on the degraded outskirts of urban life. Nevertheless, alt.country characteristically downplays and/or ironizes the near inescapability of the commodity form, already a persistent trope of earlier country music, in several new ways.[28]

AUTHENTIC AESTHETIC

While notoriously resistant to defining the genre, those who produce and promote the music resort to a discourse of cultural capital, evoking notions of discernment, art, and authenticity to distinguish this music from the mere "products" of the mainstream music industry. Blackstock and Alden, for instance, have famously struggled to articulate their "vision" of alt.country's sound and aims. For the first ten years of its publication, *No Depression* featured a subtitle announcing that it covered "alt.country (whatever that is)." The "Frequently Asked Questions" portion of its Web site still insists on the indefinite: "Do you still cover alternative country music? Whatever that is, we still cover it."[29] They note that the "definition is elusive precisely because, as with all true art, this music pays no mind to strictures or bounds."[30] They express similar aims in the preface to the anthology commemorating *No Depression*'s tenth anniversary, insisting that "it is not our purpose to identify, quantify, and codify a subgenus called alt-country. . . . We are writers, minor-league historians, fans. . . . It *is* our purpose to write and assign articles about artists whose work is of enduring merit."[31]

Even more vexed and slippery than concepts such as "enduring merit" and "art," emotional authenticity is also pressed into service when people attempt to articulate what is "alternative" about this music. For example, in the notes to another compilation disc, Blackwood and Alden intone, "At its core, country music and its distant cousin, punk rock, value emotional honesty above all other virtues."[32] The concept itself has prompted a long and vociferous debate in a number of scholarly fields pertinent to our project here, including sociology, anthropology, and literary/cultural studies. All grapple with the paradox that "authenticity" is a *cultural* construct, a set of *ideas* about "*natural*" states, experiences, or artifacts that are shaped by social structures and forces.[33] In fact, emotional authenticity is closely tied to what Hugh Barker and Yuval Taylor, in a book entirely devoted to defining authenticity in popular music, call "cultural authenticity."[34] Much discussion of musical authenticity posits a site or space of a "real" yet vanishing culture where music genres such as hip-hop and country appear to originate from a noncommercial source (the urban "street," the Appalachian "holler").[35] Thus, country music scholar and sociologist Richard Peterson argues that the meaning of authenticity "is renegotiated in a continual political struggle."[36] Examining formulations of authenticity in 1950s country music—the Hank Williams era routinely invoked in alt.country music and commentary—he notes that, for influential publications such as *Billboard*, "authenticity . . . was based in the history of a people and was drawn from the experiences of those who lived in the everyday world."[37] Such associations pervade the foundational and more recent materials that purport to describe—if not define—alt.country, yet that music often transforms the rural location into a psychological state where experiences of rural hardship and pastoral ease become symbolic journeys to interior spaces. The producers and owners of Bloodshot records amplify these sentiments in their Web site manifesto, which describes the kinship between country and punk as a "DIY ethic of *expression;* we all appreciate that music is only innovative and interesting when you're willing to take chances with it, to follow your *instincts*" (emphasis ours). As genuine "art," then, alt.country evokes authentic "feeling" in songs that touch its listeners' emotions and imaginations—an account of authenticity in accord with the social construction of most popular music's authenticity, which almost inevitably relies on spatial metaphors. Simon Frith defines this as "a quality not of the music as such (how it is actually made), but of the story it is heard to tell, the narrative of musical interaction in which the listeners *place* themselves" (emphasis ours).[38]

TRADITION

In addition to developing an aesthetic position, alt.country casts its relationship with traditional country music (Frith's "narrative of musical interaction") as a zealously cherished inheritance. Indeed, the hip imprimatur of Uncle Tupelo's imaginative bond with the Carter Family and rap impresario Rick Rubin's repackaging of Carter in-law Johnny Cash for his American Recordings label could be seen as the key events of alt.country in the 1990s. Alt.country nomenclature also underscores legacies to the key stars in the country pantheon: hence, "Risin' Outlaw" Hank Williams III, grandson of the ultimate alt.country icon; Shooter Jennings, son of the original 1970s outlaws Waylon Jennings and Jessie Colter; and claims to family ties in band names such as the Bastard Sons of Johnny Cash. Those who weren't born to the "manner" express their adoptive fealty via countless tribute projects. Hear, for a decade-spanning start, *Tulare Dust: A Songwriters' Tribute to Merle Haggard* (1994), featuring Iris DeMent, Dave Alvin, Lucinda Williams, and others; *Return of the Grievous Angel: Tribute to Gram Parsons* (1999), featuring Lucinda Williams and Steve Earle; *Timeless: A Hank Williams Tribute* (2001), featuring Lucinda Williams, Hank Williams III, and Ryan Adams; *Dressed in Black: A Tribute to Johnny Cash* (2002), featuring Robbie Fulks and Rodney Crowell; or *Anchored in Love: A Tribute to June Carter Cash* (2007), featuring Emmylou Harris, Elvis Costello, and Willie Nelson. This continual engagement with illustrious forebears allows alt.country to present itself not as a commercial product but as a beloved family sing-along.

A CONTEMPORARY COMMUNITY

Now that the alt.sound is established enough to warrant its own radio format, the rhetoric also emphasizes a forward-looking vision, highlighting creativity and innovation alongside its commitment to tradition. Sugar Hill Records explains its mission in just these terms: "Sugar Hill . . . has never bowed to any trend in country music. The focus has always been *contemporary music with traditional roots* and Sugar Hill has always remained true to its motto."[39] XM Radio claims that its X Country programming "honors the roots of country while infusing a sonic personality that is unmistakably NOW! . . . Today's musicians are taking the sound of Country, reinterpreting its spirit, and taking it places where it's never been." But significantly, while the "sound" and "spirit" of country are continuously transformed for the contemporary moment, "the feeling never changes: it's music of real life." When XM 12 imagines how its listeners respond to the music, it promises, "It twangs, it rocks, and it burns a hole in your soul."[40] In this hyperbole, XM 12's publicists join alt.country's other promoters in celebrating purportedly organic communities grounded in connections between the artistic voices of singer-songwriters and the ears of discerning listeners who long to express themselves through good music.

The listeners, too, publicize their communities. Twangville.com, a blog featuring a group of writers from around the United States, explains that it started "as a place to post playlists for our friends" but expanded into reviewing with an emphasis on "the alternative side of alt-country." They invite readers to become "a part of our community" by simply registering and submitting posts. However, the labeling of participation levels reveals the taste policing that alt.country entails.

> [A]nyone who registers will automatically be authorized as a "Hooligan" (Contributor) and can submit any post to be reviewed and approved by our town "Posse" (Editors). As we get to know our "Hooligans," we'll invite them to become "Vigilantes" (Authors) so that posts can be made at any given time. . . . Over time, we'll elevate select "Vigilantes" to the "Posse" based on criteria we're bound to make up along the way.[41]

The more anonymous Cheezeball.net, with a mailing address in Mobile, Alabama, and a concert photo page dominated by performances taking place in Iowa City, states in its manifesto that its purpose is to protect "our punk 'do it yourself' ethos" and "our hillbilly inheritance." To that end, the manifesto lists twenty-one constituent elements for "producers and would-be musicians." While many points on the list articulate sonic preferences (no key changes, no backup singers, etc.), most interesting is a compulsive insistence on an ironic approach to life's most intense emotions. About love songs, for example, it advises, "As Jay Farrar so succinctly put it, 'Watch out for love like ipecac.' Love songs require irony and sarcasm (or at least an unexpected turn of phrase)." It takes a similar approach to religious sentiment: "Go ahead, record 'Satan, Your Kingdom Must Come Down'—if we think you mean it, we'll be off-put. If we think you're just kidding, well, then Jesus is just all right."[42] The file-sharing page (the "Digital Victrola") offers 1920s recordings, reformatted as MP3s, by the likes of Vernon Dalhart, Hobo Jack

Turner, and the Carter Family. The writers also post playlists ("our ongoing series of carefully chosen, obsessively ordered compilations") and link their selections are linked to an iTunes download.

CULTURAL POLITICS AND NATIONAL POLITICS

Ultimately, if the differences between alt.country and mainstream country seem fluid (if not arbitrary), this fluidity can be traced to the importance of taste distinctions and to an ironic form of sophistication prevalent among fans of the genre. While our definition of alt.country has thus far stressed the views of producers and promoters, Richard Peterson and Steve S. Lee go so far as to suggest that alt.country is a "collage of quite different sorts of music that *fans* find sound well together and that expresses much the same range of sensibilities for them. In effect, alternative country music is a prime example of an emergent class of musical genres not based in an aesthetic of music production but in an aesthetic shared by *consumers*."[43] While most aesthetics of music production need to appeal to consumers to subsist, alt.country promotional rhetoric often equates purchasing with cultural activism. The publicist at Burbank-based Little Dog records uses just such an appeal to flatter potential customers: "Be sure you're part of the F.O.L.D. (Friends of Little Dog). For over ten years, Little Dog Records has brought you the best in American roots music—rock, country, blues, folk, and honky-tonk. As an independent label, we have been able to sign and develop the most creative artists, unfettered by the pressures faced by the majors. Little Dog needs your help as we nip at the heels of the big dogs."[44] The closing flourish of Bloodshot's manifesto similarly emphasizes the role of the discerning music fan: "[H]elp us keep our steel-toed boots on the throats of the forces responsible for the free fall decline of the contemporary music scene. As [Clash cofounder] Joe Strummer taught us, search out the good stuff, go underground and don't buy what's shoved in front of you."

Finally, the refusal to automatically accept mainstream music also connects alt.country to a critique of majority politics, particularly since September 11, 2001. Chris Willman poses the logic as a rhetorical question: "Is there a natural equation that follows that . . . alt.country = alt.politics?"[45] Unsurprisingly, alt.politics is often articulated as a question of taste. For example, Steve Earle has hosted a weekly show on the progressive Air America radio network since 2004 where the Web site description of the show equates sophisticated taste in food with an appreciation for both alt.country and liberal politics: "It's like tapas for the musical soul."[46] Left-leaning tunes also garner industry approval: James McMurtry's political songs such as "We Can't Make It Here" (2005), a protest about working-class economic struggle in the Bush era, and "God Bless America" (2007), an attack on gas-guzzling Republicans, garnered him awards from the Americana Music Association.[47] The political sentiments of a song can even trump the "sound" in Jessie Scott's mind: in November 2005, she was debating whether to add Merle Haggard's "Rebuild America First" (2005), which is critical of the Iraq War, to the X Country playlist. The sound, she noted, was not "rocky" enough for the station although the sentiments it expressed fit well with the other music being played.[48] Within weeks, the station began to play the song. The saga of the Dixie Chicks, explored at greater length in our volume's conclusion, also indicates that adopting a leftist/liberal political stance can render what was once a mainstream country music alternative. After the record burnings and Clear Channel radio station banning that followed from lead singer Natalie Maines' denunciation of President Bush and the war in Iraq, *No Depression* coeditor Grant Alden proclaimed the Dixie Chicks' album *Home* the best record of 2002 and announced that he was going to buy it from a record store (such as Wal-Mart) that tallies sales with Nielsen SoundScan (and forwards the data to the *Billboard* charts) so that "we liberals" could show support for the Chicks' dissent.[49]

II. Alt.Cosmopolitanism

As the song lyrics, journalism, and record label promotional materials we have cited indicate, alt.country's self-conscious position outside of the mainstream manifests itself in the kind of hip intellectualism that country music has historically rejected. As Willman puts it, "Country: It's where the elite don't meet." Or, as Sasha Frere-Jones, the music critic for the *New Yorker*, recently noted, "[T]here are still too many places that country music can't get into to get thrown out of."[50] In other words, country music itself is not mainstream music as measured by commercial success or cultural cachet. It is marginal to fans of hip-hop, rock, and every other kind of better-selling music. Thus, given the long-lived lowbrow stigma attached to country music, alt.country strives to be cool when country isn't.[51] This manner of "appreciating" country music turns it into a contemporary form of cultural capital, what Richard Peterson and Roger Kern, drawing on Pierre Bourdieu, call "discriminating omnivorousness." They argue that sophisticated country music fans can be distinguished from, say, stereotypical Opry listeners, by the critical discourse in which they engage: "[T]hey appreciate and critique [country music] in the light of some knowledge of the genre, its great performers, and links to other cultural forms, lowbrow and highbrow."[52] Marian Leighton Levy observes this dynamic at work in Rounder's customers, noting that alt.country names a "critical category" for listeners rather than a set of stylistic traits and that "after a feature [about a Rounder artist] on NPR [National Public Radio] we see a big spike in sales."[53] The mainstream press now manipulates this rhetoric of distinction and discernment to flatter alt.country fans. The November 2006 issue of *Vanity Fair*, for instance, captioned a group photograph of several alt.country stars by defining their version of country music as "cerebral, devoid of anything hick."[54]

Significantly, many alt.country signature songs dramatize such a critique. In songs such as Jason and the Scorchers' "Greetings from Nashville" (1983), Robbie Fulks' "Fuck This Town" (1997), Heather Myles' "Nashville's Gone Hollywood" (2002), and Dale Watson's "Nashville Rash" (1995), alt.country accuses Nashville not only of rejecting its rustic roots but also of failing to recognize new artistic merit. Fulks' song tells the tale of a sophisticated male songwriter who initially dreams of artistry on Music Row only to be disillusioned by the "moron market" he's being asked to please.[55] In Houston Marchman's "Viet Nashville" (1999), the writer has been reduced to a "whore" writing for a prototypical "eighth-grade-level divorced housewife." Dallas Wayne, singing another Robbie Fulks composition, sneers at mainstream country's female demographic with "I ain't sayin' that suburban moms ain't fun, but I don't think that's the way Hank [Williams] wanted it done" ("If That Ain't Country," 2000).

In their public statements, the artists similarly underscore their sophistication. Steve Earle, justifying his decision to leave Nashville in order to live in New York City, explains "I quit being proud of being from Texas a long time ago. . . . I feel like a . . . Martian in Tennessee at this point. . . . I'd like to be able to see any movie and get any book and see good theater."[56] Other musicians display their cultural capital by comparing themselves to poets and writers. Lucinda Williams, the daughter of Arkansas poet Miller Williams, says that some of her songs are like "little short stories." She also notes that she "grew up around a bunch of poets . . . Charles Bukowski, e.e. cummings, and all that stuff."[57] Explaining his sources of inspiration to Monte Dutton, Robert Earl Keen cites novels, naming Graham Greene's *The Heart of the*

Matter as an example.[58] Both Steve Earle and Rosanne Cash have published fiction, and James McMurtry is the son of novelist Larry McMurtry.[59]

Visually, too, alt.country marks its hip difference from its mainstream counterparts by its low-key or campy album covers. Three approaches predominate. The grainy and blurry photograph may be the most prevalent, as seen here ranging from Uncle Tupelo's 1990 *No Depression* (fig. 1) to Sarah Borges' 2007 *Diamonds in the Dark* (fig. 2). Unlike the glamorous and glossy photographs found in *Rolling Stone,* this genre of cover shot could have been taken by fans, as Richard Peterson and Bruce Beal note in their

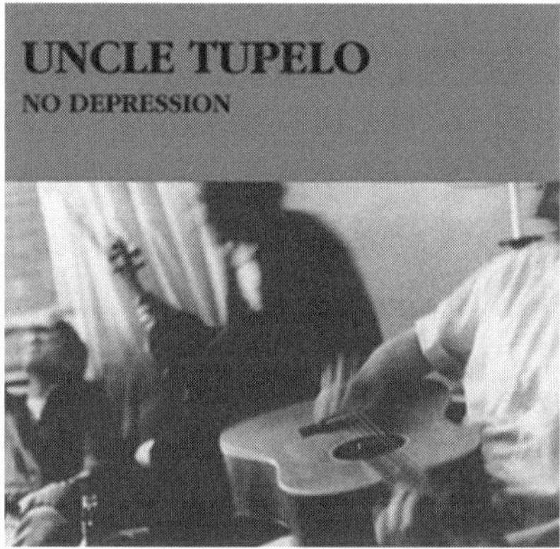

Fig. 1. Cover of Uncle Tupelo's *No Depression* (Rockpile, 1990).

Fig. 2. Cover of Sarah Borges' *Diamonds in the Dark* (Sugar Hill, 2007).

Fig. 3. Cover of Steve Earle's *Copperhead Road* (MCA, 1988).

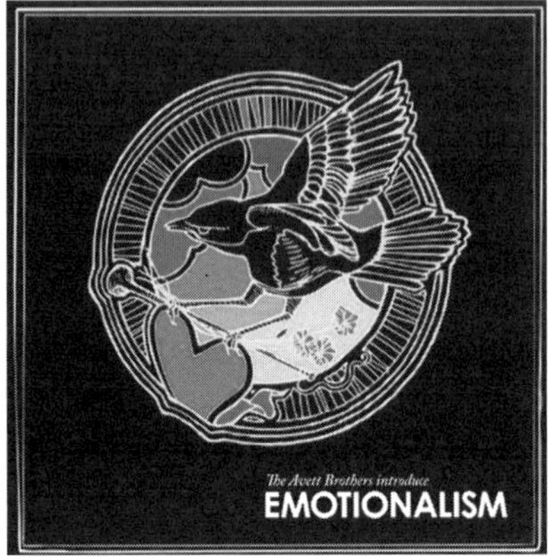

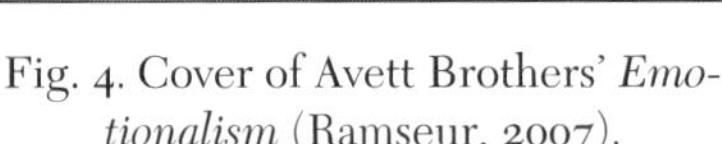
Fig. 4. Cover of Avett Brothers' *Emotionalism* (Ramseur, 2007).

Fig. 5. Cover of Robbie Fulks' *Revenge* (Yep Roc, 2007).

discussion of alt.country visuals.[60] Almost as long-standing is the folk-artsy cover evoking fantasies of the primitive, pre-Sunbelt South, as in Steve Earle's 1988 *Copperhead Road* (fig. 3) and the Avett Brothers' 2007 *Emotionalism* (fig. 4). Finally, the ironic illustration can also signal that the music separates itself from contemporary music and consumption practices. The graphics and grimace on Robbie Fulks' 2007 *Revenge,* for instance, conjure up a more innocent and easily thrilled age at the same time that they invite consumers to ironize their purchase of the record (fig. 5).

From Backwater to Mainstream

Although it is a multifaceted style and practice proudly occupying the cultural margins, alt.country has also paradoxically operated from the mid- to late1990s as a mass cultural force influencing popular music, film, and forms of fandom, culminating in the phenomenal success of the Coen Brothers' film *O Brother, Where Art Thou?* (2000) and its accompanying soundtrack. As we will explore further in this collection's conclusion, such an appeal indicates that what started as a rebellion against the hegemony of Music Row and its "prepackaged dreck"[61] has arguably transformed the Nashville industry itself—so much so that many a Top 40 country artist is opting for a "rootsier" sound and image (Lee Ann Womack, Brad Paisley, Dierks Bentley, and, most recently, Miranda Lambert)—and engineered a powerful infusion of alt.country performers into the mainstream (Kasey Chambers and Alison Krauss).[62] This blurring of prior, seemingly distinct boundaries—commercial versus artistic, hegemonic versus oppositional—serves as a key point for analysis, demanding an approach that neither blindly applauds (as cultural change) nor condemns (as selling out). Much alt.country discourse has been guilty of both, in the process inevitably reproducing binary categories that divide country's hallowed traditional past from its corrupt, fallen present and establishing a "counter" roster of artists who wrest the banner of authenticity from their platinum-selling Others (i.e., Shania Twain/Lucinda Williams and Faith Hill and Tim McGraw/Buddy and Julie Miller).

But in fact, like most borderlines, the point of separation between alt.country and the mainstream also functions as a law of attraction. Alt.country may make a point of resisting codification and celebrating diversity, but that openness often entails fraternizing with the enemy. Take, for example, the triangulation among Willie Nelson, alt.country, and mainstream country. Alt.country songwriter Bruce Robison deified the 1970s outlaw hero in his "What Would Willie Do" (2001) while Gary Allan, one of mainstream's hat-wearing hunks, recorded his version of it that same year. *No Depression* featured Willie's grizzled face on the cover of its September–October 2004 issue, yet Top 40 juggernaut Toby Keith, alt.country's favorite whipping boy, sang a duet with him the year before ("Beer for My Horses"). Alt.country thus faces its own "crisis" as its recent acceptance *as* country music threatens its hip marginal status and eclipses the edgier rock, punk, and grunge strains of its formative years.

Equally important, its much-ballyhooed reverence for history offers no real alternative if it does not engage with the material conditions that create the need for change. As Raymond Williams reminds us, notions of "tradition" are intimately tied to the *contemporary* moment, defined by "the interest of the dominance of a specific class."[63] In other words, alt.country's representations of tradition could work equally well to "ratify" rather than disrupt hegemonic sites of power. As its tribute projects suggest, alt.country's devotion to a distinctly patriarchal rustic heritage produces its own disturbingly "selective" history—straighter, narrower, and whiter than that of Music Row. Singer Shooter Jennings' recent "Put the O Back in Country" also exemplifies this trend: although *O* ostensibly stands for *outlaw,* without the letter *o* the word *country* contains a misogynist vulgarity. The song begins with a voice-over from George Jones announcing that he's there to help Shooter "put the *O* back." The song itself is a rewrite of daddy Waylon's version of Neil Young's "Are You Ready for the Country" and invokes the roster of male country stars who typically comprise the alt.country fraternity: George Jones, Johnny Cash, and Merle Haggard. Clearly, in this scenario, only men—and particularly those connected to country music's past "family tradition" of raw violence, despair, and excess—can revive this genre as an authentic alternative to commercial country.[64] Alt.country's ties to mainstream ideology thus also produce a more regressive kind of "irony" unanticipated by its ostensibly progressive listeners.

The Twenty-first Century Alternative: Keeping on the "Sunny Side"?

As suggested in our opening vignette, alt.country has not forsworn the cultural cachet of rock's urbane modernity even as it seeks to revitalize older strains of country music. Nostalgia and hope for the cultural resonance of both rock and pre-1990s country continues in the early years of the twenty-first century. As examples, Son Volt's *The Search* and Southern Culture on the Skids' *Countrypolitan Favorites,* both of which topped the charts of XM Radio's alternative country station in June 2007, demonstrate what alt.country sounds like and aspires to now. While *The Search* sounds dramatically different from early Son Volt albums such as their first, the banjo-packed *Trace* (1995), leader Jay Farrar (an erstwhile Uncle Tupelo member), with his trembling and tentative vocal style, ghosts Neil Young on each.[65] Likewise, in 1995, Son Volt had Young's crunchy guitars and reverb mixed with country strings. In 2007, the band relies less on banjos and fiddles but echoes the hesitant piano of Young's *After the Gold Rush.* Throughout, Farrar's songs favor typically alt.country midtempo melodies and meditative, cranky lyrics borrowed from Young's sonic tool kit. Even as it notes the 1970s echoes, *Blender*'s negative review of *The Search* takes aim at alt.country's political aspirations: "[T]he saggy country-rock complaints about corporatization and alienation . . . sound like submissions to an Air America poetry contest."[66] It is important to recognize, however, that critique is not the only tone struck in *The Search.* The opening cut, "Slow Hearse," introduces the transportation for the search party alluded to in the album title, yet the album's sequencing indicates that no funeral takes place. The title song and closing cuts celebrate the journey and the hope that drives us to take to the road and look to the future. The chorus of the last song, "Phosphate Skin," states it plainly: "[I]t can only get better from here."

While *The Search* epitomizes the seriousness and nostalgic creativity of alt.country's new material, Southern Culture on the Skids' *Countrypolitan Favorites* plays to the genre's love of cover songs, mixing country and rock selections mostly from the 1960s and 1970s. Although this band is more campy and parodic than most, out-retroing Nashville media darlings BR–549, their style highlights alt.country's double-edged covering techniques. Like many alt.country covers of country classics, Southern Culture's "Let's Invite Them Over" (a duet about a loveless marriage and the consolations of spouse swapping made famous by George Jones and Melba Montgomery in 1963) marks its modernity by rocking the arrangement—in this case using a busy bass line and loud, Latin-tinged percussion to mask the waltz rhythm (and the pathos). True to rock style, the instruments overpower the vocals. Alt.country covers as far back as Uncle Tupelo's 1990 take on the Carters's "No Depression" (via the New Lost City Ramblers' 1959 version) often work this way, kicking up the volume, picking up the beat, and frequently making an anachronistic instrument choice.[67] Conversely, Southern Culture's inspired cover of the Kinks' "Muswell Hillbillies" (1971) decelerates the sulky original with a twangy, relaxed bass line. While Ray Davies' lyrics tell the story of a Cockney who prefers dreaming of American hills and hollers to an image makeover from an encounter with Henry Higgins, the Southern Culture version replaces the Kinks' sad defense of "Cockney pride" with affirmation, singing instead that nothing can "kill my country pride."

III. Essay Overview

Diane Pecknold's comparison of the music business in the 1950s with alt.country's emerging institutions opens our collection by pointedly demonstrating that alt.country's marketing strategies are embedded in the very history of commercial country music. Alt.country's future, then, could replicate Nashville's own commercial practices, leading its artists and fans straight to the seat of power. In a similar vein, Jon Smith discusses alt.country as a form of cultural capital amassed by generation X in an attempt to distinguish its taste (and all the social meanings that come with it) from that of the still dominant, rock-loving baby boomers. Taking the career of Neko Case as his model, he argues that in alt.country's future, the fans' and performers' need for irony, and even the trope of "country" itself, may fall away as generation X ages out of youth culture and into full adulthood. Focusing on alt.country mecca Austin, Texas, and its outskirts, Aaron Fox's extensive fieldwork with Texan musician Justin Treviño underscores the irony of alt.country's curatorial nostalgia, particularly for a working-class Mexican-American artist whose hard country apprenticeship and business acumen have led him to make uneasy compromises with alt.tastemakers at the risk of sacrificing his traditional fan base. Focusing on films that introduced many listeners to alt.country, Barbara Ching's essay on *Songcatcher* and *O Brother, Where Art Thou?* explores alt.country's mythologies as they are crafted for public consumption. In these late-twentieth-century film narratives set in the early twentieth century, alt.country's revered traditional music and its (fictionalized) makers metamorphose from unrecognized musical royalty into royalty-collecting stars. Thus, both films close as comedies of commercialization and joyful plunges into the mainstream rather than discoveries of down-home places without depression.

Our last essays further explore how alt.country's construction of the past informs its place in the present, especially its claim to be a genuinely alternative cultural form. Pamela Fox's essay on Gillian Welch and the group Freakwater demonstrates how authenticity discourse can function to support a gendered, as well as classed, dominant culture. She analyzes these artists' contrasting performances of "old-time" rusticity in order to point to the complex dangers inherent in alt.country's fetishizing of a seemingly obsolete musical past. Likewise, Olivia Carter Mather's essay on alt.country's infatuation with Gram Parsons underscores the role of selective memory and even a tendency toward fantasy in describing the discursive transformation of this country rocker hailing from a wealthy southern family into a "hillbilly" in touch with gothic portions of heartache. Aaron Smithers demonstrates the importance of studying local interactions within the music industry as he rethinks the relationship between punk rock and "old-time" arrangements in alt.country music. He proposes that for some artists (such as the Bad Livers and the Meat Purveyors) punk actually serves as a more uncontaminated signifier of authenticity than country, but country elements ironically make their music more accessible and acceptable to their fans. Similarly, Stevie Simkin's examination of Jay Farrar's musical career, both with and beyond his post–Uncle Tupelo band Son Volt, identifies the uses and limitations of country and rock traditions for an artist who has served as both alt.country icon and dissident and who self-consciously explores the role of technology in undermining and creating the experience of musical authenticity. Finally, in the conclusion we look at three artists (Gretchen Wilson, Miranda Lambert, and the Dixie Chicks) whose work successfully floats on the edges of the mainstream in order to call attention to the shifting discourses that define, and even police, the taste-making irony of this alternative.

As academics in the interpretive fields of ethnomusicology, musicology, folklore, history, and literary/cultural studies, we hope to offer our readers—be they alt.country fans, omnivorous music lovers, and/or scholars of alternative culture—a more comprehensive understanding of how alt.country functions as a musical genre: from one individual's CD choices to multiple artists' signature sounds and the marketing of a cultural brand.

NOTES

1. See also Jon Langford's account of how his punk rock band the Mekons became disillusioned with the commodification of punk and discovered country music in *Nashville Radio: Art, Words, and Music* (Portland, OR: Verse Chorus Press, 2006), 28–37.

2. Herbert Marcuse, *One Dimensional Man: Studies in the Ideology of Advanced Industrial Society* (Boston: Beacon, 1968), 70. Marcuse borrows the expression from the nineteenth-century French novelist Stendhal.

3. We thank Robert A. Russell for bringing this image to our attention.

4. http://www.nodepression.net/admin/readerfaq.html (accessed June 14, 2007). For more on the "virtual scene" of the discussion board, see Steve S. Lee and Richard A. Peterson, "Internet-Based Virtual Music Scenes," in *Music Scenes: Local, Translocal, and Virtual*, ed. Andy Bennett and Richard A. Peterson, 187–204 (Nashville: Vanderbilt University Press, 2004). Although this article uses the alt.country Internet discussion board as a case study, it does not claim that virtual scenes in and of themselves are unique to alt.country or constitutive of the genre.

5. For a concise statement of this concern, see Raymond Williams: "[N]early all initiatives, . . . even when they take on manifestly alternative or oppositional forms, are in practice tied to the hegemonic: . . . the dominant culture . . . at once produces and limits its own forms of counter-culture." *Marxism and Literature* (Oxford: Oxford University Press, 1977), 114. Marcuse's theory of "repressive desublimation," articulated in *One Dimensional Man*, claims that capitalism simply recuperates (and commodifies) new developments that threaten to destabilize the status quo (56–83). For recent applications of this theory, see Thomas Frank, *The Conquest of Cool: Business Culture, Counterculture, and the Rise of Hip Consumerism* (Chicago: University of Chicago Press, 1997); and Thomas Frank and Matt Weiland, eds., *Commodify Your Dissent: Salvos from the Baffler* (New York: Norton, 1997).

6. Langford, *Nashville Radio*, 35.

7. Russell Jacoby, *The End of Utopia: Politics and Culture in an Age of Apathy* (New York: Basic Books, 2000), xii.

8. Jessie Scott, interview with Barbara Ching, XM Studios, Washington, DC, November 2, 2005. Scott named three other songs in response to this question: Lucinda Williams' love song "Righteously" (2003), Cross Canadian Ragweed's pot-smoking anthem "Boys from Oklahoma" (1999), and Chris Knight's blue collar murder-revenge story (but also a triumph) "Down the River" (2001).

9. Timothy D. Taylor, *Beyond Exoticism: Western Music and the World* (Durham: Duke University Press, 2007), 118.

10. As Simon Frith has noted, "[T]he fact that the objects of judgment are different doesn't mean that the processes of judgment are." *Performing Rites: On the Value of Popular Music* (Cambridge: Harvard University Press, 1996), 17. For more on the masculine exclusivity of this taste culture, see Barbara Ching's "Going Back to the Old Mainstream: *No Depression*, Robbie Fulks, and Alt.Country's Muddied Waters," in *A Boy Named Sue: Gender and Country Music*, ed. Kristine M. McCusker and Diane Pecknold, 178–95 (Jackson: University Press of Mississippi, 2004); Aaron A. Fox's "'Alternative' to What? 'O Brother,' September 11th, and the Politics of Country Music," in *Country Music Goes to War*, ed. Charles K. Wolfe and James E. Akenson, 164–91 (Lexington: University of Kentucky Press, 2005); and Pamela Fox's forthcoming *Natural Acts: Gender, Race, and Rusticity in Country Music* (Ann Arbor: University of Michigan Press), especially chapter 5, "Revivals, Survivals, and the Future: Alt.country's Reclamation of Rusticity."

11. On this dynamic, see Juliet B. Schor, *The Overspent American: Upscaling, Downshifting, and the New Consumer* (New York: Basic Books, 1998), 58–59. For a case study, see Barry Shank's perceptive analysis, "Daniel Johnston and the Fetishization of Sincerity," in *Dissonant Identities: The Rock 'n' Roll Scene in Austin, Texas*, 153–59 (Hanover, NH: Wesleyan University Press, 1994). Indeed, as the recent documentary *The Devil and Daniel Johnston* reveals (Dir. Jeff Feuerzeig, 2005), Johnston's deteriorating mental health has rendered his participation in the music industry nearly impossible; therefore, his work has become an even "hotter" commodity.

12. Linda Hutcheon, *Irony's Edge: The Theory and Politics of Irony* (London: Routledge, 1994), 26, 37.

13. Marian Leighton Levy, interview with Barbara Ching, Rounder Records Warehouse, Burlington, Massachusetts, August 6, 2007.

14. Jedediah Purdy, *For Common Things: Irony, Trust, and Commitment in America Today* (New York: Vintage, 2000).

15. For a sampling of the many titles available, see Lawrence Grossberg, *We Gotta Get Out of This Place: Pop, Conservatism, and Postmodern Culture* (New York: Routledge, 1992); Kevin J. H. Dettmar and William Richey, eds., *Reading Rock and Roll: Authenticity, Appropriation, Aesthetics* (New York: Columbia University Press,

1999); Richard Middleton, ed., *Reading Pop: Approaches to Textual Analysis in Popular Music* (Oxford: Oxford University Press, 2000); Andrew Ross and Tricia Rose, eds., *Microphone Fiends: Youth Music and Youth Culture* (New York: Routledge, 1994); Simon Frith and Andrew Goodwin, eds., *On Record: Rock, Pop, and the Written Word* (New York: Routledge, 2000); Lori Burns and Mélisse Lafrance, eds., *Disruptive Divas: Feminism, Identity, and Pop Music* (New York: Routledge, 2002); Murray Forman and Mark Anthony Neal, eds., *That's the Joint! The Hip-Hop Studies Reader* (New York: Routledge, 2004); Imani Perry, *Prophets of the Hood: Politics and Poetics in Hip Hop* (Durham: Duke University Press, 2004); Tricia Rose, *Black Noise: Rap Music and Black Culture in Contemporary America* (Middletown, CT: Wesleyan University Press, 1994); and Gwendolyn D. Pough, *Check It While I Wreck It: Black Womanhood, Hip Hop Culture, and the Public Sphere* (Boston: Northeastern University Press, 2004).

16. Focusing on the last five years, for example, see Mary A. Bufwack and Robert K. Oermann, *Finding Her Voice: Women in Country Music, 1800–2000* (Nashville: Country Music Foundation Press and Vanderbilt University Press, 2003); Richard Carlin, *Country Music: A Biographical Dictionary* (New York: Routledge, 2003); Jeffrey J. Lange, *Smile When You Call Me a Hillbilly: Country Music's Struggle for Respectability, 1939–1954* (Athens: University of Georgia Press, 2004); Douglas B. Green, *Singing in the Saddle: The History of the Singing Cowboy* (Nashville: Country Music Foundation Press and Vanderbilt University Press, 2002); Richard Kienzle, *Southwest Shuffle: Pioneers of Honky-Tonk, Western Swing, and Country Jazz* (New York: Routledge, 2003); and Charles K. Wolfe and Ted Olson, *The Bristol Sessions: Writings about the Big Bang of Country Music* (Jefferson, NC: McFarland, 2005). It might be possible to argue that alt.country's interest in the "old masters" has further encouraged this positivist emphasis in country music scholarship.

17. In addition to the collections previously cited, see Brian Hinton, *South by Southwest: A Road Map to Alternative Country* (London: Sanctuary, 2003).

18. In addition to the essays by Barbara Ching and Aaron A. Fox cited in note 10, see S. Renee Dechert, "'Oh, What a Life a Mess Can Be': Uncle Tupelo, Bakhtin, and the Dialogue of Alternative Country Music," in *Country Music Annual, 2001*, ed. Charles K. Wolfe and James E. Akenson, 70–91 (Lexington: University of Kentucky Press, 2001).

19. Grant Alden and Peter Blackstock, eds., *The Best of No Depression: Writing about American Music* (Austin: University of Texas Press, 2005); Steve Harris, *Texas Troubadours: Texas Singer Songwriters* (Austin: University of Texas Press, 2007); Monte Dutton, *True to the Roots: Americana Music Revealed* (Lincoln: University of Nebraska, 2006).

20. Shank, *Dissonant Identities*, 219.

21. Susan Sontag, "Notes on Camp," in *Against Interpretation* (New York: Farrar, Straus and Giroux, 1966), 276.

22. Gerald W. Creed and Barbara Ching, "Recognizing Rusticity: Identity and the Power of Place," in *Knowing Your Place: Rural Identity and Cultural Hierarchy*, ed. Barbara Ching and Gerald W. Creed, 1–38 (New York: Routledge, 1996).

23. David Goodman explains that "by 1994, . . . the term alternative country was being used regularly to describe the music. . . . Several other names were suggested including 'No Depression,' 'Insurgent Country,' 'Twangcore,' 'Western Beat,' 'Rural Contemporary,' 'Hillbilly Noir,' and 'Y'alternative.' And while Americana . . . ran a close second, 'Alternative Country' became the most widely accepted term." David Goodman, *Modern Twang: An Alternative Country Music Guide and Directory* (Nashville: Dowling, 1999), v. It is worth noting, however, that the Americana Music Association remains the name of the primary institutional organization of the record labels, artists, and radio station executives involved in this genre.

24. http://www.twangfest.com/about.html (accessed January 26, 2007).

25. Barry Mazor, "Where the Twang Finally Met: How New York's Short-Lived Country Craze Spawned the Stars of Americana," *Journal of Country Music* 24, no. 1 (2006): 34–39.

26. Alden and Blackstock, *The Best of No Depression*, 1.

27. Raymond Williams, *Keywords: A Vocabulary of Culture and Society* (New York: Oxford University Press, 1985), 314–15.

28. See Barbara Ching, "Acting Naturally: Cultural Distinction and Critiques of Pure Country," *Arizona Quarterly* 49 (1993): 107–25; and Aaron A. Fox, "The Jukebox of History: Narratives of Loss and Desire in the Discourse of Country Music," *Popular Music* 11 (1992): 53–72.

29. http://www.nodepression.net/admin/readerfaq.html (accessed June 14, 2007).

30. Liner notes to *No Depression: What It Sounds Like*, vol. 1, Dualtone Records 1153, 2004, emphasis ours.

31. Alden and Blackstock, *The Best of No Depression*, 2.

32. Liner notes to *The Best of Alt.Country: Exposed Roots*, K-tel Records 6428–2, 1999, emphasis ours.

33. See, for example, such varied texts as Lionel Trilling's seminal *Sincerity and Authenticity* (Cambridge: Harvard University Press, 1972), which draws on highbrow literary examples to argue that Western culture has shifted from valuing the "sincere" ("a congruence between avowal and actual feeling," 2) to the "authentic," a distinctly modern concept ("a more exigent conception of the self . . . and a less . . . genial view of the social circumstances of life," 11); postmodern theorist Jean Baudrillard's *Simulations*, trans. Paul Foss, Paul Patton, and Philip Beitchman (New York: Semiotext[e], 1983), which coined the term *hyperreal* to reflect the late twentieth century's preference for, and inability to distinguish, the reproduction from its "real" referent; James Clifford's *The Predicament of Culture* (Cambridge: Harvard University Press, 1988), which deconstructs the concept of authenticity via his critique of primitivism, the Western practice of fetishizing tribal peoples and cultures; and cultural anthro-

pologist Richard Handler's brief treatise "Authenticity," *Anthropology Today* 2, no. 1 (February 1986): 2–4, which essentially makes the case for a postmodern methodology in anthropology.

34. Hugh Barker and Yuval Taylor, *Faking It: The Quest for Authenticity in Popular Music* (New York: Norton, 2007), 22.

35. The literature on rap and hip-hop is vast. For just a few examples focused specifically on authenticity, see Mark Anthony Neal's *What the Music Said: Black Popular Music and Black Public Culture* (New York: Routledge, 1999); Murray Forman's *The 'Hood Comes First: Race, Space, and Place in Rap and Hip-Hop* (Middletown, CT: Wesleyan University Press, 2002); Paul Gilroy's "Sounds Authentic: Black Music, Ethnicity, and the Challenge of a 'Changing' Same," *Black Music Research Journal* 11, no. 2 (autumn 1991): 111–36; and Kembrew McLeod's "Authenticity within Hip-Hop and Other Cultures Threatened with Assimilation," *Journal of Communication* 49, no. 4 (December 1999): 134–50, which explicitly points to parallels with country music: "As is the case in this study of hip-hop, authenticity is invoked within country music as a referent to a past that is constructed to fit the needs of the present community. Constructions . . . center around . . . an acknowledgement of a rich cultural heritage, a close connection to its audience, and a genuine expression of one's inner feelings" (147).

36. Richard A. Peterson, *Creating Country Music: Fabricating Authenticity* (Chicago: University of Chicago Press, 1997), 220.

37. Ibid., 210. Peterson is at pains to point out, however, that "this unaffectedness was itself an affectation" (211).

38. Frith, *Performing Rites*, 275, emphasis ours.

39. http://www.sugarhillrecords.com/content/pagemaker.cgi?about (accessed June 13, 2007), emphasis in original.

40. http://www.xmradio.com/programming/channel_page.jsp?ch=12 (accessed March 24, 2006).

41. http://twangville.com/about-us/ and http://twangville.com/contribute/ (accessed December 29, 2007).

42. http://www.cheezeball.net/Manifesto.htm (accessed December 29, 2007).

43. Lee and Peterson, "Internet-Based Virtual Music Scenes," 190, emphasis ours.

44. http://www.littledogrecords.com/news.php (accessed June 13, 2007).

45. Chris Willman, *Rednecks and Bluenecks: The Politics of Country Music* (New York: New Press, 2005), 208.

46. http://www.airamerica.com/steveearleshow/about (accessed June 9, 2007).

47. http://www.jamesmcmurtry.com/ (accessed June 9, 2007).

48. Jessie Scott, interview with Barbara Ching, XM Studios, Washington, DC, November 2, 2005.

49. Grant Alden, "Hello Stranger," *No Depression* 45 (May–June 2003): 2.

50. Willman, *Rednecks and Bluenecks*, 7; Sasha Frere-Jones, "Red-Hot Pop," *New Yorker*, October 4, 2004, 108.

51. This is a deliberate play on Barbara Mandrell's 1981 song title, "I Was Country (When Country Wasn't Cool)," recorded as Mandrell was establishing her own authenticity credentials after the pop-infused 1970s.

52. Richard Peterson and Roger M. Kern, "Changing Highbrow Taste: From Snob to Omnivore," *American Sociological Review* 61, no. 5 (1996): 904. See also Pierre Bourdieu's *Distinction: A Social Critique of the Judgement of Taste,* trans. Richard Nice (Cambridge: Harvard University Press, 1984).

53. Marian Leighton Levy, interview with Barbara Ching, Rounder Records Warehouse, Burlington, MA, August 6, 2007.

54. "The Country and Western Music Portfolio," *Vanity Fair,* November 2006, 291.

55. While mainstream country also features songs critical of selling out, the singers usually don't recount their own adventures. For example, Alan Jackson's "Gone Country" (1994) and his duet with George Strait, "Murder on Music Row" (2000), don't purport to reflect any personal experiences.

56. Cited in Willman, *Rednecks and Bluenecks,* 216.

57. Keith Zimmerman and Kent Zimmerman, *Sing My Way Home: The Voices of the New American Roots Rock* (San Francisco: Backbeat, 2004), 209, 213.

58. Dutton, *True to the Roots,* 51.

59. Another indication of alt.country's preference for "deep" lyrics is the extensive glosses provided on the Old 97s' Web site: http://www.old97s.com/biography/factoids.html (accessed June 11, 2007).

60. Richard A. Peterson and Bruce A. Beal, "Discographic Essay: Alternative Country—Origins, Music, Worldview, Fans, and Taste in Genre Formation," *Popular Music and Society* 25, nos. 1–2 (2001): 233–49, http://people.vanderbilt.edu/~steve.s.lee/country.htm (accessed June 18, 2007).

61. http://www.bloodshotrecords.com/manifesto/ (accessed January 26, 2007).

62. Womack's *There's More Where That Came From* (2005) explicitly invokes the sound and look of mid-1960s country music; Paisley recorded a haunting alt.country duet with Alison Krauss, "Whiskey Lullaby," and has begun to feature Little Jimmy Dickens in his music videos; Bentley was recently featured in *No Depression* as a kind of "closet" alt.country artist; and Lambert, as our conclusion explains, is currently topping the Nielsen Country Chart, though, similar to Bentley, she is also gracing *No Depression*'s coveted cover as "Country's New Alternative."

63. Williams, *Marxism and Literature,* 116.

64. We borrow the phrase "family tradition" from Hank Williams Jr.'s song "Family Tradition," which itself contributes to the macho, hell-raising model of country music history.

65. The Son Volt Web site makes a broader claim, defining "Son Volt's bedrock sound" as "an amalgam of the Byrds, Neil Young & Crazy Horse, the blues, murder ballads, old-time country and other indigenous elements." http://www.sonvolt.net/

(accessed June 11, 2007). Son Volt is not unique in its reverence for this country, punk, grunge and everything else rocker: Young is also name checked in Lucinda Williams' "Ventura" (2003), and Cross Canadian Ragweed has covered several Young songs.

66. http://www.metacritic.com/music/artists/sonvolt/search (accessed June 11, 2007).

67. Many of the Carter Family selections on *Keep on the Sunny Side* (1993), a tribute album organized by Freakwater and others, feature fuzz guitar. The most influential Carter Family member, Johnny Cash, demonstrates the second mode of alt.country covering: drawing out the agony of a song, whether it has a country or rock pedigree, also washes it out of the mainstream. Cash's new versions of his old songs, as well as his covers of songs such as Trent Reznor's "Hurt" on his *American Recordings* series (1994–), rely on little but his acoustic guitar and hauntingly moribund voice. Lucinda Williams' 2001 version of Hank Williams' "Cold Cold Heart" also slows the pace, and her voice cracks more audibly than Hank's did. Ryan Adams' "Wonderwall" (2003), drawn from the widest point of the mainstream, provides the most dramatic example. In "Wonderwall," which was a number-one hit for the British pop group Oasis for nine weeks in 1996, Adams offers a more meditative and sticky, as opposed to slick, rendition as his voice cracks and fades on the last lines.

DIANE PECKNOLD

Selling Out or Buying In?: Alt.Country's Cultural Politics of Commercialism

The standard story of alt.country's genre formation has been well rehearsed. Downstate Illinois punk rockers start out playing hard-core but eventually combine their punk sensibilities with country music, writing songs about the decay of small-town life and America in general and delivering them with an abrasive DIY aesthetic that flies in the face of Nashville's slick, celebratory country pop. Their first album, *No Depression,* triggers the development of a loyal audience that coalesces especially by way of an Internet mailing list, Postcard2 (P2). Realizing that they are part of a larger community that rejects Nashville but loves "real" country, fans begin forming and looking for other, similar bands. A genre is born or perhaps reclaimed.

But for those who were listening to alternative music in the 1980s, the sudden emergence of "alt.country" as a genre, and particularly the myth of origin that begins in 1990 with the release of Uncle Tupelo's *No Depression,* seems singularly illogical. Uncle Tupelo's fusion of country and punk was not particularly revolutionary, and the idea that a sustainable audience with shared aesthetic values emerged immediately around the sound of a single record is somewhat suspect. Although it summarizes the genre's vox populi outlook, the standard story of alt.country's origins obscures a more complex process that relied as much on institutional and commercial forces as on audience demands for a renewal of the raw grit of both alternative and country. The timing of alt.country's emergence—and especially its transformation from a constellation of disconnected local scenes into something even a well-informed participant-observer could have recognized as something more than "all these great bands that were doing something with the theme of country music"—can only be understood in relation to the business infrastructures that have shaped the genre and defined its boundaries: record labels, the critical and trade music press, live venues and festivals, and ultimately the Americana radio format and Americana Music Association (AMA).[1] Beginning with a chronological narrative that explores why alt.country became particularly visible and significant to the music industry during the 1990s, this essay argues that, rather than responding to a preconstituted audience, alt.country's business structures developed coterminously with its audience and responded to the needs of the industry as well as the desires of its fans.

In spite of its oppositional aesthetic, alt.country has followed a relatively predictable path of institutionalization that mirrors quite closely the early development of mainstream country. And while it defines itself in large part as the antithesis of Nashville commercialism, the shared values and aesthetics of alt.country artists, entrepreneurs, and fans rely as much on discourses of commercialism as do Music Row's more obvious commitments to celebrity and profit. In the second half of the essay, I compare alt.country's discourse of commercialism with that of mainstream country during the 1950s, a moment when the latter, like alt.country in the 1990s, had begun to cohere as a genre but when its artists and entrepreneurs faced significant challenges in maintaining their control over the production and distribution of the music in a mass marketplace. Alt.country may or may not turn out to be as tenacious as its mainstream alter ego, but its institutional development and its followers' mobilization of commercial discourse to claim both cultural authority and cultural power follow some well-worn paths.

Creating Alt.Country Music

While a comprehensive history of alt.country has yet to be written, those who have addressed the subject generally agree that the stylistic elements and outsider aesthetic of alt.country have been around for decades.[2] From the Southern California country rock of Gram Parsons to the cowpunk pyrotechnics of Jason and the Scorchers to the roots revivalism of Uncle Tupelo, Wilco, and Son Volt, concerted efforts to provide an alternative to Nashville-produced commercial country have been under way almost from the moment Music City won out as the undisputed production center for country. In spite of this long history of self-conscious oppositional movements, though, it was not until the mid-1990s that a full-blown process of genre formation began to take place, first around the label alt.country and then in a more sustained way around the Americana moniker and radio format.[3]

Whittling the definition of alt.country down from its most encompassing country rock definition to a more historically specific description that characterizes it as a combination of punk or alternative rock and country aimed primarily at an audience of alternative music listeners doesn't help to explain this paradox of genre timing; even the latter, more restrictive definition can't support a narrative that makes stylistic change or audience formation the key triggers for the genre's emergence. By the mid-1980s, Jason and the Scorchers, Rank and File, the Long Ryders, Lone Justice, the Mekons, Giant Sand, the Knitters, or any of a dozen other bands that can now be recognized in retrospect as progenitors of the alt.country style had already reached sizable audiences and had begun to be described as constituting a coherent body of work, however loosely connected.[4] The relatively widespread stylistic melding of punk rock and country thus preceded by at least a decade the emergence of alt.country as an identifiable genre. Why, then, did alt.country appear as a genre when it did?

David Goodman, whose *Modern Twang: An Alternative Country Music Guide and Directory* offers the most inclusive description of the bands that make up the alt.country tradition, sees the emergence of alt.country as a process of stylistic and audience accretion. The country-rock experimentation of the late 1960s, he suggests, metamorphosed and grew until it reached the critical mass of a genre, "gradually expanding into other musical genres, joining several generations, and crossing geographical boundaries until, in the late 1990s, it was possible to speak of alternative country not just as a tradition but a full blown musical movement."[5] Richard Peterson and Bruce Beal look instead to technological differences between the 1960s or 1980s and the 1990s. They see in alt.country the emergence of what they call a "consumption based aesthetic" made possible by the Internet. In their formulation, the most important feature of alt.country is the way its audience has circumvented the industrial systems through which genres have traditionally been constructed and maintained. They argue that the alt.country aesthetic, like the teen music aesthetic, "is determined by the audience."[6]

Yet the most striking difference between the mid-1980s and the mid-1990s was not primarily one of sound or technology, or even of audience activity, but rather one of business infrastructure. With the notable exceptions of the Mekons and Giant Sand (the only bands, not coincidentally, to remain productive across the late 1980s divide), the early groups that combined elements of alternative and country music were signed to major labels or their subsidiaries and were dropped after generating weak sales. In contrast, by the mid-1990s, when alt.country appeared to spring full-grown from the imaginations of disgruntled postgrunge indie-rock fans, bands whose sound and influences paralleled the mid-1980s country rock boom had found homes on independent labels with more modest sales expectations such as Rockville, a subsidiary of the early indie behemoth Dutch East Records (Uncle Tupelo), Bloodshot (*Insurgent Country*, volumes 1 and 2, Waco Brothers, Robbie Fulks, etc.), Quarterstick (Bad Livers), and Drag City (Will Oldham). Similarly, country-influenced acts began to tap into the national network of live music venues seating two to eight hundred that had grown up to accommodate the burgeoning indie rock scene. Rock clubs such as Schuba's in Chicago, the Middle East in Boston, Café du Nord in San Francisco, and the 9:30 Club in Washington, DC, provided live avenues of exposure for DIY country.

In addition to obscuring the immediate stylistic antecedents of alt.country, a founding mythology that begins with the release of *No Depression* also privileges the formation of a specific audience community centered around the Postcard and Postcard2 e-mail lists, the AOL No Depression folder, and the magazine *No Depression* that it inspired. Indeed, this privileging is probably one reason why the myth has been so durable in spite of widespread agreement that the movement's musical roots extend back much farther than 1990. But by focusing attention on the spontaneous response of a particular generation of listeners to a single musical event, this story elides the institutional factors that made alt.country's emergence possible. In this telling, the audience constitutes itself, sui generis, and calls into being a production and distribution system to fulfill its needs. In truth, however, the audience and the business emerged in tandem rather than sequentially, and the establishment of labels and press organs helped to delineate the alt.country aesthetic as much as the social community generated by Internet communication.

Many who followed alt.country in the days before it bore a name remembered that bands and their respective audiences remained relatively disconnected, even within local contexts, until labels such as Bloodshot and Diesel Only started to define an aesthetic by issuing compilation records in the early 1990s. Rob Miller, one of the cofounders of Bloodshot, recalls the catalyzing effect the label's first compilation, *For a Life of Sin* (1994), had on the Chicago scene. While a number of local bands were combining rock, punk, and country in new ways, he asserts that putting the compilation together created a new synthesis rather than a reflection of an existing community. "Back then there was no scene to speak of. A lot of these bands didn't know about each other. Some would be playing at Phyllis', others Lounge Ax, others Schubas."[7] Kelly Kessler, a member of one of the bands that appeared on the compilation, agrees with Miller's analysis. "As far as I'm concerned, the only reason Chicago and country music are thought of together is because of Bloodshot," Kessler said at a 2002 Americana Music Association panel. "I was in a band [the Texas Rubies] that preceded Bloodshot and we had a good following and had a great time but it wasn't busting through until Bloodshot came along."[8] Once the CD came out, word-of-mouth connections between bands and fans "helped to delineate and define (if not exactly name) a burgeoning scene in Chicago."[9] As the label expanded its sales reach beyond consignment arrangements with local record stores, it also worked to map and codify a national retail network that could support alt.country releases. "I was in [the band] Moonshine Willy when this first record came out, we went on a tour and in every town I was like, where is the cool record store, let's see if they'll take some?," Miller recalled of the way the label pieced together its distribution list. "It was basically building a database from zero. We couldn't go online and search for 'cool record store.' It was all trench work."[10] The creation of Bloodshot helped to define the Chicago scene as a coherent whole and linked it, through touring and retail distribution, to scenes in other cities.

Thus, by 1995, when the creation of the Postcard2 mailing list marked the transformation of the largest online alt.country community from an Uncle Tupelo fan club into a genre-based audience forum, several independent labels were already bringing together a diverse group of musicians who, though all "doing this weird thing with country music," were linked most prominently by their status as label mates.[11] A similar definitional process was also under way in radio. Jon Grimson, who had worked as a publicist for Dwight Yoakum, Iris DeMent, and Uncle Tupelo at Warner Brothers Nashville, left the label in 1994 to start his own promotion company and began working with Rob Bleetstein, an editor at the radio trade publication the *Gavin Report,* to create an Americana radio chart. Just as Bloodshot had reshaped a group of disconnected audiences and artists into a cohesive local scene, the appearance of the Americana chart in January of 1995 lent the national alt.country scene a recognizable identity and a structural point of reference that both fans and the industry could organize around. It bears noting that the *Gavin* chart started well before Americana was firmly established as a genre. *No Depression* did not begin publication until September of 1995, and P2 had not yet been established. Still, thanks to the left-field success of grunge, which had also emerged from stations and labels unmonitored by the mainstream music industry, *Gavin* and other trend scouts for the industry were willing to invest in an emerging style that seemed to have the potential for a similar breakthrough. When *Gavin* announced that it would stop publishing the chart in October of 2000, its managers alluded to the fact that they had started the chart with the hope that it would help stimulate the consolidation of a new format. "It has been a gratifying five years of watching the format grow," the press release read, acknowledging that the commercial development they had hoped to encourage had not materialized. "But as yet, it has not made inroads significant enough to allow it to continue as part of *Gavin* in the present business climate."[12]

Gavin's concern over the economics of Americana broadcasting was well founded. By 1999, just before it was dropped, there were about a hundred stations reporting to the Americana chart, a healthy number in its own right but one that paled in comparison with the twenty-six hundred stations broadcasting mainstream country. The broadcasters who reported to the *Gavin* chart—like those who continued to report to a successor chart compiled by the Americana Music Association—were largely college, public, and other nonprofit stations. Nonetheless, during its five-year run, the chart essentially functioned as an alternative to a full-fledged radio format, drawing connections between disparate artists and sounds, stitching together a genre identity, and providing a cross-regional index of popularity and a contact list for local concert promoters, retailers, and labels looking to get exposure for their artists. For the coalescing Americana industry, the chart became "a graphical representation to point at when someone asked the dreaded question, 'What is Americana?' "[13] When *Gavin* announced that it would no longer publish the chart, bluegrass festival organizer Art Menius argued that it had been largely responsible for generating the energy that surrounded alt.country in the late 1990s. "Before the *Gavin* Americana chart started in 1995," he wrote to the P2 list, "alt-country releases were few and far between, and I don't think it's any accident that the mid-to-late 1990s explosion of alt-country releases coincided with the *Gavin* Americana chart."[14] Certainly online e-mail discussion, P2 spin-off concert series, "best of" album lists, and fan-organized festivals such as Twangfest served to help solidify the genre identity of alt.country, but these efforts were parallel rather than prior to mutually reinforcing trends within the recording and broadcast industries.

The timing of *Gavin*'s cancellation announcement was somewhat ironic, coming as it did just a month before the first full meeting of the Americana Music Association, an organization that arguably had its roots in the sobering aftermath of the industry frenzy created by the Americana chart. In keeping with a pattern of institutional growth rooted in the indie/alternative infrastructure, the group that would evolve into the AMA met first at South by Southwest (SXSW), the annual conference and bacchanal that brings together the indie and mainstream music industries for a week of talent scouting, mutual courtship, and deal making. In 1996, as the impact of the Americana chart began to be felt, the atmosphere around the conference's alt.country panel and showcases had been "electric." "The best part," reported Jim Caligiuri of the *Austin Chronicle,* was that

> everyone in the room seemed united in one cause—making sure this music actually broke through to the masses this time. Musicians, label heads, publicists, journalists—it was a gathering of the tribes. . . . It looked as if the day we'd all been waiting for had finally arrived. Twangcore/Americana/*No Depression*/insurgent country/roots-rock/y'alternative—whatever you wanted to call it—was, at last, *the next big thing.* The buzz was deafening.[15]

By 1999, however, the giddy aura that permeated the 1996 meeting had dissipated substantially. In spite of the industry's rush to embrace Americana, the genre remained without a breakthrough artist or album and, indeed, without any clear indication of its retail strength, audience size, or demographics. Attempts to bring such alt.country acts as Robbie Fulks through the major label pipeline that had broken grunge fell victim to the wave of corporate consolidation that swept through the industry during the 1990s. Several tentative efforts at establishing commercial Americana format stations in major markets had failed. (Even as late as 2004, an examination of the Americana Music Association's reporting stations turned up only four commercial stations that billed themselves as offering an Americana format.)

The "town meeting" of fifty or so Americana businesspeople that took place at the 1999 SXSW conference was thus an expression of a generally felt need to retrench and find a means of "coordinating, sharing, and developing resources to expand the audience for Americana music" as a business and artistic community independent of whatever whims or commercial imperatives might cause the spotlight of industry attention to settle momentarily on Americana. After a second meeting in October of 1999, the AMA's organizational structure was formalized and plans got under way for the first general membership meeting and conference to be held in Nashville in November of 2000. The core group of organizers that sustained the organization during its first year, not surprisingly, represented the institutional base that Americana had already developed: Jon Grimson, now president of Americana Entertainment; Grant Alden of *No Depression;* Jessie Scott, program director of XM Radio's alternative country station and former editor of the *Gavin* Americana chart; Marie Arsenault of Twangfest; record label representatives from Rounder, Sugar Hill, Dualtone, E-Squared, and others; and the most prominent e-tailer of Americana, Miles of Music.

The alt.country phenomenon had been driven both by the formation of an audience community and by the ability of its artists and entrepreneurs to inhabit institutional spaces opened by the success of alternative rock. But several trends within the mainstream country industry, and in broadcasting and popular music more generally, also encouraged the genre's growth. With the establishment of the Americana Music Association there arose a full articulation between the mainstream and alternative country businesses in which Americana was welcomed as a replacement for the mainstream industry's withered middle-market sector.

Joli Jensen has demonstrated that the country boom that began with the unprecedented success of Garth Brooks in the early 1990s was at first embraced as a sign of the genre's vigor and its fundamental appeal to a new audience demographic of middle-aged suburbanites alienated from hard rock and rap.[16] By the mid-1990s—not coincidentally the same moment when alternative country became salient to the business at large—the climate of opinion had shifted, and the boom was widely regarded, even within the industry, as undermining Nashville's ability to experiment with new (or old) sounds and as having decimated the business' "middle class."[17] The boom, however, might be interpreted not as a cause but as a symptom of a larger reorganization within the music and broadcasting businesses that has made it increasingly difficult for those in the music business to operate according to the old rules. Beginning in 1988, the mainstream recording industry underwent a remarkable consolidation. Large labels bought smaller labels, which were in turn bought by even larger multinational entertainment groups, often for sums that exceeded yearly earnings by multiples of ten or more, until, by 1999, just over 80 percent of the worldwide market in popular music was controlled by five companies: Sony Music, Universal Music Group, Warner Brothers, EMI, and BMG.[18]

Just as this reorganization of the recording industry was under way, the decision of the Federal Communications Commission (FCC) to remove federal limitations on the number of radio stations a single company could own prompted a similar consolidation in the radio industry. Broadcasting megaliths Clear Channel and Cumulus quickly emerged to control the majority of the major markets in the United States with tightly managed playlists of only a few dozen songs and a business strategy dictating that stations either turn a profit immediately and consistently or change their formulas.[19]

The combination of sales expectations raised by the success of artists such as Garth Brooks and Shania Twain, the dwindling number of labels, the rising rate of investment required to promote and distribute a small handful of superstars, and the increasingly limited range of playlists on most major-market radio stations had combined by the end of the 1990s to create a profound sense of unease about the foundations of the mainstream country business. Thus, for example, in 1999 the editor of one online industry magazine predicted that the multiplatinum sales of Faith Hill's album *Breathe* would perpetuate the panic to reach for even larger markets. "The sales bar has been raised again and the only way to meet the challenge is to turn in a more pop/rock direction. That's where the teen buyers are and they're the people who drive platinum sales."[20] Executives at Warner Brothers and its subsidiary Asylum agreed that the health of the genre depended on Nashville's ability to restore its middle market—artists whose albums sell by the hundreds of thousands rather than by the millions—but they also agreed that this would never be the aim of the major labels. "My charge is to play in the big leagues," the president of one Disney-owned label told an interviewer. "I don't want to be in the middle. I want to be No. 1."[21] However condescending her tone, when an Asylum executive told reporters in 2001 that "so much is falling through the cracks, and there is business out there for people who are content to pick up the crumbs," she was making an earnest argument in favor of a stronger base of independent labels.[22]

At the dawn of the new millennium, then, the Americana Music Association found space for more than just its offices in Nashville. Far from challenging the very foundation of mainstream country's commercialism, alternative country's politics of anticommercialism and its independent institutional base positioned it perfectly for a symbiotic relationship with the Nashville establishment. Americana, many in the mainstream industry believed, could become a way to reinvigorate the middle market, develop new audiences, and allow for modest investment in new artists and give them time to grow.

Buying In: Alt.Country's Politics of Commercialism

The parallels between the consolidation of the mainstream country industry in the 1940s and 1950s and the institutional development of alt.country are striking in a number of ways. Both were marginal musics fostered by alternative business structures: small start-up publishing houses and independent radio stations in the case of early mainstream country; independent record labels, college and community radio stations, and midsize live venues in the case of alt.country. Artists and entrepreneurs associated with both fledgling genres emerged from an initial industrywide frenzy of investment and attention to discover a larger crisis of sustainability related to the unsettling power and limitations of popularity charts and sales figures. Both groups faced a broadcasting atmosphere, created in the late 1950s by the development of Top 40 programming and in the late 1990s by corporate consolidation, in which fewer and fewer artists were able to reach the public. And both groups ultimately responded to these challenges in part through the development of a professional association devoted to promoting a cohesive genre identity, primarily within the music industry itself but also as a "brand" to audiences.[23] Perhaps the most interesting parallel, though, is the paradoxically similar way in which the business communities surrounding each genre mobilized discourses of commercialism as a way to establish an independent genre identity and, within that process, as a tool for staking out particular institutional spaces within the music business.

The linguistic struggles that accompanied the emergence of both mainstream and alternative country hint at the way institutional dynamics shaped the genre identities of each in its own historical moment. Like current reporting on the Americana trend, mainstream music trade coverage of country in the late 1940s and early 1950s evinced more confusion than clarity over just what was being described and what made it unique. *Billboard* wrangled for a decade with category names ranging from "Hillbilly and Foreign Record Hits," "Western and Race," and "Western, Race, Polkas," before settling on "Folk (Country and Western)" in 1949, a move that reflected the growing use of "country" as a catalog heading among labels and publishers.[24] Even with the emergence of *country* as the clear standard for naming the music, the word *folk* remained part of the *Billboard* definition of country music into the 1960s, and the Country Music Association continued to grapple with the idea of trying to rename the genre from the time the organization was founded in 1958 until well into the mid-1960s.

The experimental names originally used to try to give institutional meaning to the group of styles that became country music indicated on their very surface how country emerged as a genre. Before it could be imagined as a cohesive style in strictly musical terms, country was imagined first as music produced through particular, and peculiar, institutional channels. The white and black rural styles categorized as "Western and Race" and characterized as a single market by *Billboard* in the 1940s were linked more by business patterns than the logic of their audiences or artists. They were affiliated with the upstart publishing rights licensing organization BMI rather than with its mainstream pop predecessor ASCAP, and they had initially become commercially popular through live performance and independent radio stations such as WLS, WSM, and KWKH rather than through the payola-driven avenues of national network exposure cultivated by Tin Pan Alley's pop music industry.

As Richard Peterson and Bruce Beal have noted, a similar struggle over naming conventions has accompanied the development of alternative country, and this contest, too, has focused on the music's place in the system of production. The best unifying definition of alt.country is that it is (or at least appears to be) "not from Nashville."[25] It is recorded and pressed disproportionately by small, independent labels and midmarket major subsidiaries, and it has become commercially popular primarily through live performance and noncommercial radio stations rather than through the consultant- and focus-group-driven avenues of national network exposure cultivated by today's closest approximation of the 1940s Tin Pan Alley system, the Nashville system. As a name, then, alternative country can be read as a description of the stylistic blend of alternative rock and country music; as a reference to the genre's institutional roots in the independent labels, small-scale venues, and college radio stations that gave rise to alternative rock; and as a marker of the aesthetic and economic differences between alternative and mainstream country.

But the name that appears most likely to be adopted as the enduring genre title for alt.country and other rock-country hybrids is Americana, a label that evinces a different institutional story. First adopted to head the *Gavin* radio chart, the moniker was a conscious attempt to put as much distance as possible between the new genre and Music Row. Bloodshot's Rob Miller suggested that Americana "is geared toward breaking through that stench that hangs over the C-word. Country music has (stunk) for so long to rock-going audiences that it takes an umbrella term like Americana for people to put away their prejudices."[26] At the same time, though, the term carefully avoided a rupture with the country music establishment in Nashville. As Rob Bleetstein later told the online magazine *Puremusic,* "I originally wanted to call it the Crucial Country chart . . . but *Gavin* thought that too big a slight on mainstream Country."[27] Even the less confrontational term *alternative country* seemed "to annoy folks on Music Row," one journalist observed, though Bleetstein said he shied away from that name mainly because he thought "both words at the time just had been used and abused."[28] When Jon Grimson suggested *Americana,* Bleetstein said, "that one stuck with me after I thought about what it meant musically, which was really nothing, so it was our chance to define it as something."[29] Thus, the Americana tag allowed a fledgling genre to declare its independence from the country business, both within the industry and for its audience, but at the same time to avoid even the insinuation of a turf war for the soul of country music. The Americana label made it clear that there would be no barricades and torches along Music Row and that this music would forever remain an alternative to the unnamed hegemony of mainstream country music.

The struggles to name both mainstream and alternative country thus revealed as much about the structure of the music industry at their respective moments as about the genres' aesthetics or audience. Similarly, while country and alt.country appear to be at opposite poles of the discourse of commercialism, both have been defined, aesthetically and institutionally, by their mobilization of that discourse. Even before mainstream country figured as a single genre, folklorists and preservationists distinguished the traditional rural string band and ballad music that would become country from what they viewed as authentic folk music less by reference to musical characteristics than by reference to its commercial modes of production. During the 1960s, Nashville inverted the cultural valence of its commercialism. The entrepreneurs who guided the industry increasingly deployed narratives of commercialism as a way to present the economic success of the denigrated audience of southern white migrants they viewed as their core market; as a way to represent a progressive narrative of southern culture and history; and as a way to establish Music Row's independence during what was, at that time, an unprecedented period of consolidation within the music industry. By embracing commercialism not only as a business strategy but also as a symbolic narrative about audience identity, the emergent country music industry attracted sufficient investment in recording and distribution and developed a level of radio advertising that allowed it to remain largely independent of the bicoastal pop and rock empire.[30]

That alt.country's discourse of commercialism comes from an oppositional stance makes it no less central to the genre's identity. The anticommercialism of alt.country, like the commercialism of mainstream country, allows those who champion the genre to identify an independent space in the music industry in very specific structural terms. By asserting that Americana is roots music, that it is not commercial enough to be played on mainstream radio, the Americana Music Association and its members lay claim to the increasingly influential domain of Internet, public, community, and college radio as their territory. By embracing an aesthetic stance, and, more important, a business plan, that criticizes mass culture and assumes sales in the tens of thousands rather than the hundreds of thousands or the millions, the record labels that sign alt.country bands bring attention to and exploit the economic weaknesses of the major labels.

Although they are wary of the excesses of commercialism, Americana's artists and businessmen do not pretend to be noncommercial or unconcerned with record sales. On the contrary, while encouraging its fans to understand and reject the inner workings of a mainstream music business it sees as being driven exclusively by profits—a discourse that parallels almost exactly the narratives offered by early country music fanzines—the Americana industry also presents its ability to sell solidly at a midmarket level as an important validation of its aesthetic worth. After all, three hundred thousand Ryan Adams fans can't all be wrong. Those fans represent the strength of the Americana insurgency and, paradoxically, provide proof of the corrupt commercialism of Nashville mainly through the phenomenon of Adams' own modest commercial success. "We're trying to maintain something we all think is commercial yet maintain integrity," Jon Grimson has said. "Americana is hip and cool and cutting edge, but it can be a well-functioning business and creatively credible at the same time."[31]

Spokespeople for the business endlessly quote sales figures, real and projected, to anyone who will listen, almost always emphasizing the more modest sales expectations that characterize the Americana industry in comparison to the mainstream country business. Sales figures can be used to criticize Nashville's exclusive focus on superstars and megahits and to demonstrate that Americana is more country than country, as when former *Gavin* Americana editor Jessie Scott remarked that Americana artists in the late 1990s were "selling at the same rate that country used to (before Garth Brooks and the other multiplatinum artists of the early 1990s)." Or they can be used as a way to promote the genre's middle-market potential, as when *No Depression*'s Grant Alden told a reporter, "Many of these records only sell between 5,000 and 30,000 records. I think those numbers could be doubled. I think the midlevel artists could go from 60,000 to 100,000. And a Steve Earle or John Prine could go from 100,000 to 250,000, or even go gold with a strong release." More often than not, though, such figure quoting emphasizes the fact that lower sales expectations allow labels and artists to experiment more freely in the creative process, as when Luke Lewis, the founder of Lost Highway Records, explained how reduced expectations could be a formula for success: "If we do a business plan and we don't say, 'Lucinda's [Williams] record, instead of doing gold, is gonna do platinum, and Ryan [Adams], instead of being 125K is gonna be half a million'—if we don't go there, and just try to make it work with the current base on paper, what do we have to lose?" (Ironically, Lost Highway is the only label to produce a blockbuster Americana record, the soundtrack to *O Brother, Where Art Thou?*)[32]

The obsession with sales figures is unsurprising in the trade press, where the genre's viability depends to a degree on promoting its profit potential even at a midmarket level, but the fixation is equally apparent in interviews given to the popular press, where one must assume that it forms part of the general effort to define the genre's aesthetic and social meaning. Indeed, spokespeople for the Americana business community deliberately focus popular attention on the specific ways in which they market their music and on how these channels differ from the routine avenues of exposure used by the mainstream country industry. Artists and businesspeople alike portray the AMA's marketing efforts as a way to make it easier for audiences to find the music they like, a way to subvert a broken industrial system that no longer responds to its own audience. In this interpretation, promoters of Americana have developed ingenious commercial alternatives to the mainstream radio exposure formula—from Americana endcaps at Wherehouse outlets to cross-marketing deals with Borders, "smart package tours" and festivals, and e-tail "virtual" genre labeling through the use of onscreen suggestions—in order to get good music past the conservative gatekeepers of the record and broadcasting industries, whose exclusive focus on the bottom line otherwise makes it impossible for fans to locate the music they want to hear.[33]

Thus, for example, an artist such as Allison Moorer has no compunction about telling a reporter, "The formation of the association [AMA], as I saw it when I got involved, was to help 'brand,' for lack of a better term, the music that this group of people wanted to promote."[34] The AMA's executive director, J. D. May, is equally frank about the fact that Americana is nothing but a marketing category, but his candor clearly implies that there's nothing inherently wrong with that. "This music has been around for 40 or 50 years," he told a reporter at the AMA's annual conference in Nashville. "It's just now being called something for the purpose of growing and marketing the format."[35]

The commercial discourse of the Americana industry accepts the notion that marketing can be a creative effort to unite audiences and music and valorizes the business of bringing "noncommercial" music to a wider public. This message is underscored by the image of Americana artists and businesspeople as living on the margins of the music industry. By emphasizing the modest expectations of those who stand to benefit from the business, popular accounts of the Americana industry simultaneously defend commercialism focused on "making a living, not a killing" and reiterate the difference between the specific form commercialism takes in the alt.country business as opposed to the mainstream.[36] The comment of Elisa Sanders, former manager of Steve Earle's ill-fated E-Squared label, that "staying in the game and being able to work with music that you love is enough" evokes a form of music capitalism with a human face. Neko Case, one of Bloodshot's most successful artists, echoes the sentiment: "I don't need to be a big star. I just want to make ends meet." And Dave Alvin, whose roles in the Blasters and the Knitters place him among the first generation of alt.country artists, also portrays himself as part of the music world's working class: "You don't get limos and Lear jets, but you can have a long career. That's not a bad trade-off."[37]

In fact, the willingness of artists and entrepreneurs to operate at this level, to participate in a business that admittedly will never reach a truly mass market, becomes a new claim to authenticity rooted in business practices rather than any kind of unifying social experience. Here again, alt.country's discourse of commercialism resembles that of Music Row's early denizens. Although the authenticity of country's early performers and entrepreneurs was frequently measured by the extent to which their personal biographies connected to a symbolically freighted rural past, during the 1950s and 1960s, discourses of authenticity shifted to emphasize the unique culture of the Nashville recording studio. The head arrangements, improvisational style, absence of formal musical training, and down-home mystique that dominated the Nashville session community were widely touted as delivering a sound that could not be replicated in the recording studios of New York or Los Angeles.[38] The shapers of alt.country's business and aesthetic world similarly substitute a specific relationship with commercialism for a specific set of social relations in its efforts to construct a notional community. In an age when country music has become thoroughly unmoored from the social experience of the generations of working-class, rural-to-urban migrants who initially composed its most influential audience, the artists and entrepreneurs who stake their claim to the middle market have voluntarily joined the postindustrial working class.

Like those in the alt.country business, many in the alt.country audience are deeply invested both in the discourses of modest commercialism associated with the genre and in the quotidian commercial activity that makes up the industry. And just as the industry's evocation of commercialism parallels that of the early mainstream country business, so alt.fan commercial engagements are strikingly similar to those of early mainstream country fans. Richard Peterson and Bruce Beal have suggested that the emergence of alt.country as a genre has been driven by a new, consumption-based aesthetic supported by the Internet and MP3 technology. According to these authors, the audience, no longer subject to the genre coding enacted by radio, television, and music industry marketing practices, is free to create its own definitions through grassroots criticism, distribution, and promotion.[39] This analysis, however, underestimates the role fans played in the constitution of mainstream country music in the decades before it achieved full articulation with the pop industry. With the exception of its gender composition, the Internet-based community that provided part of the organizational impulse for alt.country as a genre bears a striking resemblance to the very active fan base that sustained mainstream country music during the 1950s and early 1960s. Both regarded their activities as functional alternatives to a mainstream commercial music business that was unwilling to serve their needs and engaged in activities from personal correspondence to concert promotion, publicity, and music distribution. Both, in short, built "a self-conscious community of like-minded people willing to work for the betterment of 'their' music."[40]

One has only to look at the pages of commercially produced fan magazines from the 1950s and 1960s to begin to understand the importance of direct communication among fans in defining the early culture of mainstream country music. Fanzines such as *Country and Western Jamboree, Country Song Round Up,* and later *Music City News* offered regular space for fan club announcements, printed registries of clubs, and encouraged fans to write to each other as pen pals. But, like the Internet-based fan communities that Peterson and Beal identify, early country fan clubs created their own networks and their own avenues of communication outside the industrial system. In fact, commercial fanzines remained secondary in many ways to the fan-produced journals distributed by the clubs themselves. When a new commercial fan magazine such as *Music City News* appeared, editors appealed to fan club presidents to mention the new publication in the next issue of their journals, tapping into existing social networks for exposure.[41]

For the most part, club presidents saw themselves as promoting not just their honored artists but country music as a genre, and they consciously viewed this activity as a response to a popular music industry that did not fit their needs because of its pursuit of profits and its cultural snobbery. The power of the "longhair" cultural elite that valued only pop and semiclassical music, and later of the station managers who capitulated to the tyranny of rock and roll, could only be defeated by vigorous consumer activism on behalf of country music. Whether or not their estimation of their ability to affect the workings of the popular music business strikes the present-day reader as naive, these fans envisioned themselves as active participants in the country music business and as helping to provide an organizational structure that would make the genre viable. Like alt.country fans in the 1990s, they created their own alternatives to the limited offerings available through the mass media.

The discourse of commercialism in the alt.country fan community differs from that of the country music fan clubs of the 1950s and 1960s in significant ways, however. The two groups are nearly diametrically opposed in their understandings of the cultural meaning of commercial success. Early country fan club activists adopted a view of the market as a democratic and effective means of assigning cultural worth. As they struggled against the cultural elite they imagined to be ensconced in the music industry, they consistently argued that country's growing economic clout was proof of its artistic value, a validation both of their "low" tastes as an audience and of their social respectability as individuals.[42] Mass popularity signaled for many in country's audience their own ascent to the middle class; the failure to achieve a similar level of popularity seems, among alt.country fans, to be a conservative claim on middle-class cultural status. The more traditional logic of taste distinctions applied by alt.country aficionados takes the music's limited (though not entirely absent) commercial appeal as a sign of its artistic value and their own familiarity with it as a form of hip capital that confirms their position of cultural and social authority.

Paradoxically, though, the alt.country audience's ability to pass more easily through the permeable border between consumers and producers also gives it a far higher stake in the genre's commercial apparatus than that felt by mainstream country's early fans. Few fan club activists of the 1960s were able to transform themselves successfully from fans into professionals in part because the music industry was defined as masculine corporate territory in which the women of the fan club world were merely interloping housewives.[43] (The most notable exceptions to this rule were Loretta Lynn's fan club organizers, the Johnson sisters, who played a pivotal role in organizing Fan Fair and who continue to sponsor a fan club monitoring organization and information clearinghouse, the International Fan Club Organization.) By contrast, a number of alt.country fans have profitably parlayed their cultural capital into financial capital. Bloodshot records, for instance, was founded by three aficionados who hoped mainly to enrich their local scene without any serious intention of turning the label into a formal business. *No Depression* magazine grew out of the AOL discussion folder of the same name, although Grant Alden and Peter Blackstock seem to have taken a more pragmatic approach to the market potential of their venture, having assessed electronica and alternative country as the two most likely candidates for "Next Big Thing" status and noted that a number of electronica magazines were already being published.[44] Participants on the P2 list have been responsible for organizing concert series and initiating one of the most prominent Americana festivals, Twangfest, and the 501 (c) (3) nonprofit organization that presents it. Marie Arsenault credits her involvement with P2 and Twangfest as having given her "the confidence to start a new professional career [in Americana booking and management]," experience she could not have gained anywhere else.[45] Ironically, in an age of overwhelmingly consolidated media power, the barriers to entry into the nonperforming side of the music business, whether in label management, the critical press, or concert promotion, may be lower than they have ever been, further obscuring the already blurry line between audiences and producers.

Bill Ivey, who was then the director of the Country Music Foundation, once proposed as a definition of *country music* "any record that a station that calls itself 'country' will play and any record that a consumer who considers himself a 'country fan' will buy."[46] This institutional principle offers commercial structures as the very definition of a musical genre not by virtue of the ideological discourse those structures can command but simply by virtue of their material logic. This cultural logic of commercialism seems to attach to alt.country as much as to more overtly commercial genres and perhaps more so. The timing of its emergence as a sustainable and recognizable genre indicates that alt.country fulfills the institutional needs of the industry as much as the desires of a new audience—that it is as much a marketing category as a cultural movement. Its artists and entrepreneurs explicitly define themselves through their relationship with commercialism, and its fans are, in general, more positively invested in the genre's commercial structure than early fans of mainstream country appear to have been (although this may be a difference of opportunity rather than philosophy). In the alt.country mythos of both industry and audience, shared social identities have been supplanted by shared commitments to specific commercial systems.

But if alt.country fails to deliver on its promise to evade the defining cultural logic of commercialism, its embrace of a commercial discourse that values success only in moderation and imagines a commercial structure that muddles the roles of producers and consumers at least reminds us of the variety of oppositional meanings and desires that commercialism can entertain. Alt.country's cultural politics of commercialism suggest that audiences, artists, and businesspeople are moving beyond the notion that there must be a fundamental antagonism between viewing the culture industries as "commercial enterprises designed to deliver cultural products to markets that they themselves construct and define" and imagining them as "ways to locate and respond to . . . diverse and evolving audience tastes and desires."[47] Both dynamics have clearly played an important role in defining alt.country, and both have been incorporated into the story the Americana business tells about itself.

NOTES

1. Rob Miller quoted in M. S. Dodds, "Insurgency Plan," *Illinois Entertainer* 30, no. 7 (May 2004): 22.

2. David Goodman, *Modern Twang: An Alternative Country Music Guide and Directory* (Nashville: Dowling, 1999); Richard Peterson and Bruce Beal, "Alternative Country: Origins, Music, Worldview, Fans, and Taste in Genre Formation—A Discographic Essay," *Popular Music and Society* 25, nos. 1–2 (2001): 233–49; Peter Doggett, *Are You Ready for the Country: Elvis, Dylan, Parsons and the Roots of Country Rock* (New York: Penguin, 2000).

3. My interchangeable use of the terms *alt.country* and *Americana* may raise hackles among fans and scholars who would argue, probably rightly so, that Americana is a broader category—including "the sorts of soft country that is such an anathema to alternative country aficionados"—into which alt.country falls. See Peterson and Beal, "Alternative Country," 238. The story of alt.country genre formation, however, is difficult to tell after 2003 without assimilating it into Americana. This is true in part because, for all of the attention it garnered in the late 1990s, alt.country never fulfilled the "next big thing" expectations of many observers except within the context of the Americana movement. Perhaps more important, whatever name they may use in promoting their own music or writing, the artists, labels, and critical press organs that originally helped to codify the emergence of alt.country subsequently became heavily involved in the constellation of social and business relationships that constitutes Americana's "art world." Jon Grimson (originally Uncle Tupelo's publicist at Warner and later president of Americana Music), Grant Alden of *No Depression,* Marie Arsenault of Twangfest, and Art Menius of Merlefest are just a few of the entrepreneurs who helped to define the alt.country aesthetic and later formed the industry network that initially underpinned the Americana Music Association.

4. Doggett, *Are You Ready for the Country,* 438–49, 491–501.

5. Goodman, *Modern Twang,* iv.

6. Peterson and Beal, "Alternative Country," 244.

7. Dave Chamberlain, "So, You Wanna Start a Record Label?" *Newcity Chicago,* April 11, 2002, http://www.newcitychicago.com/chicago/1620.html (accessed September 16, 2005).

8. Dave Hoekstra, "Chicago: America's Music City That Works," press page, The Hideout, http://www.hideoutchicago.com/press/musicCityThatWorks.html (accessed February 4, 2004).

9. Dodds, "Insurgency Plan," 22.

10. Chamberlain, "So, You Wanna Start a Record Label?"

11. Ibid.

12. Jessie Scott, press release, "Death of *Gavin* Americana Charts," archived at http://web.archive.org/web/20040610122628/www.insurgentcountry.com/home.htm (accessed July 3, 2007).

13. Jim Caligiuri, "Where Idealism Is Still Alive: The First Annual Americana Music Association Meeting," *Austin Chronicle,* November 24, 2000, http://www.austinchronicle.com/issues/vol16/issue17/music.altcountry.html (accessed July 3, 2007).

14. Art Menius, "The Death of Americana," e-mail message posted to Postcard2, October 13, 2000.

15. Jim Caligiuri, "The Americana Chart, Alternative Country, and Austin: The Great Roots-Rock Scare of '96." *Austin Chronicle,* December 27, 1996, http://www.austinchronicle.com/issues/vol16/issue17/music.altcountry.html (accessed September 16, 2005).

16. Joli Jensen, "Taking Country Music Seriously: Coverage of the 1990s Boom," in *Pop Music and the Press,* ed. Steve Jones, 183–201 (Philadelphia: Temple University Press, 2002).

17. Richard Lawson, "The Great Divide: Nashville Music Industry Separating into the Rich and Poor," *Nashville Tennessean,* February 13, 2000, 1E.

18. Reebee Garofalo, *Rockin' Out: Popular Music in the U.S.A.,* 2nd ed. (Upper Saddle River, NJ: Prentice Hall, 2002), 455–56; Keith Negus, *Music Genres and Corporate Cultures* (New York: Routledge, 1999), 35–45.

19. Lawson, "The Great Divide"; Eric Boehlert, "Radio's Big Bully: A Complete Guide to Salon's Reporting on Clear Channel," *Salon.com,* http://www.salon.com/ent/clear_channel/index.html (accessed July 3, 2007).

20. Quoted in Ted Olson, "Country Music at the Millennium: Three Recent Studies of a Remarkably Resilient Musical Genre," *American Music* 18, no. 2 (summer 2000): 222.

21. Lawson, "The Great Divide."

22. Deborah Evans Price and Phyllis Stark, "Country Music Leaders Predict Trends for the New Year," *Billboard,* January 13, 2001, 35, 37.

23. Richard A. Peterson, *Creating Country Music: Fabricating Authenticity* (Chicago: University of Chicago Press, 1997); Joli Jensen, *The Nashville Sound: Authenticity, Commercialization, and the Nashville Sound* (Nashville: Country Music Foundation and Vanderbilt University Press, 1998); Diane Pecknold, *The Selling Sound: The Rise of the Country Music Industry* (Durham: Duke University Press, 2007).

24. David Brackett, *Interpreting Popular Music* (New York: Cambridge University Press, 1995), 103–5; Ronnie Pugh, "Country Music Is Here to Stay?" *Journal of Country Music* 19, no. 1 (1997): 32–38.

25. Peterson and Beal, "Alternative Country," 233–35.

26. Ben Wener, "Americana, What Art Thou?" *Orange County Register*, July 29, 2001, http://www.ocregister.com/ocregister/archives (accessed December 28, 2007).

27. *Puremusic*, "Americana Conference 2001," http://www.puremusic.com/am2.html (accessed February 4, 2004).

28. Caligiuri, "Where Idealism Is Still Alive"; *Puremusic*, "Americana Conference, 2001."

29. *Puremusic*, "Americana Conference, 2001."

30. Pecknold, *The Selling Sound.*

31. Jeanne A. Naujeck, "Nashville Is at the Root of Americana's Growth," *Nashville Tennessean*, September 19, 2003, E1.

32. Craig Havighurst, "Carrying the Torch for Twang," *Nashville Tennessean*, November 16, 2000, 1E; Jim Farber, "A Fresh Country Fusion, Americana, Has Legs," *San Diego Union-Tribune*, April 15, 2001, F7; Tom Kielty, "Lost Highway Hopes Independence Is Route to Success," *Boston Globe*, July 7, 2001, http://www.boston.com/dailyglobe2/188/living/Lost_Highway_hopes_indepedence_is_route_to_success+.shtml (accessed Aug. 13, 2003).

33. Wes Orshoski, "Labels Strive to Make Most of Americana Tag," *Billboard*, June 30, 2001, 1.

34. Bob Townsend, "Americana Rising: Rock-Country beyond Its Roots," *Atlanta Journal-Constitution*, November 2, 2003, M1.

35. Naujeck, "Nashville Is at the Root of Americana's Growth."

36. Phil Gallo, "Music Biz Mows the Grassroots," *Variety*, February 16–22, 1998, 1.

37. Wener, "Americana, What Art Thou?"

38. Jensen, *The Nashville Sound*, 81–88.

39. Peterson and Beal, "Alternative Country," 243–44.

40. Ibid., 244.

41. Pecknold, *The Selling Sound*, 124–32.

42. Ibid., 120–24, 175–76.

43. In this regard, too, the gender dynamics of alt.country culture are suspiciously similar to early mainstream and arguably more conservative and exclusionary than contemporary country. See Barbara Ching, "Going Back to the Old Mainstream: *No*

Depression, Robbie Fulks, and Alt.Country's Muddied Waters," in *A Boy Named Sue: Gender and Country Music,* ed. Kristine M. McCusker and Diane Pecknold, 178–95 (Jackson: University Press of Mississippi, 2004).

44. Richard A. Martin, "King of the Road," *Seattle Weekly,* September 2, 1999, 59.

45. Jayne Cravens, "Connecting Humans: Twang in Cyberspace: How One Music-Related Online Community Blurs the Line between 'Real' and 'Virtual'" (2000), http://www.coyotecommunications.com/culture/twang.html (accessed January 3, 2008).

46. Bill Ivey, "The Bottom Line: Business Practices That Shaped Country Music," in *Country: The Music and the Musicians,* ed. Paul Kingsbury and Alan Axelrod (New York: Abbeville, 1988), 407.

47. Jensen, "Taking Country Music Seriously," 201.

JON SMITH

Growing Up and Out of Alt.Country: On Gen X, Wearing Vintage, and Neko Case

> In our final year of high school, my best friend, Lan Ying, and I passed the time with morbid discussions about the meaninglessness of life when everything had already been done. The world stretched out before us not as a slate of possibility, but as a maze of well-worn grooves like the ridges burrowed by insects in hardwood. Step off the straight and narrow career-and-materialism groove and you just ended up in another one—the groove for people who step off the main groove. And that groove was worn indeed (some of the grooving done by our own parents). Want to go traveling? Be a modern-day Kerouac? Hop on the Let's Go Europe groove. How about a rebel? An avant-garde artist? Go buy your alterna-groove at the secondhand bookstore, dusty and moth-eaten and done to death. . . . To us it seemed as though the archetypes were all hackneyed by the time our turn came to graduate, including that of the black-clad deflated intellectual, which we were trying on at that very moment. Crowded by the ideas and styles of the past, we felt there was no open space anywhere.
>
> —NAOMI KLEIN, "ALT.EVERYTHING" (2000)

> Can't seem to fathom the dark of my history,
> I invented my own in Tacoma.
>
> —NEKO CASE, "THRICE ALL-AMERICAN" (2000)

People who aren't of Naomi Klein's generation and class may feel little sympathy or even patience toward the bourgeois anomie she chronicles at the opening of "Alt.everything," the third chapter of her popular book *No Logo*. "After college, should I travel in Europe? But it's *so* been *done!*" Particularly troubling, perhaps, are the elevation of styles to the level of ideas (or the reduction of ideas to the level of styles) and the apparent absence in these girls of any idea that a good, worthwhile, happy, ethical life might be lived regardless of its stylistic novelty. The idea that becoming a teacher has been "done to death" or that being an intellectual bears some necessary connection to wearing black will strike many older or younger and/or less privileged readers as false, beside the point, and shallow. It might seem thus even to the figurative older siblings of Klein and Ying, the hundreds of my own college classmates from the 1980s who dove headfirst into investment banking.

It is no accident, however, that "false, beside the point, and shallow" is also how alt.country fans and performers, heavily Generation X, have sometimes appeared to fans and performers of more traditional country music. As Johnny Cash put it:

> [W]hen music people today, performers and fans alike, talk about being "country," they don't mean they know or even care about the land and the life it sustains and regulates. They're talking more about choices—a way to look, a group to belong to, a kind of music to call their own. Which begs a question: Is there anything behind the symbols of modern "country," or are the symbols themselves the whole story? Are the hats, the boots, the pickup trucks, and the honky-tonking poses all that's left of a disintegrating culture? Back in Arkansas, a way of life produced a certain kind of music. Does a certain kind of music now produce a way of life?[1]

As he worried about the apparent devolution of country into a vacuous kind of stylistic commodity consumption, Cash was, in fact, talking about "the 'country' music establishment," but his musings, redolent of class—"I wonder how many of those people ever filled a cotton sack"—apply at least as well to the alt.country music establishment—and, I think, to the bourgeois ennui of Naomi Klein.[2] What Klein's adolescent dilemma has to do with branding, the subject of her book, might seem obscure, but the connection may undergird a large portion of the appeal of alt.country. Two pages later, Klein explains, "my frustrated craving for space wasn't simply a result of the inevitable march of history, but of the fact that commercial co-optation was proceeding at a speed that would have been unimaginable to previous generations."[3] She goes on to argue that earlier "scenes were only half-heartedly sought after as markets. In part this was because seventies punk was at its peak at the same time as the infinitely more mass-marketable disco and heavy metal, and the gold mine of high-end preppy style."[4] However, Klein and Ying's anomie may have resulted from the fact not so much that various alt.identities had already been branded as that the pervasive cultural logic of branding had led Klein and Ying by their teens to confuse, as it were, hats and boots with the land and the life it sustains and regulates. Ironically, punk itself may also have contributed, both as a style politics with a depressingly minimal real-world political effect and as the nevertheless dominant bourgeois post- (and anti-) hippie mode of "rebellion."

Like most of the others in this volume, however, the present essay does not attempt to distinguish, yet again, between "authentic" country and "inauthentic" alt.country—or vice versa. Indeed, Cash himself seems to signal that by the 1990s neither was "authentic" in the traditional sense—a sense somewhat to the effect of "validated by its association with the performance of extremely difficult physical, chiefly agricultural, labor." Cotton sacks get filled by machines these days, and across the South (as has long been the case around the Bakersfield of Merle Haggard and Buck Owens) the most difficult, most unpleasant, lowest-paying work, especially in agriculture (e.g., peach picking in Alabama, tobacco picking in North Carolina, chicken processing in Arkansas), is performed overwhelmingly by migrant Hispanic laborers—not exactly an image lionized on Country Music Television (CMT) or in the pages of *No Depression,* although it should be.[5]

Instead, this essay attempts to unpack the (implicitly white) generational rhetoric and structures of feeling that underlie the authentic/inauthentic, deep/shallow distinction. This rhetoric, I believe, draws on two questionable temporal conceits. The first, which has recently been exploded by new southern studies work such as Leigh Anne Duck's *The Nation's Region,* concerns the relationship between the nation and "the South." It partakes, that is, in what Duck calls "the paradoxically frenetic production of southern backwardness . . . placed in dialogue with equally assertive accounts of national progressiveness."[6] By associating the South with the authentic, cotton-pickin' past and "the nation" (including Canada as the ultimate progressive "North" and the source of much alt.country) with youth culture and the future, country/alt.country rhetoric tends to lend country music an aura of maturity it does not especially deserve while simultaneously both valorizing and infantilizing alt.country in terms necessarily similar to those used, as we shall see, to valorize and infantilize Generation X. Such valorization and infantilization represent the second temporal conceit, for the oldest Xers are in their forties now. Yet, while scholarship on "the South" is finally growing up, scholarship not only on what anthropologist Sherry Ortner has called "the public culture on Generation X" but also on alt.country as well may, in contrast, still be treating their subjects as a contemporary "youth culture." In any event, as Ortner herself first noted, we would continue to do well to ask whose interests have been served—whose guilt assuaged, whose narcissisms fueled—by the discourses that have circulated about Xers, and about alt.country, in North American public culture for nearly two decades.[7]

To understand alt.country, that is, it helps to understand the peculiar myths circulating around the generation that more than any other has produced it. That means not only acknowledging Ortner's argument that Generation X is a cultural construct addressing complex cultural needs (particularly the needs of older demographic groups) but also complicating her primarily monocausal explanation of those needs, that is, her reliance on increasing income inequality, which she figures as an "abyss" opening in the middle class. Particular additional or alternative factors to consider include (a) the fact that the cultural logic of branding that Klein so rightly notes became omnipresent in the 1990s and (b) the fact that the legacy of punk, in which so many of alt.country's major figures—Ryan Adams, Neko Case, Alejandro Escovedo, Jay Farrar, Jeff Tweedy, and so many others, most of them Generation Xers—began their musical careers. (Although Douglas Coupland claims that the link is coincidental, even the term *Generation X*, popularized by Coupland's 1991 novel of the same name, appeared first in punk as the name of Billy Idol's old band.) Identity for both punks and Generation Xers has tended to be highly oppositional, a matter in both overlapping cases of "distinction" (in sociologist Pierre Bourdieu's sense) chiefly from baby boomers, their music, and what is perceived as their culture of narcissism (in Christopher Lasch's famous phrase). When Generation X hipsters "discovered" country music in the late 1980s and early 1990s, they thought they had found an ally, an entire genre that loathed hippies-cum-yuppies as much as punks did. But the situation was more complicated than that and not simply because in Muskogee folks still don't take ecstasy or sport fauxhawks. Barbara Ching has compellingly argued that much traditional country music—by emphasizing countriness as a choice rather than some naive lack of "cultural capital"—resists middle-class and college-educated people's attempt to distinguish themselves from the masses by the sorts of things one learns in college.[8] By using country music as a way to distinguish themselves from the boomers, however, postpunk bourgeois alt.country fans and performers actually reintroduced this kind of distinction into the equation. In short, they made country into a form of what Sarah Thornton calls "subcultural capital," a marker chiefly of their own hipness and putative authenticity.[9] More than a few of the tensions between traditional and alternative country can thus be traced to the differing ends to which country style was deployed and performed in each. As Generation X ages out of being a youth market, however, alt.country fandom and performance are no longer markers of hipness. At the turn of the century, Trent Hill, writing within the dominant terms of cultural studies, was precisely right to ask, "Why isn't country music youth culture?"[10] But today there is no obvious wave of twenty-somethings swelling up to replace the Ryan Adamses and Gillian Welches who at the end of the last century defined alt.country cool. (Even Conor Oberst, for example, who was born in 1980 and so is technically still an Xer, is not so easily classifiable. Bright Eyes' MySpace page just calls the music "indie"; many of my students just call him "emo.") Because Neko Case not only was one of the most talented performers in that bygone hip country music youth culture but also continues, as it were, to grow up in public, a consideration of her career might offer a useful entrée into the Gen X–style politics of alternative country even as Gen Xers grow out of needing either.

Generation X

Now a lamentable cliché, even in its 1990s prime the term *Generation X* seems to have appealed most to people who are drawn to oversimplified generalizations: Search Amazon.com or Barnesandnoble.com for books with the phrase in the title and the overwhelming majority concern how to evangelize the demographic.[11] The second-largest category comprises books about how to manage them; next come books about how to market to them. (Tellingly, many from the 1990s are already out of print.) Famously hostile to evangelists, managers, and especially marketers (hence the need for all the books), Gen Xers themselves unsurprisingly seem rarely to embrace the appellation. As Coupland put it in *Wired* as late as 1997, "Regarding Generation X, well, the whole point is that there never was or will be a definition. . . . Nothing could be less X than wearing a T-shirt saying 'Generation X'."[12] Appropriately enough, then, six chapters in Stephen Craig and Stephen Earl Bennett's 1997 collection *After the Boom: The Politics of Generation X* define the group five different ways: those born from 1965 on (two chapters) or 1961, 1963, 1964, or 1972 (one chapter each).[13]

It was Ortner, however, who in 1998 offered the most provocative definition of Generation X. Referencing Althusser and writing self-consciously from the subject position of Generation X's parents—her initial ethnographic sample was her own 1958 high school graduating class—she concluded that

> the idea of Generation X tells us as much about the anxieties of upper-middle-class parents as it does about some set of young people out there in the world. Indeed, we may think of the public culture on Generation X in part as the product of a cultural scouting expedition on behalf of these people, a trip to what to them is the edge of social space, and a set of postcards from that edge.[14]

If this seemingly somewhat narcissistic interpretation held true, however, we might expect Generation X rhetoric to continue, for the edge of social space—what Ortner calls the "abyss" of income inequality—has only grown in the decade since she first published her article. Instead, our business-oriented public culture has moved on quickly (and with seeming indifference to the parental concerns of Ortner's cohort) to discussions of the *next* next big thing: the subsequent (and much larger) "Generation Y," or the "Millennial Generation," whose members are figured as optimistic, can-do, even heroic congeries of tech-savvy multicultural multitaskers with no time for whining—a near-perfect set of incoming capitalist employees, although as consumers they, too, apparently leave some things to be desired. (Among other things, they do too much free downloading and fail to watch enough television.) Given this pressure from below, Generation X's time in the sun may have been pretty well restricted to the decade or so in which, while fewer in number than the baby boomers or the Millennials, they nevertheless benefited from being North America's youth market—and, as such, trendsetters despite themselves. This period might also be measured as stretching from 1991, when Coupland's novel *Generation X* made being a Gen X hipster cool; to around 2002, when LCD Soundsystem's single "Losing My Edge" suggested a redirection of Gen X energies from looking angrily back at boomers to looking nervously forward at Millennials; or to 2003, when Robert Lanham's *The Hipster Handbook,* following on the heels of Aimee Plumley's Web site hipstersareannoying.com, mocked hipsters' consumption patterns as just as shallowly conformist as everybody else's. In alt.country terms, the period might be measured from 1990, the year Uncle Tupelo's *No Depression,* which shares several themes with Coupland's novel, appeared, to around 2006, when the Jayhawks broke up and Jesse Fox Mayshark, drawing on a fairly wide range of other evidence (including the fanzine *No Depression*'s dropping the term from its tagline), eulogized "the twang that was alt-country" in the *New York Times.*[15] When Ortner's article reappeared, essentially unrevised, as a chapter of her 2006 book *Anthropology and Social Theory,* she wisely conceded in an endnote that "there is some question as to whether the idea of Gen X is still alive."[16] Not coincidentally, that year the same could have been said—and was—for the idea of alt.country.

Perhaps the single biggest theme running from Coupland through Klein to Lanham and energizing a generational identity politics or sense of "distinction" is a feeling of betrayal and nihilism once pithily expressed by the Sex Pistols: "No future." Coupland's book appeared early enough that one reason for such an attitude in the novel remains a fear of nuclear Armageddon, but the bigger reason is a generational rage at the boomers for having used everything up. As is often noted, for example, Gen Xers in the United States tend to believe there will be no Social Security left for them after the boomers get through with it. More broadly, as boomer Constance Alexander wrote in reviewing Coupland's novel, "Reading the book forced me to acknowledge some uncomfortable truths about my generation, the Baby Boomers. The sheer numbers of us alone create a tyranny of the aging. It's no wonder the young generation, as portrayed in *Generation X,* feels cheated."[17] Coupland's running glossary includes such terms as *bleeding ponytail* ("an elderly sold-out baby boomer who pines for hippie or pre-sell-out days") and *boomer envy* ("envy of material wealth and long-range material security accrued by older members of the baby boom generation by virtue of fortunate births").[18] While saving her greatest ire for multinational corporations, Klein (who appears to be no stranger to fortunate birth) registers a similar resentment of generational tyranny, however "grooving," in the epigraph to this essay. "Embrace the fact that baby boomer bashing is fun," advises Lanham.[19] Bennett and Craig begin their scholarly introduction with a modified epigraph from a men's room stall at the University of Cincinnati:

"The Baby Boomers [mucked] up the entire planet!"[20] Even scholars do it. In her early essay "Subcultural Identity in Alternative Music Culture," Holly Kruse laments that "the lived experiences of the post–baby boom generation seem especially neglected" in cultural studies. She identifies herself in 1992 as "a member of the twenty-something generation"—the favored term before *Generation X* appeared—and proceeds to examine how "college music scenes . . . allow their members to define themselves as separate (though not unproblematically so) from mainstream culture."[21]

Kruse's carefully qualified reference to "college music scenes" notwithstanding, such generational distinctions too often elide class—specifically educational—issues. As early as the late 1960s, Andrew Greeley "observed greater differences of political outlook between college-educated and lesser-schooled baby boomers than between boomers as a whole and older Americans."[22] To this day, when one thinks of a baby boomer, one's imagination rarely conjures the lesser-schooled sort. Similarly, the Generation X complaint that their fancy college degrees have gotten them nothing but McJobs (another Coupland coinage) and massive student debt is largely lost on working-class Americans who never got the fancy degrees in the first place and not infrequently see collegians and the so-called creative classes as parasites on their "real" working-class labor—a theme of no small number of traditional country songs from the same period, including Brooks and Dunn's "Hard Workin' Man" and Aaron Tippin's "Working Man's Ph.D." Such posturing, however, contains more than a little narcissistic defensiveness as well, and Alan Jackson's recent "The Talkin' Song Repair Blues" is unusual in country music in that it stands up a bit for intellectual work. Nevertheless, to most commentators the whole boomer/Generation X debate appears to be a profoundly middle-class one, a debate, perhaps, between North America's last upwardly mobile bourgeoisie and its first downwardly mobile one.

Within public culture, then, one might rather sweepingly suggest that those contesting the meanings of *Generation X* and *alt.country* tend to fall into three camps. The first, favoring *country* over *alt.country*, seems narcissistically invested in overstating the value of its semiskilled labor and in distinguishing itself from collegians; this attitude is frequently associated with masculinity issues, as in Toby Keith or Robbie Fulks, although it can take milder forms, as in the earlier acts Ching analyzes. The second camp, in contrast, seems narcissistically invested in Gen X's distinction from the baby boomers. While avoiding the term *Generation X*, Trent Hill's 2002 discussion of alt.country in "Why Isn't Country Music Youth Culture?" deploys familiar Gen X rhetoric in at least two ways. First, he argues that "the cultural politics of alternative country are premised less on the possibilities of flight, freedom, and mobility than on immobility or downward mobility."[23] Second, he claims distinction from hippies-cum-yuppies, thus overstating, I think, the links between alt.country fans and Ching's traditional country fans. For Hill, alt.country's "musicians are not, unlike the urban, college-graduate hillbillies of the folk revival, interested in recovering an authentic past so much as articulating a set of connections and alliances within a marginalized present." As oxymoronic "urban, college-graduate hillbillies," that is, the boomer folk revivalists are inauthentic; alt.country fans, on the contrary, are, like country fans, authentically grounded in labor. They "imagin[e] an alternative culture, . . . one that might allow new affective and political alliances to understand the experience of 'working man's blues,' regardless of whether that working man is a truck driver or an office temp, a college-town bohemian or army vet."[24] While this fantasy of alliance may not have been totally repudiated by the divisive Bush years, it has certainly been deferred, and in any event Neko Case—whom Hill cites to bolster his argument—was in her early career nothing if not an urban, art-college-educated hillbilly.

The third camp is represented in the scholarly realm by Ortner and in the business realm by the media she most often cites, for example, *Business Week*. Like the traditional country gang, both subcamps have little patience with the "whining" of people like Hill, but their arguments are narcissistically invested not in working-class labor but in a kind of paternalism toward Generation X, for what is inadmissible to both is the idea that Xers' complaints might be objectively justified. (If they are, then Ortner's generation has failed as parents and/or neoliberalism is not a rising tide lifting all boats.) Ortner at points seems to deflect attention from the former potential failure by examining the latter. The "abyss" on which her analysis depends takes the form of a remarkably neat binarism—the sort literary critics, if not anthropologists, deconstruct almost reflexively—between lower-middle-class Xers and upper-middle-class ones. To her credit, she finds the former's *ressentiment* eminently comprehensible, for "it makes sense that people who feel that they are slipping economically, despite their best efforts, would be frustrated and angry. It is more of a puzzle to hear Gen X–type noises from the other side of the abyss."[25] Weirdly conflating the cultural capital of a graduate education in anthropology with actual capital, she continues:

> Yet every time I gave a talk arguing that the real embodiment of Generation X was the children of the lower middle class, and that the children of the upper middle class had been in effect terrorized by the media, there were howls of pain from the numerous Gen Xers (that is, graduate students) in my audiences. Finally I reminded myself of the cardinal rule of ethnography: the informant is always right. Even if, "objectively," these kids had nothing to worry about, there was something experientially real to them about the doomsaying forecasts of the Gen X literature.[26]

The condescension here—which presumably derives at least in part from Ortner's parental transference issues—is troubling. Graduate students—adults in their twenties and early thirties—are not simply figured as "children" and "kids" but infantilized as ones who "howl" and make "noises." Yet only one-third of them will ever land the tenure-track jobs for which they are ostensibly being trained (they know full well, however, that their "teaching assistantships" enable the 2–2 teaching loads of professors such as Ortner) and that two-thirds of them will end up entering the nonacademic workforce. All of them will begin to save for what they may well be right in believing are Social Security–less retirements—eight to ten years later than their college classmates, armed with hypertrophied skills in ethnography and atrophied skills in most everything else. "Objectively," those adults had *plenty* to worry about—and financial security is in any event hardly the only measure of happiness or success. How do you give someone back his or her twenties?

Punk (as) Style

So it should not surprise us that some of those Xers, depressed or angry at the twin infantilizing forces of capitalism and boomers, might seek to affiliate themselves with musical genres that seem depressed or angry at the same things—or that seem to offer a way out, if only symbolically or stylistically. For nearly two decades after its inception in the mid-1970s, critics from what Rupert Weinzierl and David Muggleton have skeptically dubbed the heroic school of subcultural studies famously saw punk as a kind of authentic and, yes, heroic working-class resistance to bourgeois capitalism.[27] As Dick Hebdige put it in the landmark *Subculture: The Meaning of Style,* "It is this alienation from the deceptive 'innocence' of appearances which gives the teds, the mods, the punks, and no doubt future groups of as yet unimaginable 'deviants' the impetus to move from man's second 'false nature' . . . to a genuinely expressive artifice; a truly subterranean style."[28] Yet this fanlike idea of punk as antibourgeois and radical drew fire from the start. As early as the mid-1970s, critics such as Angela McRobbie and Jenny Garber were pointing out that things were more complicated, that, for example, "female participation in youth cultures can best be understood by moving away from the 'classic' subcultural terrain marked out as oppositional and creative by numerous sociologists."[29] McRobbie would go on to argue for the importance of consumption to subcultural identity formation, noting that "sociologists of the time perhaps ignored this social dimension because to them the very idea that style could be purchased over the counter went against the grain of those analyses which saw the adoption of punk style as an act of creative defiance far removed from the act of buying."[30] Sarah Thornton in her 1995 book *Club Cultures* may have put the last nail in the coffin of subcultural heroism, arguing that the dance-oriented youth subcultures she studies "are *taste cultures*" that "embrace their own hierarchies of what is authentic and legitimate in popular culture—embodied understandings of what can make one 'hip'."[31] Bourdieu has argued that intellectuals in France accrued "cultural capital" (knowledge of wine, art, literature, classical music, etc.) to distinguish themselves from the masses since they lacked the old-fashioned kind of capital with which rich people achieved distinction: money. Thornton applies this approach to subcultures by famously redescribing hipsters' embodied understandings as "subcultural capital": the taste decisions by which they attempt to distinguish themselves from an alleged "mainstream." She thus has little patience for Hebdige and others' ideas about "genuinely expressive [working-class] artifice."

> Authenticity is arguably the most important value ascribed to popular music. It is found in different kinds of music by diverse musicians, critics, and fans, but it is rarely analysed and is persistently mystified. Music is perceived as authentic when it *rings true* or *feels real,* when it has *credibility* and comes across as *genuine.* In an age of endless representations and global mediation,

> the experience of musical authenticity is perceived as a cure both for alienation (because it offers feelings of community) and dissimulation (because it extends a sense of the really "real"). As such, it is valued as a balm for media fatigue and as an antidote to commercial hype. In sum, authenticity is to music what happy endings are to Hollywood cinema—the reassuring reward for suspending disbelief.[32]

Whether in music or fashion, in other words, one does not get outside inauthenticity or the market simply by buying or associating oneself with items that predate, or appear to predate, the ages of mechanical reproduction or corporate branding. One is still involved in commodity fetishism, what McRobbie calls "the magical exchange of the commodity."[33]

Unfortunately, McRobbie's 1989 essay hasn't stopped people from trying. Consider V. Vale's decidedly heroic-phase account of the origins of the swing revival—there but for the grace of God went alt.country—in his 1998 *Swing! The New Retro Renaissance.*

> At first glance this movement seems to be more about nostalgia than social criticism, but a closer look will reveal a different form of rebellion. . . . The swing movement is about cultural rebellion in its most subversive form: one that uses the symbols of the status quo for its own intents and purposes. This is achieved through the simple means of rejecting corporately-dictated consumption and embracing forgotten and/or ignored aspects of the American experience (e.g., music, dance, manners, clothing). . . . People consciously seek out older forms of music that have not been put through the corporate music industry's sanitized and stilted face-lift. . . . Judging by the number of morose models in the ad campaigns, the nineties have also been a kind of Great Depression *of the spirit.* . . . Depression may be caused by "mental" factors but ultimately resides in the body. So the body must provide the cure. [Hence swing dancing.] . . . The 90s have been described as the "decade of past decades."[34]

Apparently, swingers, too, thought they were going where there's no depression. The genealogy from punk that alt.country shares with swing is clear here, if implicit. The heroic DIY symbolic rebellion of that movement, its focus on style, gets transferred over to "rejecting corporately-dictated consumption and embracing forgotten and/or ignored aspects of the American experience." Vintage "music, dance, manners, clothing" are embraced as both a punk and a postpunk alternative to, well, the Gap. Of course, the swing revival has the curious distinction of also having been, like alt.country, easily commodified in a Gap ad. Despite, or perhaps because of, the swing revival's ephemerality, the Louis Prima "Jump, Jive, 'n' Wail" ad of spring 1998, with its *Matrix*-style graphics, was far more successful than the Dwight Yoakam "Crazy Little Thing Called Love" ad that followed, not to mention the short-lived one featuring Willie Nelson and Ryan Adams covering "Move It on Over." However, one cannot draw too sharp a distinction between the swing and alt.country scenes: at one point these overlapped considerably in the music of, for example, Big Sandy and his Fly-Rite Boys. In both, too, vintage music and vintage clothing come to take on the same aura of being somehow "outside the market," even as Vale notes that "the proliferation of new 'roots' musicians and bands . . . was facilitated by the invention of the compact disc, which brought about the massive re-release of thousands of obscure recordings in every genre which were formerly impossible to locate, or prohibitively expensive. Basically, our American roots music heritage was restored to us."[35] Vale's syntax conceals the fact that the agents of such re-release and restoration, for alt.country as for swing, were music corporations.

In fact, the political poverty of punk-cum-retro style, once allegedly so transgressive, may lie precisely in its rather art-school assumption that stylistic gestures have ipso facto real-world consequences. The logic behind the idea that by buying and displaying something one can cure alienation and dissimulation—no depression, indeed—is also precisely the logic of corporate branding, which in the terms of marketing theorist David Aaker offers a "value proposition" about the "emotional benefits" of a commercial relationship with a particular brand.[36] In such terms, "vintage" operates as a brand every bit as much as, say, Diesel or Fluevog—or Nike. As Ted Polhemus implies, subcultures and their accoutrements had by the 1990s very much taken on the attributes of brands: "Clubland is a Supermarket of Style where every world and every era you ever dreamed of (and these are, of course, all mythologized places and times) is on offer like tins of soup on a supermarket shelf."[37]

When Generation X, coming of age in the 1990s with the apparent triumph of "late" capitalism, set out to distinguish itself from baby boomers, it thus initially tended to make its choices not by constructing a "counterculture" or voting or protesting—such actions seemed useless, unoriginal/unhip, and foredoomed to boomeresque sellout—but by using the logic of branding, commodity fetishism, and graphic design (the field that makes corporate logos and elevates visual style to or above the level of content).[38] In such a context, it is no wonder that Klein and Ying seem to imagine career choices as tired brands competing for their attention and commitment. Unsurprisingly, too, the most visible X-voxes uniformly possess exquisite visual senses. Coupland is a sculptor who has won two major Canadian industrial design awards; *Generation X* begins with an epigraph from an Xer that runs, "Her hair was totally 1950s Indiana Woolworth perfume counter. . . . But the dress was early '60s Aeroflot stewardess. . . . *And such make-up!* Perfect '70s Mary Quant, with those little PVC floral appliqué earrings. . . . She really caught the sadness—she was the hippest person there. Totally."[39] Klein acknowledges "the ever-fabulous Sara who insisted that *No Logo* must have a design that matched the spirit of its content."[40] Lanham's book is about almost nothing *but* style, and even Dave Eggers is nearly as respected (or reviled) for his graphic design work at *McSweeney's* as for *A Heartbreaking Work of Staggering Genius.* And in 1998, a different kind of generational voice, Neko Case, would earn her bachelor of fine arts degree from the Emily Carr Institute of Art and Design in Vancouver, a school whose most famous recent alumnus at the time was Douglas Coupland.[41]

Neko Case

In her teens and early twenties when she frequented the Seattle music scene, Case (born, like Klein, Eggers, and even LCD Soundsystem's James Murphy, in 1970) was such an avid fan that in 1990 the Tacoma band Girl Trouble (which is not a "girl" group, although it has a female drummer) actually recorded a song called "Neko Loves Rock 'n' Roll."[42] Her style politics as fan-cum-performer became more apparent on her recording debut as part of the punk girl group Maow. Writing about the sleeve of the 1979 Buzzcocks album *A Different Kind of Tension,* designed by Malcolm Garrett, Rick Poynor notes of Garrett's borrowing from an El Lissitzky poster:

> What gets overlooked, when the past is treated as a quarry from which useful visual material can be extracted at will, are the changes of meaning—the drainage of meaning—that occurs when visual ideas with specific purposes are applied in new contexts. In Lissitzky's *Red Wedge* poster, the triangle and

> circle stand for political factions and progressive visual form underscores a progressive political message. The Buzzcocks' sleeve treats similar motifs as super-stylish product packaging that benefits from a historical association with a radical moment, without representing anything of comparable significance, if it represents anything at all.[43]

On the sleeve of Maow's only album, *The Unforgiving Sounds of Maow* (1996), Case sports a big, furry, Russian-looking hat with a big gold hammer and sickle. The band's name had recently been changed from Meow, but there is still nothing Maoist about Maow, whose sound, look, and subject matter recall nothing so much as those of the pre–*Beauty and the Beat* Go-Gos. Whereas the Go-Gos sang punky, transgressive-for-the-times tunes such as "Johnny, Are You Queer?" Maow steps into the ring with "Wank" ("I'll tease you till you think you'll explode / You'll have to go home to blow your load") and, like their predecessors, a plethora of other songs about boys and partying. I don't mean to be humorless here, as the Mao motif could be construed as a complicated gendered joke about music and politics, lending the band a faux seriousness that the merely catty "Meow" does not, only to undercut that seriousness with that oft-cited Gen X irony. But irony only gets you so far, and when all is said and done the Maow name and sleeve, like the Buzzcocks sleeve, remain "super-stylish product packaging that benefits from a historical association with a radical moment, without representing anything of comparable significance." Or, as Case put it in a 1999 interview, "I'm not really country. I just like things to be incredibly archaic all the time. Like pinhole cameras and knee high socks."[44] As she observed after winning *Playboy*'s poll for the "hottest woman in indie rock" and gently declining to pose for the magazine, if she *did* pose, "a retro pictorial would be the most fun. I don't want it to be campy, though."[45]

The Go-Gos—as their name suggests—themselves made more than a nod to 1960s retro. The point where Maow's retro differs from the Go-Gos' may lie chiefly in Case's contribution of a couple of covers from the late 1950s and mid-1960s: Wanda Jackson's rockabilly "Mean Mean Man" and Nancy Sinatra's country pop "How Does That Grab You, Darlin'?" Both artists were gutsy, sexy women who by the 1990s were obscure enough that covering their works advertised a kind of subcultural capital, a connoisseurship of female rock history. (Hipness index: Sinatra's "Bang Bang" would years later serve on the soundtrack to Quentin Tarantino's *Kill Bill, Vol. 2*.)

The gender politics here are admirable. As Case puts it on one of her Web pages:

> A pivotal moment in my life was when I realized that Poison Ivy, a hot sexy lady, played that dirty, evil, titillating guitar in the Cramps. I had "Songs the Lord Taught Us" and I loved it. One day, poring over the cover as I'd done a million times, it hit me. I was filled with shame. I loved music. How come I didn't think women played it?
>
> From that day on, I was on a mission to find them all. Punk rock didn't have enough voices I could relate to at that time in my life, except X and a few others. That experience opened up a vast world to search through. All genres, all cultures, all eras. Most important to me was gospel and country.[46]

Lest this sound too earnest and hence uncool, however, Case begins her narrative with, "People always ask me 'is it hard to be a woman in rock?' and upon much forced reflection I can only site [*sic*] two things that make it difficult: (1) repeatedly being asked that question; and (2) finding a clean toilet seat in a dirty rock club."[47]

In Maow's original tune "Very Missionary," which Case sang and cowrote, Case's performance of gender is inextricable from a very clear performance of *generation:* in a typical Gen X move, Case dismisses the "flaccid" songwriting, among other things, of baby boomer icon Eric Clapton (whether or not she intends it, überboomer Ann Beattie's short story "Eric Clapton's Lover" is a subtext here) in favor of preboomer Hank Williams Sr. Some of "Very Missionary" is itself pretty flaccid songwriting (apostrophizing Williams, for example, Case awkwardly declares, "to heartache you're the host"), but the song still offers a surprisingly complex performative fusion involving gender, fandom, generational identity, punk, and country. The desire of fans for (male) performers that Warren Zanes, drawing on his own appreciation of the Rolling Stones' Brian Jones, has to construct as "queer" isn't exactly queer when the fan is a straight woman, and the song straightforwardly, if metaphorically, rejects a fantasy missionary encounter with Clapton in favor of one with Hank.[48] Female agency is complicated here. To some degree, a fan's relation to a performer is always passive, the missionary "bottom." On the other hand, Case, like any number of other consumers, expresses agency in her choice: in this case, her choice of which male performer she'd like to get missionary with. As noted earlier, Case's is a postpunk move as well. The turn to Hank, like other 1990s turns to preboomer genres such as swing, lounge, and surf, ironically enough represents an attempt to get out from under "the ideas and styles of the [boomer] past": the 1990s evolution of 1970s punk's minimalist and retro abhorrence of the pretentious, narcissistic guitar solos of "classic" boomer rock.[49]

In fact, one of the central draws of country for youthful Gen Xers in the 1990s seems to have been simply that it *wasn't* boomer music, that it wasn't yet even "the groove for people who step off the main groove." After all, the terms of contrast offered by Case's lyrics are largely subjective, describing the singer's response much more than they describe the music itself. Though apparently an exercise in name-calling, the song nevertheless seems, almost against itself, to reinforce the arbitrariness of its own contrasts. Although she ultimately more than resolves any ambiguity with "Clapton, you're the shits" and "Hank, you are the most," for much of the verses Case actually employs could-go-either-way phrasing ("the hair stands on my neck," "make tears roll down my face") to describe each performer's effect; complementarily, in the chorus she uses the same word, *missionary*, to suggest both "possessing the attributes of a banal sexual position" in Clapton's case and "righteous" in Williams'. In the absence of objective reasons for differentiation, the turn to country becomes what Cash called "a way of talking about choices—a way to look, a group to belong to, a kind of music to call [one's] own": an exercise in what Bourdieu calls "distinction," an attempt to amass what Thornton calls "subcultural capital." If Case's choice seems to have, despite itself, a certain Coke versus Pepsi arbitrariness, it may be because both Eric Clapton and Hank Williams operate as metonyms, musical logos for Brand Classic Rock and Brand Hard Country. Case's agency, like that of so many music fans, is not just feminized (or, in Zanes' terms, "queer"); it is also literally and figuratively that of a consumer. In the context of 1990s consumption as protest, professing to want to get missionary with Hank Williams instead of Eric Clapton is much more than a matter of taste: it's a matter of self-definition.[50]

Yet unlike her performance of gender and generation, Case's performance of *country* in Maow, especially on "Very Missionary," retains a decidedly kitschy and ironic, almost yee-haw, aspect even as she proclaims her country fandom. At the end of the song, she repeats the phrase "makes me feel so fine" four times, pronouncing "fine" a bit like "fahn" and interjecting a fairly ludicrous "c'mon, now" after the third. Case is playing a kind of vocal dress up, and the phrase is the vocal equivalent of a big, furry, Russian-looking hat. Steve Bailey observes of the spate of what he calls "ironic covers":

> The new versions tend to ridicule the originals, often exaggerating particularly dated or embarrassing aspects of a given song, but, at the same time, they tend to celebrate the continued vitality, despite these shortcomings, of the music and its importance to the rock audience. This is not "making fun" in a monolithic sense, nor is it pure validation, but rather an often uneasy and thoroughly ironic hybrid.[51]

After an analysis of 1970s precursors of the present wave of irony, he concludes:

> Much as [Bryan] Ferry's work betrays the heavy influence of his art-school background and fascination with pop art, and [Todd] Rundgren's evokes his antipop, elitist sensibility, the recent wave of ironic discourse across a wide variety of media reflects the dissemination of an avant-garde sensibility to the domain of the popular. As a general phenomenon, the process begins with the work of liminal figures who work within popular art forms—rock music, Hollywood cinema, mass market novels—but who situate themselves within a relative elite in these fields.[52]

Case's "Very Missionary" belongs in this ironic tradition.

As noted earlier, Barbara Ching has rightly argued that *all* country music is "performative" and that much of the best of it is, in fact, campy. While camp and irony bear some similarities, something different from camp—and I think genuinely new—was going on with early Case and early alt.country more broadly. For Ching, "country music plays in the space of white Americans who are on the whole less educated and hold low status jobs. . . . This is a population that lacks, again in Bourdieu's terminology, 'cultural capital'."[53] Thus, she concludes, "instead of legitimating the cultural choices that create the distinction of the privileged, country music underlines the production and dubiousness of such distinctions."[54] By recasting country as subcultural capital for punky Gen X hipsters, however, *alt.country reinscribed these distinctions.*

Yet as Generation X individually and collectively ages, the situation is growing more complicated. Boomer journalist Ann Hulbert recently observed in the *New York Times Magazine:*

> You may remember all the hard-bitten qualities that once gave young Gen X'ers a bad name: their disillusioned pragmatism and underachieving fatal-

ism. The tables have turned. Those traits have now metamorphosed into a welcome antidote to the boomers' competitive, perfectionist brand of "hyperparenting."

America's debt-burdened younger parents . . . embrace their prospects of downward mobility with equanimity—even enthusiasm. Unlike their elders, they value family time over money and status.[55]

In many ways, the article is predictably depressing. Hulbert draws most of her evidence from market research and, with a familiar if still breathtakingly un-self-aware boomer narcissism, manages in the final paragraphs to make the article really about boomers after all. ("Make room for us, Gen Xers"!) Still, the article draws on a body of research suggesting (in the usual sweeping terms) that, while the boomers started out idealistic and veered rapidly toward the shallow and self-indulgent, Gen Xers may be moving in the opposite direction. If so, one might expect factors other than "distinction" to arise in their aesthetic choices; one might expect their creative cultures to be something other—more—than mere "taste cultures." We might expect Generation Xers to become something like post-hip.[56]

Although she seems unlikely to embrace parenting anytime soon—her 2004 live album *The Tigers Have Spoken* closes with a modest proposal about feeding children to tigers—a similar evolution is taking place in the career of Neko Case. Her early post-Maow work remains haunted by a diminishing punky, ironic, narcissistic, "look at me I'm singing country" affect. On *The Other Women,* the live acoustic album she recorded with Carolyn Mark as the Corn Sisters in 1998, the two perform, among other things, a cover of "Long Black Veil." However, while Mark and Case—unlike, say, Emmylou Harris' changing the words of Steve Earle's "Guitartown" to create a ramblin', don't tie me down, female speaker, thereby inverting some stereotypes—do not change the gender words, the result does not subvert "heteronormativity," as one might expect. In *Performing Rites,* Simon Frith rightly notes that "gay and lesbian singers can subvert pop standards by *not* changing the words: Ian Matthews bubbling that 'I met him on a Monday and my heart stood still'; Mathilde Santing realizing that 'I've grown accustomed to her face'."[57] Mark, the lead vocalist on this number, indeed sings, "The judge said, *son,* what is your alibi," but she does change another word, continuing, "if you were *somewheres* else, then you won't have to die." Performers as diverse as Johnny Cash, the Country Gentlemen, and Jason and the Scorchers all sing "somewhere," which is what Wilkens and Dill originally wrote. To have the judge, a presumably educated authority figure, instead say "somewheres" is, in a 1998 recording to overdo the countriness, to suggest that the South is a land of unremitting redneckness. What one hears when two female Pacific Northwest hipsters sing "Long Black Veil" is thus an ironic, almost Brechtian performance of country in which one can't fully suspend disbelief (and a story told by a dead man demands some suspension) not least because the gender terms foreground the fact that a female hipster is singing country. Similar ironies abound on Case's first solo album, *The Virginian.* Even the title both claims and ironizes a kind of southern/country authenticity for Case. The title song, though sung in the third person, is pretty clearly autobiographical, but Case is a Virginian in name only: she was born there (in Alexandria, which many Virginians consider to be less Virginia than a deregionalized suburb of the nation's capital), but the family moved soon after.

Yet things start to change for Case on *Furnace Room Lullaby.* The opening track, "Set Out Running," itself sets out with the sheer spectacle of Case's voice, heavy on the reverb and unaccompanied till the rhythm section kicks in on the second measure. At least since punk, and perhaps since early Dylan, rock music concerned with "authenticity" has tended (pre-irony) to embrace what Hal Foster dubbed "the anti-aesthetic," presuming that what was pretty was fake and that authenticity lay in the gritty voice of a Bob Dylan or a Joe Strummer. Of Poly Styrene's famous vocal performance on X-Ray Spex's "Oh, Bondage, Up Yours," Simon Frith writes, "[I]t is not 'feminine'; it is not sweet or controlled or restrained. Such rawness also serves to register the track's punk authenticity . . . [and] its 'unmusicality' is crafted. It is necessary for the song's generic impact."[58] Yet, as so many other awed critics have noted, Case has in just a few years matured into what they call a "big" voice; here one luxuriates—on top of the reverberation, the tempo is a slow waltz—in both its depth and force and *beauty.* Her voice, gorgeous and vaguely Reba-ish in the country context, is rendered even more powerful in the context of punk: its radical "generic impact" lies, paradoxically, in its beautiful old-fashionedness. Instead of "look at me, I'm singing country," her voice is now starting to say "listen to me, I'm *singing.*" In Case's ironic vocal performances, the "dated or embarrassing aspects" tend most often to be played up by the accents and embellishments ("c'mon, y'all," "fahn"—precisely those elements fetishized by fans, critics, and some musicians as "twang") while the "continued vitality" is carried in large part by the power of her voice. As the accents and embellishments fall progressively away, the irony diminishes and the performances approach instead an unapologetic vitality.

Such *singing* is, I think, what the later Case means by wanting to be retro without being campy. When Robert Christgau, reviewing the New Pornographers' CD *Electric Version,* remarks, "I wish the sparingly deployed Neko Case would abandon her faux-country career," he misses the point.[59] As Ching argues, "[C]ountry songs are often about being a hick, about being unable to participate in urban culture even while being bombarded by it. Country music songs are about why hicks—whether they be remote rustics or urban newcomers or perennially alienated city-dwellers—listen to country music."[60] But Case's music offers no winking pact between performer and audience about (their) performed rusticity. To a traditional country audience, Case's adoption of a "country" or southern accent on "Set Out Running"—how she pronounces *me* "muh-ee" or puts a sob in *cry*—will probably still seem "faux," especially if one hears her accent-free singing with the New Pornographers on *Mass Romantic,* released the same year. Yet I suspect the problem here lies less with Case's twang than with the country audience's narcissistically expecting a performer to flatter their countriness through camp, not mock it through irony. (Like costume—nudie suit or furry hat—the accents and embellishments seem to be the medium of both camp and irony, as of "country" itself.) Ching also points out that "the only way for a critic to really start thinking about this music is to escape this double-bind of authenticity that can so readily dismiss or celebrate it,"[61] but even her argument threatens to let authenticity in by—what else?—the back door: country is, properly, music of "hicks," playing "in the space of white Americans who are on the whole less educated and hold low status jobs";[62] Ching herself is proudly from Dubuque, "the classic hick town."[63] The argument, that is, could replace the perception of country as the music of stupidly unself-conscious hicks with an image of it as the music of cleverly (and sometimes angrily) self-conscious "hicks."[64]

Case, on the other hand, starts out as a Gen X hipster singing for other Gen X hipsters.[65] Yet if as an audience we refuse the discourse of authenticity, as Ching rightly argues we should, then the absence of either kind of authentic countriness must not matter. Frith, citing David Brackett's analysis of how the Bing Crosby version of "I'll Be Seeing You" sounds to Billie Holiday fans and vice versa, points out that "'truth' is a matter of sound conventions, which vary from genre to genre. . . . [I]t is almost impossible to hear both of them as sincere: the assumptions behind a reading of Holliday's voice as 'witheringly' sad entail our hearing Crosby's voice as 'shallow' . . . while someone hearing Crosby as reassuringly direct and friendly could only hear Holliday as mannered."[66] Such neat binarisms are always suspect, of course: listening groups (what Stanley Fish might call musical "interpretive communities") are rarely as segregated as this obviously race-inflected example from the 1940s imagines, and there are no doubt plenty of hip hicks and hick hipsters.[67] Either way, however, Case makes no bargains with hicks.

The way to approach Case's music from *Furnace Room Lullaby* onward is therefore not—despite the obsessions of *No Depression*—to see it as something that tries to be "authentic" country and largely fails, as Christgau implies, nor as yet more 1990s hipster art-school irony, but as music that tries to expand the generic boundaries of postpunk hipster music—and succeeds admirably,[68] as *Lullaby*'s hitting number 36 on the *Village Voice*'s list of the top 100 albums of 2000 might indicate. Indeed, Case's twangy hipster irony has lessened with each record. Irony might be seen as among the forms of specifically *youth* "distinction" Sarah Thornton critiques.

> The material conditions of youth's investment in subcultural capital (which is part of the aestheticized resistance to social ageing) results from the fact that youth, from many class backgrounds, enjoy a momentary reprieve from necessity. . . . Without adult overheads like mortgages and insurance policies, youth are free to spend on goods like clothes, music, drink and drugs.[69]

As Case starts to outgrow hipster irony, her authority as a performer must come from more enduring sources. Part of it now comes, of course, from the force, control, and sheer *ambition* of her voice. Part of it comes from the first words of *Furnace Room Lullaby:* "[I] want to," a straightforward act of female self-assertion even, as it will turn out, in the face of apparent self-abnegation. Part of it comes from the fact that Case wrote the song, rightly or wrongly suggesting a note of first-person autobiography.[70] Frith notes that "as listeners we assume that we can hear someone's life in their voice—a life that's there despite and not because of the singer's craft, a voice that says who they really are, an art that only exists because of what they've suffered."[71] Hipsters tend to be a little less sentimental than this—the whole irony thing again—but in Case's case something similar still goes on. The hickness of "Set Out Running"—by which the song might live or die for traditional country music fans—comes off as largely beside the point. Given the emotional power of that voice portraying the imagined situation of a speaker who "just can't shake this feeling / that I'm nothing in your eyes" (when she is everything in "your" ears), the country affectations appear to hip and post-hip listeners, I think, as mere examples of "the singer's craft." Perceived authenticity of feeling trumps perceived authenticity of accent. (And, admittedly, when it comes to the latter many hipsters can't tell the difference.)[72] Such perceived authenticity also means that Case, and perhaps other graduates of alt.country, are moving beyond hats-and-boots dress up, beyond the mere stylishness of being "incredibly archaic," or—in Coupland's words—"the hippest person there. Totally." By 2002's *Blacklisted*, which hit number 23 on the Pazz and Jop poll, Case was singing with almost no visible or audible stylistic props and with virtually no diminution of authority.

And that's a good thing. Jesse Fox Mayshark writes of 2006's *Fox Confessor Brings the Flood* that "the twang and two-steps that colored [Case's] early efforts have been subsumed by noirish pop."[73] Pitchfork Media calls the album only "shaded" by "finely-tuned, country-noir twang"; the *Onion A/V Club* gets it just right: "Case has finished paying homage; she's making Neko Case music now."[74] Doing so has been a good career move: *Fox Confessor* landed way up at number 8 on Pazz and Jop, and three weeks after its release I heard a track from it being played—for better and worse—in the Anthropologie store in Atlanta's posh Lenox Square Mall. Over a year later, when on May 15, 2007, I checked Amazon.com to see what else people who bought *Fox Confessor Brings the Flood* were buying, Case's fan base appeared to have widened well beyond even what remains of alt.country, as her move from Bloodshot to Anti-might have predicted. The only alt.country record listed was Lucinda Williams' *West.* Instead, people buying *Fox Confessor* bought other Case albums (*Furnace Room Lullaby* and *Blacklisted*), the New Pornographers' *Twin Cinema,* and albums by the Decemberists, the Shins, Cat Power, and Jenny Lewis. Even people who were buying Case's earlier albums weren't buying other alt.country anymore; they were just buying more Neko Case (including, again, the New Pornographers).

At the risk of sounding harsh: it's called growing up. In 2007, I listened again to the 1999 K-tel anthology *Exposed Roots: The Best of Alt.Country* (edited by Grant Alden and Peter Blackstock of *No Depression*), which is dominated by urban, twenty-something hipsters who, usually in the early

1990s, had begun listening to less punk and more "roots music" and then making music of their own that, a decade later, sounds pretty innocuous, even homogeneous, despite the genre's oft-asserted indefinability. The double CD felt like an artifact, like watching *Pulp Fiction* (remember the surf revival? the Clinton administration?), and, however subjectively, I felt compelled to agree with Mayshark: alt.country—as the kind of youth culture phenomenon (the subcultural capital) in which both cultural studies scholars and the music industry prefer to invest—is over.[75] Of course, Bloodshot will keep sending bands to South by Southwest, and of course journalists—both mainstream and "indie"—keep using the term, as Ching has reminded me, and no doubt will continue to do so. In the May 8, 2007, *New York Times*, Kelefa Sanneh, covering the Stagecoach country music festival in California, refers casually to one of the four stages, the Palomino, as the "alt.country" one,[76] the other three being the "Mane" (main) stage, where Sanneh spent most of his time, which featured Kenny Chesney, Alan Jackson, and so on; a bluegrass stage called the "Appaloosa"; and a sort of western swing catchall stage, the "Mustang," which featured everything from Asleep at the Wheel to Garrison Keillor. With the exception of the Railbenders, however, not a single act on the Palomino stage—where Neko Case headlined and, according to Sanneh, "seemed out of place"—was under thirty. Some—reclaimed oldsters such as Emmylou Harris, Willie Nelson, and Kris Kristofferson—were twice that.

Of course, much alt.country, like other 1990s retro movements, wanted to be about getting beyond the boomer dead end of a self-proclaimed youth culture aging gracelessly by refusing to admit that youth's window has been slammed shut. Hence the reclamation, back then, not only of Merle Haggard, Loretta Lynn, and Johnny and June Carter Cash, but of Mel Tormé, Tony Bennett, Dick Dale, vintage dresses, and on and on. As early as 1992, Lawrence Grossberg observed that "for the baby boomers, youth is something to be held onto by cultural and physical effort,"[77] and the giant Gen X and alt.country reclamation project was a response to that effort. ("Interestingly enough," bubbled V. Vale, "much of the backbone of the new swing movement is provided by people who are in their 50s–80s. . . . This underground is *de facto* combating society's vile obsession with the cult of perpetual youth.")[78] In general, though, you can't be forty and still proclaiming your hip subcultural distinction from people in their sixties, even if one element of that distinction is the reclamation of people even older. As Hulbert implies—and to their credit—Gen X seems to be about as okay with aging as they have been with other forms of downward mobility, and one nice thing about growing old is that you no longer have to mourn your lack of authenticity by buying some old Johnny Cash record and getting off on *his* melancholy. You *are* old. A 2006 interview suggests Neko Case knows just that.

> PITCHFORK: So you're saying that people shouldn't believe some of the rumors about there being dissension within [the New Pornographers]?
>
> CASE: I think that those things came from the fact that we're incredibly boring. None of us are drug addicts or alcoholics. All we do is work. I'm sorry that we're not the Rolling Stones getting busted at the border for heroin. People just fill in the blanks. It's not easy to be a rock writer and I don't envy that position because what kind of exciting sex angle are you going to put on a middle-aged rock'n'roll band that works all the time?[79]

It is comments like this—happily contrasting "boring" adult behavior by "middle-aged" people in their late thirties with "exciting" adolescent behavior by boomer idols a good deal older—that make me think Case has a real shot at *not* becoming her generation's Eric Clapton.

Not that it matters. What has come to pass may be just what Jameson predicted back in the 1990s as he contemplated an observation by Simon Frith in the *Cultural Studies* anthology.

> "[I]f, as variously suggested in this book, fans are 'popular' (or organic) intellectuals, [writes Frith,] then they may well have the same anxieties about being fans (and take comfort from the same myths) as the rest of us" (182). This is to underscore a peculiarly Derridean turn in the transformation of the "people" into "fans": where the first of these was a primary substance, calmly persisting in its essence, and exercising a powerful gravitational effect on the insubstantial intellectuals who fluttered near it, the new version opens up a hall of mirrors in which the "people" itself longs to be a "people" and be "popular," feels its own ontological lack, longs for its own impossible stability, and narcissistically attempts, in a variety of rituals, to recuperate a being that never existed in the first place. That would, to be sure, lead us on to a more psychoanalytic view of groups and ethnic conflict (perhaps along the lines proposed by Slavoj Žižek); but it would also considerably dampen the enthusiasm of popular intellectuals for a collective condition not much better than their own.[80]

If the grown-up Neko Case no longer flutters insubstantially near Girl Trouble, Hank Williams, Wanda Jackson, or Johnny Cash (or big, furry, Russian hats), she offers a model not only for (and perhaps of) Gen Xers as they move into real adulthood but also for intellectuals tempted to flutter insubstantially around trailer-dwelling Texans, rustic Appalachians, Wicker Park or Williamsburg hipsters, or Case herself. What I find so delightful about so many of the essays in this collection, then, is their refusal to valorize the narcissistic ontological lacks of youth culture that fandom, hipness, and subcultural capital seek so vainly to fill: their strong suggestion that cultural studies, like Neko Case, is finally growing up.

NOTES

1. Johnny Cash with Patrick Carr, *Cash: The Autobiography* (New York: Harper, 1997), 12–13.

2. Ibid., 13.

3. Naomi Klein, *No Logo,* 1st rev. ed. (New York: Picador, 2002), 65.

4. Ibid., 67.

5. See Kim Byrd, "Chilton County: Where Peaches Are Tops!" unpublished graduate paper, University of Montevallo, 2006; Sandy Smith-Nonini, "Federally Sponsored Mexican Migrants in the Transnational South," in *The American South in a Global World,* ed. James L. Peacock, Harry L. Watson, and Carrie R. Matthews, 59–79 (Chapel Hill: University of North Carolina Press, 2005); and Steve Striffler, "We're All Mexicans Here: Poultry Processing, Latino Migration, and the Transformation of Class in the South," in *The American South in a Global World,* ed. James L. Peacock, Harry L. Watson, and Carrie R. Matthews, 152–65 (Chapel Hill: University of North Carolina Press, 2005).

6. Leigh Anne Duck, *The Nation's Region: Southern Modernism, Segregation, and U.S. Nationalism* (Athens: University of Georgia Press, 2006).

7. Ibid., 9; Sherry Ortner, "Generation X: Anthropology in a Media-Saturated World," *Cultural Anthropology* 13 (August 1998): 414–40.

8. Barbara Ching, "Acting Naturally: Cultural Distinction and Critiques of Pure Country," *Arizona Quarterly* 49 (autumn 1993): 107–25; *Wrong's What I Do Best: Hard Country Music and Contemporary Culture* (New York: Oxford University Press, 2001).

9. Sarah Thornton, *Club Cultures: Music, Media, and Subcultural Capital* (Hanover, NH: Wesleyan University Press, 1996). In 1998, Grant Alden and Peter Blackstock actually boasted that "the phrase 'No Depression' is now tossed around by many of the same hands that dealt 'grunge' when we started the magazine." "Out

there in the margins," they went on, "that's where some of the most rewarding music is to be found." Grant Alden and Peter Blackstock, *No Depression: An Introduction to Alternative Country Music, Whatever That Is* (Nashville: Dowling, 1998), 8. Aaron A. Fox's essay on Justin Treviño in the present collection simultaneously critiques this gesture and replicates it.

10. Trent Hill, "Why Isn't Country Music Youth Culture?," in *Rock over the Edge: Transformations in Popular Music Culture*, ed. Roger Beebe, Denise Fulbrook, and Ben Saunders, 161–90 (Durham: Duke University Press, 2002).

11. As the term *Generation X* moved rapidly from marking resistance to a marketing buzzword, thereby illustrating how quickly style politics can be co-opted, it fell out of favor among Gen Xers. I use it deliberately and unfashionably to attempt to resist the logic of branding and style. *Not* to use it would be to endorse the illusion that style politics offers meaningful rebellion: it would be, that is, at least marginally "hip" in a way this essay attempts to resist.

12. Douglas Coupland, "Picking Brains," *Wired*, April 1997, http://hotwired.wired.com/hardwired/wiredstyle/97/04/pickingbrains.html (accessed July 30, 2004).

13. Stephen Craig and Stephen Earl Bennett, eds., *After the Boom: The Politics of Generation X* (New York: Rowman and Littlefield, 1997), 18.

14. Ortner, "Generation X," 434.

15. Jesse Fox Mayshark, "Recalling the Twang That Was Alt-Country," *New York Times*, July 16, 2006, B26.

16. Sherry Ortner, *Anthropology and Social Theory* (Durham: Duke University Press, 2006), 160. In 2000, Neil Howe and William Strauss, whose 1993 book *13th Gen: Abort, Retry, Ignore, Fail* (New York: Vintage, 1993) served as the starting point for Ortner's argument, published *Millennials Rising: The Next Great Generation* (New York: Vintage, 2000), whose title pretty much says it all. They followed it up in 2006 with *Millennials and the Pop Culture* (New York: LifeCourse Associates, 2006), which was aimed directly at entertainment industry executives. My thanks go to Matt Roth, one of my students and Millennial informants, for directing me to "Losing My Edge"—and for suggesting his own generation's embrace of the single's impatience with struggling to feel "hip."

17. Constance Alexander, review of *Generation X*, *Louisville Courier-Journal*, April 3, 1993, http://www.geocities.com/SoHo/Gallery/5560/genx15.html (accessed July 30, 2004).

18. Douglas Coupland, *Generation X: Tales for an Accelerated Culture* (New York: St. Martin's, 1991), 21.

19. Robert Lanham, *The Hipster Handbook* (New York: Anchor, 2003), 159.

20. Craig and Bennett, *After the Boom*, 1.

21. Holly Kruse, "Subcultural Identity in Alternative Music Culture," *Popular Music* 12, no. 1 (1993): 33.

22. Greeley is cited in Stephen Earl Bennett and Stephen C. Craig with Eric W.

Rademacher, "Generations and Change: Some Initial Observations," in *After the Boom: The Politics of Generation X,* ed. Stephen C. Craig and Stephen Earl Bennett (New York: Rowman and Littlefield, 1997), 9.

23. Hill, "Why Isn't Country Music Youth Culture?"

24. Ibid., 183.

25. Ortner, "Generation X," 425.

26. Ibid., 427.

27. Rupert Weinzierl and David Muggleton, "What Is 'Post-subcultural Studies' Anyway?," in *The Post-Subcultures Reader,* ed. David Muggleton and Rupert Weinzierl, 3–23 (New York: Berg, 2003).

28. Dick Hebdige, *Subculture: The Meaning of Style* (New York: Methuen, 1979), 19.

29. Angela McRobbie and Jenny Garber, "Girls and Subcultures," in *Resistance through Rituals,* ed. Stuart Hall and Tony Jefferson (London: Routledge, 1973), reprinted in *The Subcultures Reader,* ed. Ken Gelder and Sarah Thornton (New York: Routledge, 1997), 120.

30. Angela McRobbie, "Second-Hand Dresses and the Role of the Ragmarket," in *Zoot Suits and Second-Hand Dresses,* ed. Angela McRobbie (London: Macmillan, 1989), reprinted in *The Subcultures Reader,* ed. Ken Gelder and Sarah Thornton (New York: Routledge, 1997), 192.

31. Sarah Thornton, *Club Cultures,* 3.

32. Ibid., 26.

33. McRobbie, "Second-Hand Dresses and the Role of the Ragmarket," 197.

34. V. Vale, *Swing! The New Retro Renaissance* (San Francisco: V/Search, 1998), 4–5.

35. Ibid., 4.

36. David A. Aaker, *Building Strong Brands* (New York: Free Press, 1996).

37. Ted Polhemus, *Style Surfing: What to Wear in the 3rd Millennium* (New York: Thames and Hudson, 1996), 91–93.

38. For a thorough discussion of this process, see old issues of the *Baffler,* many of whose better articles were collected in Thomas Frank and Matt Weiland, eds., *Commodify Your Dissent: Salvos from the* Baffler (New York: Norton, 1997); and Alan Liu's remarkable description of resistance and resignation among knowledge workers in *The Laws of Cool: Knowledge Work and the Culture of Information* (Chicago: University of Chicago Press, 2004). At the risk of providing too much information, in 1998, when Ortner's article first appeared, I had (I thought) left a tenure-track academic job to teach middle school English in the city where my wife was an English professor rather than endure the nine-hundred-mile commute forced on us by "the market." I had to sign out whenever I went off campus, I was using my sojourn at the School of Criticism and Theory at Cornell and my degree from a top-five doctoral program in English to teach *To Kill a Mockingbird* and participial phrases, and I had to wear a tie every day. I wore skinny ones. I sported a mustache that could have been

interpreted as ironic. I could go on. The point is to admit guiltily that I am no stranger to Gen X–style politics, even if I no longer feel the need to deploy them. And I must admit they *did* make me feel better about my sense of downward mobility and lack of autonomy even if they did nothing to ameliorate them.

39. Coupland, *Generation X,* vii.

40. Klein, *No Logo,* x.

41. *No Depression* is as thoroughly steeped in Generation X–style politics as any other aspect of 1990s alt.country. Coeditor Grant Alden is a graphic designer with his visual sense firmly rooted in retro. As he writes on one of the magazine's Web pages, "Initially *No Depression*'s visual identity was meant to update the look of a magazine you might have found laying around in the waiting room of a muffler shop in the late 1950s. As a younger generation of designers has begun to plunder the modern style of the 1950s, and as I've begun to develop new respect for the sounds of country music in the early 1960s, I have sought to move the magazine's visual identity a few years forward, say, to the Kennedy years." Grant Alden, "A Few Words about Philosophy," http://www.nodepression.net/adfaq.html (accessed July 30, 2004). As soon as "a younger generation" of bourgeois creative-class professionals starts "plundering" the same visual vocabulary and look, Alden must move on, in his creative-class work at *No Depression,* to "update the look" of the early 1960s. And when those kids catch on to the 1960s gambit, he'll have to move again to stay on the graphic design cutting edge. It's all a bit reminiscent of the origins of the magazine itself. In an interview with *Seattle Weekly,* Blackstock argues that, having grown up in Austin, he was a bit more into alt.country than Alden, who, however, was "tired of documenting the whole grunge thing—this was the early, mid-1990s in Seattle, remember, and Grant had written a *lot* about that." Eric Waggoner, "Profile: Radio Cure," *Seattle Weekly,* April 2, 2003, http://www.seattleweekly.com/2003–04–02/arts/radio-cure.php (accessed June 12, 2004). And in an article in the *Puget Sound Business Journal,* Alden himself notes, "It just felt to me, based on music I'd been hearing, [and] the aging of the college radio audience, it felt like something that was right. I felt like I had been early on things in my life, with Seattle rock bands at *The Rocket,* and I looked around and decided to trust my instincts on this." Rob Smith, "Founders Upbeat over *No Depression*'s Growth," *Puget Sound Business Journal,* July 24, 2000, www.bizjournals.com/seattle/stories/2000/07/24/focus2.html (accessed December 13, 2003).

42. Peter Blackstock, "Destiny Rides Again," *No Depression* 26 (March–April 2000): 54.

43. Rick Poynor, *No More Rules: Graphic Design and Postmodernism* (New Haven: Yale University Press, 2003), 76.

44. Neko Case, interview with Gabino Travasos, *Mote,* August 1999, http://www.moregoatthangoose.com/interviews/neko.htm (accessed July 30, 2004).

45. "Country Love Song," n.d., http://www.playboy.com/sex/features/indierock/ (accessed July 30, 2004).

46. Neko Case, "Neko's Ladies," http://www.nekocase.com/ladies.html (accessed July 30, 2004).

47. Ibid.

48. R. J. Warren Zanes, "A Fan's Notes: Identification, Desire, and the Haunted Sound Barrier," in *Rock over the Edge: Transformations in Popular Music Culture*, ed. Roger Beebe, Denise Fulbrook, and Ben Saunders, 291–310 (Durham: Duke University Press, 2002).

49. For the definitive account of punk's roots in 1950s and 1960s surf and garage music, see Bill Osgerby, "Chewing Out a Rhythm on My Bubble-Gum: The Teenage Aesthetic and Genealogies of American Punk," in *Punk Rock: So What?*, ed. Roger Sabin, 154–69 (New York: Routledge, 1999).

50. Consumption as protest carried over into the 2000s. Rob Walker writes about hipsters embracing Pabst Blue Ribbon beer precisely because they believed it was *not* being marketed to them: "The Plan B analysis even says that P.B.R.'s embrace by punks, skaters, and bike messengers make it a political, 'social protest' brand. These 'lifestyle as dissent' or 'consumption as protest' constituencies are about freedom and rejecting middle-class mores, and 'P.B.R. is seen as a symbol and fellow dissenter.' Eventually all of this sounds like satire, but the punch line is that it isn't really that far off from P.B.R.'s strategy." Rob Walker, "The Marketing of No Marketing," *New York Times Magazine*, June 22, 2003, 44.

51. Steve Bailey, "Faithful or Foolish: The Emergence of the 'Ironic Cover Album' and Rock Culture," *Popular Music and Society* 26, no. 2 (2003): 142.

52. Ibid., 155.

53. Ching, "Acting Naturally," 108–9.

54. Ibid., 109.

55. Ann Hulbert, "Look Who's Parenting." *New York Times*, July 4, 2004, http://www.nytimes.com/2004/07/04/magazine/04WWLN.html.

56. The earliest use of the term *post-hip* I have found comes from Andrew Boyd's *Life's Little Deconstruction Book: Self-Help for the Post-Hip* (New York: Norton, 1998); it has also been applied to the ethos of the *Baffler*. I do not mean the term in John Leland's sense of "hip with ironic quotation marks"; I mean postcommodified distinction. See John Leland, *Hip: The History* (New York: Ecco, 2004), 338–56.

57. Simon Frith, *Performing Rites: On the Value of Popular Music* (Cambridge: Harvard University Press, 1996), 195.

58. Ibid., 196.

59. Robert Christgau, "Diffusion Rools," *Village Voice*, June 16, 2003, http://www.villagevoice.com/music/0325,christgau,44871,22.html (accessed July 30, 2004).

60. Ching, "Acting Naturally," 109.

61. Ibid., 111.

62. Ibid., 108.

63. Ibid.

64. When Ching wrote "Acting Naturally," the angriest such performer she mentioned was Hank Williams Jr., who "enacts a grotesque country dandyism that may be one of the last effective ways to 'épater le bourgeoisie'" (116). In the new century, as a grotesque country dandyism runs the nation, Williams seems decidedly middle-of-the-road compared to performers such as Toby Keith and Darryl Worley. The tendency of country's once benign camp to morph, when in power, into bullying is, however, outside the scope of this essay except for a note that such a tendency in country's camp casts alt.country's irony, such as it is, in a somewhat better light. Speaking truth to power now appears to require that one *épater les hicks.*

65. Amazon.com's "Customers who bought this CD also bought" feature is useful here. When I checked on July 28, 2004, customers who had bought Case also bought the New Pornographers' two CDs, other Neko Case records, and an assortment of alt.country, chiefly Calexico. People who bought the New Pornographers also bought Death Cab for Cutie, the Shins, the Strokes, Fountains of Wayne, and so on. No traditional country musician appeared.

66. Frith, *Performing Rites,* 197.

67. Robert Lanham identifies one sort of hipster as the "Bipster": "Blue-collar Hipsters who shun art-school pretension and have little patience with leisure-class Hipsters. . . . Bipsters are usually from middle-class to lower-middle-class backgrounds. They are a very common breed of Hipster and often grow up in the South or the Midwest." Lanham, *The Hipster Handbook,* 112.

68. This is also, I suggest, how one should read, perhaps generously, the core of postpunk Gen X 1990s alt.country: Gillian Welch, Whiskeytown and its descendants, Uncle Tupelo and its descendants, Freakwater, the Gourds, Lambchop, and so on. However, as I have implied by contextualizing my argument in 1990s Generation X consumption politics, it is *not* the way to read late boomer acts that got their country starts in the 1980s and were retroactively labeled alt.country by the tastemakers in *No Depression:* Steve Earle, Dwight Yoakam, Lyle Lovett, and, most important, Jason and the Scorchers, each of whom, however hip, makes some kind of campy bargain with hickness.

69. Thornton, *Club Cultures,* 103.

70. No longer flaccid, her songwriting gets better with each album. "Set Out Running" contains the great country couplet, "If I knew heartbreak was comin', I would've set out runnin'," and on other parts of *Furnace Room Lullaby* she seems to have been listening to a good bit of early Dylan. "We've Never Met" recalls "I Don't Believe You (She Acts Like We Never Have Met)"; "Whip the Blankets" invokes the humorous tall-tale surrealism of *The Freewheelin' Bob Dylan.*

71. Frith, *Performing Rites,* 185–86. Although Case has moved largely toward telling stories, her seemingly more autobiographical songs continue to forge bonds with many listeners. On *Fox Confessor,* one thinks of "Hold On, Hold On," "That

Teenage Feeling," and "The Needle Has Landed." Lauded for a certain inscrutability, such songs' lyrics nevertheless tend to contain at least one universal, hooky sentiment, for example, "If I knew then what's so obvious now, you'd still be here."

72. In England, for example, the fashion magazine *The Face* offered its readers only the latest fashions in verbal as well as visual style. In September 2003, it helpfully explained to its readers that "fuck all y'all" was "classic Deep South abuse—use 'fuck y'all' to two or three people, but for a whole room you need this." See "Arrivals/Departures," *The Face,* September 2003, 51.

73. Mayshark, "Recalling the Twang That Was Alt-Country," 26.

74. Ryan Dombal, "Neko Case: *Fox Confessor Brings the Flood,*" *Pitchfork Media,* April 10, 2006, http://www.pitchforkmedia.com/article/record_review/16041-fox-confessor-brings-the-flood (accessed October 31, 2007); Keith Phipps, "Neko Case": *Fox Confessor Brings the Flood,*" *Onion A/V Club,* March 7, 2006, http://www.avclub.com/content/node/46067 (accessed October 31, 2007).

75. As my informant Matt Roth put it in a 2007 e-mail, "Some of the sites I read still use the term to describe albums or artists occasionally, but I really feel as though it's more often than not in an attempt to describe the music's feel ('such and such . . . an artist is a talented songwriter with alt-country sensibilities' or whatever.) So most young music listeners will recognize the term, but not necessarily as a movement or genre." Anti-'s eclectic catalog (capacious tagline: "Real artists creating great recordings on their own terms") seems to be a more appropriate marker of where things are today than Bloodshot's. None of this is to suggest that alt.country is gone for good; indeed, one might reasonably expect to see, as with ska, "second-wave" and "third-wave" alt.country popping up over the next couple of decades.

76. Kalefa Sanneh, "In the Desert, a Festival of Country and Its Kin," *New York Times,* May 8, 2007, E1.

77. Lawrence Grossberg, *We Gotta Get Out of This Place: Popular Conservatism and Postmodern Culture* (New York: Routledge, 1992), 183.

78. Vale, *Swing!* 5.

79. Ryan Dombal, "Interview: Neko Case," *Pitchfork Media,* April 10, 2006, http://www.pitchforkmedia.com/article/feature/31252-interview-neko-case (accessed October 31, 2007).

80. Fredric Jameson, "On Cultural Studies," *Social Text* 34 (1993): 43.

AARON A. FOX

Beyond Austin's City Limits: Justin Treviño and the Boundaries of "Alternative" Country

Introduction

AF: Do you have any opinion on the label "alternative country"?

JUSTIN TREVIÑO: Well (laughing). . . . The way I see it is, what I do is country, and the Dixie Chicks and Shania and all of that as far as I'm concerned, THAT's alternative, 'cuz it ain't country, but that's what's so screwed up about it all.

In the winter of 2001, Justin Treviño, a twenty-six-year-old country musician from Martindale, Texas, was putting the finishing touches on the third album of his career, *Loud Music and Strong Wine.* Justin had enjoyed unexpected success with his previous self-produced CD—*Texas Honky Tonk*—the year before.[1] That 1998 recording had made a respectable showing on a relatively new commercial metric, the "Americana" format chart published by the (now defunct) Gavin Corporation.[2] *Texas Honky Tonk,* which Justin had recorded, mastered, and marketed entirely from his own home, had achieved widespread airplay on FM-band college radio stations and the small number of commercial stations around the United States that programmed the Americana format and targeted listeners described at the time by the Americana Music Association as "professional, affluent, and educated."[3] This success was due largely to word-of-mouth (and e-mail) and the active support of a few college radio disc jockeys (DJs) on influential stations. Importantly, the record was also well received on "country gold" format AM (and some FM) stations serving rural and working-class listeners, especially in

Texas and Oklahoma, markets where Justin had often appeared as a sideman with traditional country stars, often former major label recording artists now in the commercial twilight of their careers.[4]

On the heels of its widespread Americana airplay and chart success, *Texas Honky Tonk* was reviewed in a number of prominent alternative country publications, in one case in the pages of *No Depression* (the most influential alternative country journal) by a major figure in Americana format radio. Don Yates, the reviewer, was the program director at Seattle's KCMU-FM (a position he retains at KEXP, as the station is now called), and he programmed cuts from *Texas Honky Tonk* frequently.[5] Yates was also a founder of the influential Postcard2 (P2) e-mail Listserv group (discussed at length in Peterson and Lee 2004),which is made up largely of Americana, bluegrass, and alternative country disc jockeys, performers, promoters, and critics. Justin's *Texas Honky Tonk* (and later *Loud Music and Strong Wine*) were both favorably discussed on P2 and made many members' "best of the year" lists. Yates set the tone for the critical—and curatorial—response to Justin's music that soon arose from many quarters when he wrote:

> Honky-tonk crooners have been serenading the Texas dancehalls since the beginnings of the genre, and while they're not as ubiquitous as they once were, 24-year-old Justin Trevino [*sic*] is a worthy upholder of the tradition. . . . Trevino's latest album . . . is the real deal.[6]

As the "real deal" and an "upholder of the tradition," Justin was suddenly generating crucial "buzz" in a discursive and commercial universe that had formerly been largely opaque to him—and tantalizingly out of reach—as a small-town country musician whose performance career had until then centered almost exclusively on working-class bars and dance halls, mostly in rural areas or blue-collar sections of cities such as San Antonio and Fort Worth. Now, with the success of *Texas Honky Tonk,* the prospect suddenly loomed of a career "breakout" into a much larger and more lucrative market and exposure to a different, more influential audience. As Yates' remarks remind us, Justin possessed a rare and ineffable resource in this market: working-class "roots music" authenticity—the "real" deal.

It is undeniable that he also possessed enormous quantities of sheer talent. This talent had made him a revered musician among "traditional" country artists and their fans since his teenage years. Indeed, reviews and fan commentary on the Internet tended to stress this one-two punch, citing both Justin's extraordinary virtuosity as a singer and his unimpeachable pedigree as a protégé of Johnny Bush and a son of rural Texas. (At least one review, on the Web site Country Standard Time [n.d.], drew on another rhetoric of authenticity when it compared Justin favorably to Freddy Fender and Johnny Rodriguez, two great Mexican American country singers from Texas, although, unlike these artists, Justin makes no explicit effort to assert his ethnicity and considers his Mexican American identity irrelevant to his art.)

The possibility not only of increased professional prospects but of a broader, serious, informed, and respectful audience for an artistic practice he takes extremely seriously had long enticed Justin, but it had also frustrated him, living and working as he had been doing all his life on the margins of the periodically explosive "Austin music scene." While Justin was no stranger on the Austin scene, his artistic presence in that entrepreneurial and musical epicenter of "alt.country" (as the genre is often called, with the medial "dot" marking deference to the crucial role of the Internet in creating this genre) had been relatively minor, although Austin is located only thirty miles north of his home in the countryside near San Marcos.[7]

It is worth pausing over the irony of Justin Treviño's relative marginality to the Austin alt.country scene of the mid- to late 1990s. Despite his youth, Justin is, as Yates says, a master craftsman of Texas dance hall swing and honky-tonk music with a deep and detailed knowledge of the history of these country subgenres—subgenres that are at the musical core of much of what has been marketed, since the early 1990s, as alternative country music. Many of the younger artists who flocked to Austin in the mid- to late 1990s were (or became) dedicated students of these subgenres, which they learned largely from re-released and vintage recordings. These styles (and the post–World War II working-class social world they emerged from and described) were increasingly minor components of the Nashville-produced "mainstream" country styles then enjoying a cyclical phase of massive national popularity. They lived on in a fragile live performance tradition in Texas (and to a lesser extent elsewhere in the Southwest and Gulf Coast regions), matched and served by an equally small-scale recording and broadcast industry committed to so-called traditional (or "hard" or "real") country artists and styles. This poorly capitalized sector of the country music industry keeps alive the fading careers of older artists who no longer merit recording contracts with major labels; its products tend to be poorly produced, and the working conditions for artists tend to be exploitative. But it is shaped by a fiercely ideological commitment to a cultural politics of conservative nostalgia for which the fate of country music's "traditions" is a matter of important allegorical significance. In that world, Justin's commitment to the styles, songs, and—in his work as a producer and sideman—ongoing careers of his "traditional" elders was a primary credential.

But, of course, alt.country works these same ideological fields. The re-released "vintage" recordings of these same older artists (often in luxurious reissued boxed sets put out by European recording labels) were a key source for the burgeoning alt.country movement of the early and mid-1990s. In Austin, stores selling vintage equipment and clothing (as well as recordings) sprouted up and down Congress Avenue as the "roots" music scene—and its alt.country sector—expanded and developed in the mid-1990s and as the growing South by Southwest festival marked the increasing importance of the city to the music industries. A certain conspicuous and respectfully ironic consumption of Texana came to define the city's public style and its image as a mecca for music tourism and youth cultural credibility.

I don't mean to overstate the distinction between the alt.country and traditional country scenes. Justin certainly has an enormous record collection from which he has learned much of his craft and repertoire. But Justin's star credentials in the world of traditional country performance and among working-class Texas country fans are as overwhelmingly due to his work experience with traditional Texas musicians as to his mastery of the recorded legacy of the honky-tonk and western swing styles. Justin has been singing country music since he was a small child and professionally since his early teens. He has apprenticed himself to a series of older musicians, at first to such local artists as Randy Meyer and Larry "Hoppy" Hopkins and, since his teens, to Johnny Bush.[8] Bush is sometimes known as the "country Caruso," and his early 1970s recordings are perhaps the apogee of Texas working-class dance-hall country's golden age. Justin has been the principal bass player in Bush's band, the Bandoleros, for years, and Bush has recorded Justin's songs and appeared as a guest artist on each of Justin's albums. Bush has been Justin's mentor and advocate since he first heard Justin sing at a San Antonio flea market when Justin was sixteen. Today Bush frequently says of Justin, "He was my biggest fan until I heard him sing; then I became his."

Apprenticing under Bush, as well as other masters of Bush's generation, Justin has developed an extraordinary vocal technique and range that allow him to emulate nearly any canonical hard country singer. His vocal style features his strong, silky tenor voice, which evokes Bush and Ray Price and Marty Robbins (and, some say, Wynn Stewart) for nearly every knowledgeable critic who has reviewed his work. His technical knowledge of singing is uncanny and would be exceptional for an artist in any genre. I have interviewed him for hours on subjects ranging from vibrato to the placement of cry breaks; he can analyze his own technique in detail and cite and perform precise comparative examples of the technical practice of other singers past and present. His skills as a bass player, vocalist, bandleader, and "front man" (a singer who opens a set for a featured artist), keep him employed full time as a sideman with artists such as Kitty Wells, Leona Williams, Frenchie Burke, Darrell McCall, and many others when he is not fronting his own band or playing for Bush or, in previous years, for the Cornell Hurd Band or the late Don Walser's Pure Texas Band, his regular employers. Justin also has a remarkable ability to manage and engineer complex recording projects. To see him work in his home studio, which has grown from a four-track cassette recorder to a room full of digital equipment in the years I have known him, you would never guess that Justin has been completely blind since shortly after his birth in 1974. And Justin would prefer that you didn't notice.

To be sure, Justin was hardly absent from the Austin scene. As astute readers may have noted while reading the résumé in the last paragraph, Justin's steady work with Don Walser and Cornell Hurd put him in regular contact with the city's clubs and audiences, though almost always in a supporting role. Indeed, Justin's ability to provide such "support" earned him a lot of work, and he was a valued sideman. With Justin onstage, directing the band from behind his bass, a band's repertoire would suddenly increase dramatically; Justin could entertain nearly any "classic country" request, and lesser musicians were improved by following his unwavering rhythmic grooves and sure knowledge of complex chord progressions. He made any band sound better.

But the transition from valued sideman to solo artist continued to elude Justin in Austin during the mid-1990s as the city's alt.country scene boomed. This was despite his growing prestige as a musician and producer, a series of strongly reviewed solo recordings, or what I used to call the "Justin effect," as fans with limited experience of country music would suddenly realize that the heavyset, conservatively dressed, blind Tejano bass player was, indeed, a virtuoso artist, often a much more compelling artist than the singer in vintage western clothing whose name was on the sign out front.

Justin often complained to me that his attempts to book his own band in the clubs he frequented as a sideman were often fruitless. Living in a rural hamlet near San Marcos and being blind and unable to drive himself certainly limited Justin's ability to network socially on the Austin scene (as other alt.country aspirants were doing) on the rare nights when he wasn't playing for his own living. And Justin had little or no experience with (or interest in) playing rock (especially punk rock) music, the lingua franca of the twenty- and thirty-something musicians who flocked to Austin in the 1990s to play some variety of country music.

This lack of experience with rock-based performance conventions and techniques, of course, reflects Justin's social difference from the majority of his Austin-based peers. Where Justin grew up, in small-town South Texas, being a musician *means* being a country musician (or perhaps a Tejano musician with the dividing line not always as clear as the distinctive genre names might imply). There were, for Justin, few "alternatives," and the politics of musical authenticity in Justin's home community devolved almost entirely around a venerable critique of "mainstream" country music's abandonment of "traditional" country styles and artists, all of which had been the latest thing in their day. It is also worth pointing out that Justin *has* been able to make a full-time living as a professional performer and producer catering to his rural and working-class fans, something that very few Austin-based alt.country musicians, relying on a handful of clubs and focused on commercial recording, have been able to do. Justin has never had to hold a "day job." He has made a living playing country music for his entire adult life. Music *is* his day job.

He was born in the right place to have this experience. The persistence of a tradition of partnered dancing to live country music in working-class and rural Texas is nearly unique in the United States, and even so this tradition is in sharp decline. However, the opportunity to practice country music as a craft and a business—indeed, the expectation that being a musician could be a *trade*, especially for a blind man—was available to Justin within his immediate social world from a young age in a way that was not true for most of the young alt.country musicians then working in the Austin scene who had not grown up working class in rural Texas or elsewhere in the rural South.

However, these are the raw materials that combine into something more subtle and ironic at work in Justin's lack of fit with Austin's hip alt.country ethos. The apparent irony concerns, as always with country music, the politics of authenticity and commodification. How is it that a virtuoso rural, working-class artist of Justin's caliber, who had approached country music as a profession from a young age, could remain relatively obscure within the alt.country music scene that emerged thirty miles from his home and was founded on the almost obsessive curation of a tradition to which Justin was a gifted living heir?

For the remainder of this essay, I explore this question. I am not sure it has a single answer any more than one can ever predict an artist's career path from evaluating his or her talents on their own merits or, for that matter, his or her social background. My answer, indeed, is in part to blame Justin's distance from the Austin scene on alt.country's cosmopolitan and historicist ideological commitments and, thus, to assert that—as with all forms of minstrelsy—Austin's alt.country scene was uncomfortable admitting an actual working-class rural musician—a great virtuoso, no less, at twenty years old easily the technical equal as a musician of nearly any country performer in Austin—with a nonironic relationship to country into its inner circles of celebrity and renown.

But to stop with this explanation would be to avoid the case I make more strongly here, which is an argument for the *agency* of artists like Justin Treviño and for the tenacity and creative force of the field of working-class cultural practice that shaped him as an artist. I am not telling a sad (or allegorical) story of Justin's neglect by hip Austinites any more than I am telling a hopeful (or allegorical) story of Austin's alt.country scene embracing and launching the career of an actual working-class, "traditional" country artist of the same generation as most of that scene's participants (as opposed to the common story of the many elder traditional country artists who have been lionized, sometimes condescendingly via "tribute," by alt.country stars). To say that Austin's alt.country scene didn't "get" Justin Treviño for a long time would be correct. But this is not because Austin-based musicians feared the overweight, blind teenager dressed in a pressed shirt and slacks—as opposed to the self-consciously grungy looks adopted by many young alt.country musicians—and playing circles around almost everyone else on the city's stages as *competition*. And, despite Justin's own interest in developing his career as a solo artist in the alt.country markets he was discovering as a sideman, he would be quick to tell you that he *also* didn't "get" a good deal of the young, edgy, subcultural formation that characterized the alt.country scene in Austin, not because he was unaware that such a subculture existed but because he actively rejected parts of it as antithetical to his own working-class tastes and values.

The actors in any adequate sociological explanation are not scenes and ideologies and musical genres and styles but individual musicians, club owners, music retailers, record company executives, critics, disc jockeys, consumers, and fans. And my argument here entails an emphasis on the motivations and understandings of one individual musician in particular with an emphasis on the ways in which this artist's class position not only enables and constrains his social agency but also shapes the *cultural* context within which such terms as *success* and *musicianship* are understood as values. My point is that class matters, not only as a structure of material constraints, and not only as an ideological structure of hegemonic difference, but also as a cultural structure of feeling (and thus value) as well, as I argue at some length in *Real Country: Music and Language in Working-Class Culture* (2004). Class experience is not (or not only) an *external* force acting on popular music and its agents; it is generative of the lifeworlds of particular social actors who create and consume popular music.

More specifically, here I suggest that Justin's ideological and practical commitment to both working-class fans and a deeply rooted Texas working-class tradition of musical craftsmanship and professionalism explain, in part, why he maintained his *own* distance from the "Austin scene" as much as that scene did not fully embrace *him.* Indeed, Justin has followed an "alternative" path to alt.country success that differs from the path followed by many prominent musicians of his generation whose careers were nurtured in Austin and other relatively cosmopolitan centers such as Seattle, Los Angeles, and New York during the 1990s. Justin has been relatively successful as an alt.country artist by many standards in the intervening years, yet he still rejects the label and disdains some of its most emblematic performers—and certainly its signature embrace of ironic distance from country music's commercial history, discussed in the introduction to this book. He would say, with some justification, that he has advanced his career in an uneasy but effective negotiation with the alt.country market. And he would say, also with some justification, that while the growth of his alt.country career has been slow, it has been on his own terms.

For the remainder of this essay, then, my point is to elucidate those "terms" in their cultural, ideological, practical, and sonic aspects and show their importance in defining the trajectory of Justin's career, thus, in effect, showing that more than one alternative form of country music (and alternative agency) remains possible even *within* the field of cultural practice this volume calls alt.country. To be more blunt, I argue here (and at more length in my book) that country can—still—be counted a "working-class" music in a noncuratorial sense. Working-class constituencies—country music's core historical market—have a stake in how intellectuals (as well as consumers and critics) think about alternative country music. Scholars should be careful to avoid assuming that the boundaries around alt.country can be discerned in real fields of sociomusical practice without ethnographic attention to particular musical worlds and their actors. Without attending to lived worlds of musical practice, or by overattending to commercial metadiscourses *about* such worlds as if they were the only real worlds of practice that matter (an approach characteristic of much popular music scholarship), we take the music industry's categorical interests as our own and reproduce its ideological categories without analysis.

Since I claim to take an ethnographic perspective on Justin's career, I should explain how I am myself an actor in this story as a musician and a DJ as well as a scholar. During the early 1990s, I worked extensively with Justin (and many other working-class singers) as a lead guitarist while conducting ethnographic field research on country music in the working-class small towns of southern and central Texas in which Justin's name is widely known. I was living in Austin then, during the early years of the alt.country explosion, and frequently found myself negotiating the sometimes blurry cultural and musical divide—as a musician, an ethnographer, and a country music fan—between the worlds of alternative and working-class country.[9]

It is not my point here to draw a sharp line between these worlds, for of course they overlap and interpenetrate extensively, and several working-class artists (such as Dale Watson, and, indeed, as I argue here, Justin Treviño) have achieved alt.country success without abandoning their commitments to working-class traditional country audiences and communities. Moreover, I do not intend to posit either side of what was, to me, a palpable cultural and ideological divide in 1990s Austin as more serious or legitimate than the other or more committed to country music's traditions. Rather, my point is to examine what happens when these worlds collide and the politics of musical authenticity become subject to negotiations that challenge and reveal the ideological commitments that continue to shape country music as a broader field of cultural practice and discourse. It is perhaps worth recalling that nearly every major development in the history of country music has entailed a staged encounter of competing class-specific nostalgias—*always* including the nostalgias of elite social classes and always with competing implications for the political significance of country music in the present.[10]

Austin: A City's Limits

Even after the success of *Texas Honky Tonk,* Justin rarely performed at Austin's hippest urban venues—the Continental Club, La Zona Rosa, or even the Broken Spoke—as a bandleader despite his steady efforts to book shows at these clubs and despite the fact that he was known to the managers of these venues through his exceptional work as a sideman for Hurd, Walser, Susanna Van Tassel, and others. On the other hand, Justin had become much better known in San Antonio, a more musically conservative city without a significant alternative country scene, and in the bars, VFW halls, and dance halls of a swath of central Texas running from Caldwell County in the east to Brady in the west and Fort Worth in the north. The vast majority of his most devoted fans were working class, and most lived in small towns or the rural exurbs of San Antonio and Austin.[11] A significant proportion of these were people over the age of forty. For most of them, as for Justin, country music, and the particular idiom of country music Justin has mastered, is the music they have loved and heard all their lives; for them, "country" is not an "alternative" genre affiliation. Most would agree vehemently with Justin's assertion in the epigraph to this essay: to them, much of the music marketed as country by the Nashville-based music industry since the late 1970s has been the real alternative. And for many of them, it's not an alternative they have embraced. Indeed, many of these fans are barely aware of the alternative country scene that is the focus of this volume or of its leading artists other than those who have "crossed over" to mainstream success (such as the band BR–549 or the singer Dwight Yoakam).

Instead, as an alternative to mainstream country, these rural and blue-collar fans prefer dancing to *live* (and local) country music, a central cultural practice and expression of an increasingly nostalgic working-class, ethnic, and regional identity. Likewise, Justin's nonironic, deeply studied, and respectful curation of traditional Texas styles, broadly characterized as honky-tonk and western swing, and his claim to an artistic pedigree by virtue of sustained personal apprenticeship, signify—certainly to Justin's working-class traditional country fans—a class-specific form of resistant nostalgia, indeed, as I discuss at length in *Real Country*, a pervasive nostalgic structure of feeling summarized in the very word *country*. Justin's art emerges from and speaks to and for working-class culture, in working-class idioms of craft and tradition, even as he has increasingly aimed at the larger and more urbane alt.country audience for whom such notions are framed differently. Indeed, like other working-class artists who move beyond their own communities and regions, Justin performs a tightrope-walking act in which his commitments to his working-class audience underpin and certify his status as an authentic Texas country musician for a (now international) audience of connoisseurs of traditional country, as well as for more casual country fans.

This mediation is a challenge of which he has become increasingly conscious as his career has progressed. His mastery of this structure of feeling is given vital currency by his age and Tejano heritage, connecting nostalgic recollections of the working-class past, keyed to a specific value placed on manual labor, with an emerging, fluid, postmodern class cultural politics in which manual labor and "blue-collar" identity are increasingly cast as undignified or archaic—and along with them the fields of sociomusical practice Justin embraces and sustains. Justin is seen by his working-class fans as a defender of a culture in decline, if not under siege, but he has transcended that role as well.

To be sure, of course, this "traditional" taste culture is not without its own irony since it embraces musical styles and sociomusical practices that were "mainstream" and "modern" (and often resisted as such) from the 1950s through the early 1970s.[12] The transformation of the "hard country" and "honky-tonk" styles from mainstream to traditional, and the concurrent transformation of industrial working-class culture, is the background story here. But my goals for the remainder of this essay remain more modest, befitting our lack of historical perspective on "alternative" country and the current state of contemporary popular musical culture. I take Justin's musical career as an example of what can happen when nostalgias collide, and I am principally interested here in the implications of this collision for Justin's own artistic project. Justin can, of course, articulate the professional and aesthetic dilemmas he faces working between two worlds of "country" music (as he does in the epigraph of this essay): many blue-collar and rural Texans—Justin's community and most loyal fans—claim a particular form of working-class cultural nostalgia as their own, for which Justin's music is a powerfully symbolic alternative to mainstream country.

But the objects of this nostalgia are also the objects of more cosmopolitan forms of nostalgia and anxiety over the future of American vernacular musical culture characteristic of alt.country and other "roots music" ideologies also situated in anxious opposition to mainstream contemporary popular culture. This nostalgia has been the basis of a massive documentary and curatorial effort on the part of elite cultural institutions.[13] The emergence of the elite curatorial effort to preserve roots musics has in turn provided resources for (and drawn resources from) a cosmopolitan constituency that asserts a competing claim to traditional musics. What happens when these ideologies encounter each other on the field of musical practice and across fluid boundaries of class experience? The answer to that question is complex and lies in part in the hands of artists such as Justin Treviño who are able to move, even if with difficulty, between sociomusical worlds and their distinctive forms of nostalgia. That Justin *has* been able to move between these worlds is worth stressing, but I stress here also that he has remained distinctly anchored in the working-class traditional country scene by both choice and perceived necessity.

The city of Austin, Texas, is a key actor in this story. Unsurprisingly, a cosmopolitan form of nostalgia permeates—indeed, practically defines—the Austin alt.country scene. Since the early 1990s, Austin has been undergoing massive growth and development. Its leading industries—technology, government, banking, education, and tourism—financed a rapid cultural and demographic transformation of the city throughout the decade, pushing working-class residents—especially but not exclusively white, working-class residents—out into the suburban and rural margins to the north, south, and west while the urban center was becoming more commercially dense, wealthy, and cosmopolitan. Under the impact of the North American Free Trade Agreement and the technology boom, the entire region became much more aware of and connected to global economic processes. Population levels and economic activity in Austin itself, and then in the neighboring small towns and cities to the west, north, and south, began to expand at an extraordinary rate. By some estimates the central Texas region was the fastest-growing region in the United States in the late 1990s.

At the same time, a significant urban—and urbanely cosmopolitan—musical scene began developing in Austin (as in several other cities under similar demographic and economic conditions such as Seattle, Los Angeles, and New York) under the genre rubrics of roots, Americana, and alternative country. Though loosely integrated with the local rock and traditional (i.e., working-class) country scenes, and, indeed, an earlier layer of "Texas music" scene building during the 1970s, alt.country in Austin consisted, in the 1990s at least, of a volatile mix of survivors of the 1970s "redneck rock" scene (epitomized by the continuing shadow cast by Willie Nelson over Austin's musical culture),[14] a lionized elder statesman with authentic but quirky traditional country credentials (the late Don Walser), several singer-songwriters whose work skirted the boundaries of a commercial country sound, rockabilly and roots rock pickers, western swing ensembles, a growing contingent of performers of ethnically marked roots musics, and an increasing number of young, mostly college-educated, cosmopolitan musicians who emigrated to Austin from places like New York, Boston, San Francisco, Athens, and Minneapolis, as well as from other cities in Texas.

What many of these émigrés (and I count myself among them) sought in Austin in the 1990s was the critical mass of a "scene"—a historically important emplaced moment and the attendant institutions that this moment spawned, many of which rapidly developed or evolved from earlier incarnations of the "Austin scene."[15] The central institutions consisted of venues and small- and medium-scale marketing concerns, the public radio stations KUT-FM and KOOP, as well as the commercial station KGSR, a spectrum of clubs ranging from blue-collar taverns rebranded as hip destinations, such as Henry's Bar and Grill, and venerable dance halls, such as the Broken Spoke, to trendsetting venues such as the Continental Club, a number of small record labels such as Watermelon Records, and a very large annual music industry conference called South by Southwest, which brought representatives of major labels to town each year. A critical mass of educated, affluent, and cosmopolitan fans provided by the University of Texas and the high-tech boom supplied an economic basis for this moment. Some of the major alt.country artists and acts in Austin during this period included the Wagoneers, the Delta Rays, the Bad Livers, the Damnations, Libbi Bosworth, Ted Roddy, Mary Cutrufello, and countless other start-up projects that never achieved a commercially recorded release.

These new alternative country artists and institutions also sought something else in Austin: the ineluctable and inchoate authenticity that a Texas address in particular imparted to their cultural practice. Austin's ideological history as an alternative to Nashville as a creative and business center for country music stretched back to the 1970s, but the roots of Texas country music—implanted more deeply in the Dallas–Fort Worth and Gulf Coast areas than in Austin—run deeper still as an alternative tradition more culturally authentic in its expression of working-class, though not necessarily rural (see Fox, forthcoming), musical and cultural values than the Nashville-centered mainstream country tradition. In the 1990s, these still palpable roots were increasingly framed in the critical and curatorial discourses of cultivated musical consumption in a manner that seemed to reach back much farther. These traditions were seen to persist in such institutions as the Broken Spoke, the famous dance hall in South Austin, and at the now defunct Henry's Bar and Grill in North Austin, where Don Walser held musical court in the early 1990s, attracting both University of Texas students and retired working-class country fans to hear and dance to his ineffably cheerful western swing (as Walser once told me, "I played for both kinds of 'blue hairs' at Henry's").

Never mind that, as the locals say, "Austin is nice, and so is Texas," an expression that captures nicely the ironic, meta-Texan flavor of so much Austin alternative culture. And never mind that the reality of the country music business had been, for decades, that Texas artists and styles were mediated by Nashville-based institutions and Nashville-produced music had been canonical for Texas musicians throughout the postwar era. Austin evoked an aura of alternativity rooted in faded, authentic, working-class cultural traditions apparently uncorrupted by the industrialized commodification of those traditions by Nashville's music business, which was achieving massive new levels of popularity at the expense of ideological and musical authenticity, for its critics, in the same years.[16]

The new alternative country acts that emerged in Austin in the 1990s—especially those created by younger and more urbane musicians—for the most part eschewed significant contact with the working-class traditional live country music scenes already in place in the city's rural environs, though shoulders did rub in fascinating ways at a handful of blue-collar bars in the city such as Henry's, the Horseshoe Lounge, and Ginny's Little Longhorn Saloon. The most interesting figures on the scene, whose Texas-rooted and working-class biographies gave them standing and rapport with working-class audiences—such as Don Walser and Dale Watson—ventured to mingle their younger, more urbane fans with older, working-class fans, a strategy Willie Nelson had used to create a vital Austin scene a generation before.[17]

But, despite the fact that the key musical reference points for the Austin scene—classic Texas honky-tonk, dance hall swing, rockabilly, hard country—were exquisitely represented in fragile but living performance traditions in the small beer joints and even some large dance halls along the highways heading out of the metropolitan area and well out into the countryside, the key sources of stylistic inspiration for most alt.country acts in Austin seemed to me, as an Austin-based musician and country fan, to be vintage recordings of canonized stars. Esoteric claims of influence and choices of cover repertoire combined with a pervasively ironic—though generally respectful—orientation toward the musical, sartorial, and performative genre conventions of these supposedly mummified styles. Period fashions and instruments often seemed to matter as much as—or more than—musically coherent references to the hard country idioms being cited. And, while many performers on the scene possessed significant levels of musical skill, these skills had rarely been acquired through apprenticeship or honed in front of highly knowledgeable audiences. Although I can only report this from personal experience, many self-identified Austin alt.country musicians of my acquaintance had little interest in visiting, let alone performing in, the working-class taverns beyond the Austin city limits. Indeed, my suggestions to fellow musicians that it might be interesting to do so were frequently met with disbelief, sometimes specifically aimed at the career value of performing in blue-collar venues, sometimes at the patrons of such places. Unpaid "showcase" gigs at the South by Southwest festival or low-paid club work in Austin clubs were far more compelling options for most of these friends; indeed, the idea of making one's living playing cover versions of hit country songs for working-class audiences (as Justin and I both did) was often seen as worse for one's creative process than working at a day job in the city.

According to my own rough personal survey, a majority of the musicians and acts that identified primarily with an Austin alt.country scene in the several years leading up to 1995, when I left Austin for Seattle, had not grown up with country music but had come to the genre through earlier careers in rock, blues, or singer-songwriter acoustic music (as I had). The common musical language of an increasing number of players included more punk rock than two-step shuffles, and many bands combined musical and performance gestures from rock and country with results that would have been unpalatable—indeed, far more unpalatable than current Nashville mainstream country—in the more exclusively working-class clubs and dance halls I knew as an ethnographer and Top 40 country musician.[18] The differences ran deep, but Justin Treviño sought to bridge them.

Craft and Compromise: Finding an Alt.Country Sound

Even as he continued to enliven the music scene he had played in for years as a sideman, Justin's success with *Texas Honky Tonk* created new opportunities for Justin to enter this burgeoning scene as a soloist and bandleader. By 2001, I had known Justin for a decade. I had played guitar in his band since he was seventeen, worked on recording projects with him, and driven thousands of miles with him over the previous few years, originally in the context of my ethnographic research into working-class and rural country music culture in Texas but increasingly in the context of a collegial friendship. We frequently consulted and assisted each other with various musical projects. I had made a short film about Justin, brought him to New York City for a performance at Columbia University, where I work, and returned occasionally to Texas to visit with him, play music with him, and work on recording projects in his studio. I was also the host of a radio show on a New Jersey college station from 2000 to 2002, playing both traditional and alternative country music on a college station that reported to the Gavin Americana charts. I had used my professional connections in radio to promote *Texas Honky Tonk* to fellow Americana radio programmers and journalists. So it was not surprising that Justin sent me, in 2000, an early trial mix of the new CD, *Loud Music and Strong Wine,* to evaluate. Before he sent me the recording, however, he told me about a problem he was encountering that was holding up a final release of the recording.

Justin had recently sent another trial mix of the CD to a prominent disc jockey at an AM radio station in San Antonio, a station that primarily played country "gold" (i.e., mostly old country hits from the 1950s through the early 1970s) for a primarily working-class market. This DJ had long been a supporter of Justin's music and had been an important mediator of the passionate support Justin had developed among the kind of country music fans who listened to AM Country Gold format stations: blue-collar manual and agricultural workers and rural and small-town dwellers, many well into middle age.

Despite his experience and talent, Justin was taken aback by the disc jockey's complaint that the "sound" of the new record was wrong—too much bass, a "boomy" kick drum, the vocals too "buried" in the mix. Justin feared that the DJ's critical view of the record would mean he wouldn't play it and that other stations serving his working-class fan base would be similarly put off by the record's mix. On the other hand, Justin had worked with some of the top musicians and studio engineers in Austin on the recording and mastering of the album, people who knew how a record should sound to appeal to the Americana market, which depended on mediation by FM radio stations because they had been successful in the past in this market. Without going into detail, I should explain that there is a significant sonic difference between AM and FM radio technologies, with AM characterized by a narrower frequency bandwidth, less dynamic range, and a noisier carrier. Thus, AM sounds "thinner" and emphasizes higher frequency lead instruments and the midrange fundamental frequencies of the human voice. Since most AM broadcasts are monophonic, whereas FM broadcasts are typically in stereo, AM signals have less presence and depth as well. From the era of World War II until the early 1970s, AM radio was a crucial format in the development of country music and it remains an ideologically and aesthetically preferred format among many rural and working-class fans who feel that it emphasizes the voice and the song text over the aural richness of the recorded sound of the ensemble, in contrast to the FM sound's ability to emphasize sonority and rhythm section dynamics.

Country music stations on the AM dial (a dying breed to be sure) tend to serve rural areas, occupational and other niche markets (such as "trucker radio" formats, though increasingly these do not feature music to the extent they did through the late 1980s), and older demographic segments of the radio market. "Clear channel" AM stations—with high-powered broadcast signals that reach across broad swaths of rural America—retain a cherished place in the memory of older rural country fans, though very little country music is now carried on the remaining clear channel stations, and the saturation of local airwaves and the emergence of other listening options (now including Internet and satellite radio) have diminished the importance of high-powered regional stations across all formats. The radio music market has been fragmented into much more demographically targeted niche formats even as the ownership of stations serving these markets has been consolidated into a small number of major corporations. And the automation of radio has made it possible for many smaller, local AM stations to be run by remote control, serving up generically uniform playlists (where music programming is retained at all) that are devoid of local character.

Conversely, Nashville's country music industry long ago embraced FM radio (and television, the Internet, and satellite radio) as the primary media for disseminating their products. And contemporary roots music, Triple A, and Americana programming is overwhelmingly associated with college- and university-based stations, almost all of which are on the noncommercial portion of the FM band (though many derive significant listenership from their streaming Internet feeds as well).[19] The AM format has become increasingly irrelevant to the evolution of the Americana music genre or mainstream commercial country except in intentional sonic references signified by the archly self-conscious use of vintage recording equipment or in song texts such as Son Volt's 1995 alt.country anthem "Windfall," which contains the telling line "switching over to AM, looking for a truer sound." This truer sound is, according to the song, like "1963, but right now it sounds like heaven."[20]

In southern, central, and western Texas, where Justin built his career as a working musician, a handful of AM stations that resisted the national trends and remained committed to local country programming (especially KNEL, in Brady) had played a crucial role in building his audience. Justin was in a quandary. His traditional market depended on promotion through AM radio; his new audience would expect an FM-optimized sound. These issues hadn't come up with the earlier CD, which had been recorded on a low budget using Fostex eight-track analog home studio equipment. Although that record had sounded passable, it arguably conveyed an intention to sound vintage. In fact, Justin recalled for me that he had approached a Nashville-based agent who specialized in more mainstream country with his first CD. This agent had hurtfully dismissed the album as "sounding like [her] worst memory of 1972." (To this agent, at least, this did not "sound like heaven.")

In fact, this accidental vintage quality may have had something to do with the recording's success among the alt.country cognoscenti. Technology is an ideologically central subject of alternative cultural discourse, and many major alt.country artists make a practice of calling attention to their use of vintage instruments and recording equipment and their preference for an analog sound. Indeed, one of the constitutive ironies of contemporary music recording is the sophistication with which digital studio equipment can mimic classic analog instruments and recording technologies. A Don Walser anecdote captures the essence of this irony from the perspective of a musician relatively unconcerned with such matters. I was present when a young disc jockey (who really did have blue hair and an impressive array of body piercings) interviewed Walser on her alt.country show on radio station

KUOW in Seattle in 1996. The interviewer rather flippantly asked Walser whether he would like to be able to record on the equipment used by Bob Wills and the Texas Playboys in the 1930s and 1940s. The elderly singer's response was forceful: "Hell no," he said, adding: "if Bob Wills were alive, he'd want to record in a digital studio!"

But even if *Texas Honky Tonk* benefited from its accidental vintage quality, its low-budget production values had drawn notice. Don Yates' review for *No Depression* ended on just such a note: "Treviño's own production is at times a bit too plain to suit the richness of his voice and the often melodramatic material."[21] Justin took such criticism seriously, and his forthcoming album had been recorded on upgraded Alesis ADAT digital studio equipment (bought with the proceeds of *Texas Honky Tonk*'s sales) and professionally mastered in a digital facility used by many Austin-based alt.country recording acts. The only vintage elements on the recording were the personnel (Johnny Bush and Leona Williams performed as guest artists) and the cover songs, many of which dated from the 1960s and early 1970s. The CD's sound had much more presence and a brighter and punchier dynamic spectrum than Justin's first album. Justin had mixed the album to take full advantage of what to him was simply a better recording studio. In so doing, he had ensured that the sonority of the recording would be relatively unmarked (as either vintage or plain) on the FM radio stations that were becoming ever more important to his career development. But, in sharp, ironic contrast, the sonority of the new CD would be marked as overly "slick" and rock-influenced on the AM country gold stations that programmed mostly vintage country music sonically optimized for AM radio.

Frustrated by the delay in releasing the album, which was widely anticipated in the alt.country world, Justin sent me the master and several alternate mixes, all unlabeled so as not to prejudice my opinion. I spent a day trying the CDs out on different systems and running A/B comparisons (playing back different recordings on matched audio systems or the same recordings on different audio systems) with other albums I knew had done well in working-class and rural markets and in more cosmopolitan Americana markets. I made notes—here a comment on a snare drum's punch, there a note about the bass level, elsewhere a suggestion to alter the equalization of a vocal track. I then flew down to Texas, where Justin and I went through the mixes with my notes, as well as through some subsequent remixes he had made in his studio. We listened to the album on cassette tapes and CDs, on a lousy boom box, a car stereo, a personal stereo, and a studio-quality monitoring system that had been used to master the original mix, trying to imagine and approximate a wide range of potential listening situations and markets.

In the end, Justin settled on somewhat moderated levels for the bass and drums and compensated by somewhat darkening the newly prominent vocal levels. There was only so much that could be done to the album's mix—the levels and equalization of different parts—to compensate for the vivid presence and dynamics—or to some ears the "brittleness" and "harshness"—of the underlying digital recording. But by foregrounding the voice slightly in the mix, Justin hoped to make the CD more palatable to his AM-oriented fans without alienating FM-oriented listeners.

The resulting CD's sound was, in effect, a compromise made in dialogue with representatives of several overlapping but ultimately distinctive social and musical worlds. The album sold quite well, thanks to a significant increase in distribution channels (especially Internet retailers) devoted to Americana and other roots music products, and it spent most of the summer of 2000 in the upper-middle region of the Gavin Americana chart, debuting at number thirty-eight for radio airplay in early June and peaking at number twenty-nine in late August, ahead of records by the likes of the British radical folksinger Billy Bragg and an elderly Porter Wagoner. The album was widely and enthusiastically reviewed, and Justin had achieved another significant step forward in establishing his credibility as an Americana and alternative country act. The compromise with the CD's sound appears to have worked; no reviewers commented on the album's overall sonority, negatively or positively, suggesting that it has been accepted as an unmarked professional recording in the alt.country community.

Mapping the Discourses: Genre, Practice, Ideology, Irony

Most of the musical distinctions Justin and I (and others such as the AM disc jockey who expressed concerns about the "sound" of Justin's CD) observed in the process I have just described would be technically obscure to a listener who is not professionally involved with music production. We were attending to minute differences in the levels of particular instruments, qualities of reverb and delay, and the tonal differences between digital and analog recording or between dynamic and condenser microphones. We deployed an extensive and explicit metamusical semiotic perspective on genre boundaries, audience demographics, marketing strategies, and technological mediation in order to make multiple, intuitive judgments about precise and elusive aspects of musical sound.

But the process was in fact remarkably unremarkable in my experience as a popular musician. Commercial popular musical production has always relied on the matching of such judgments to the intuitive gestalts—the structures of musical feeling—that the producers and mediators of popular music as a commercial product and an artistic craft understand as key contexts for their work as a form of capitalist cultural practice. Attributes of class-marked taste and distinction adhere, as Bourdieu famously showed,[22] to musical genres in toto but also to the ramifying subgeneric variations spawned by mature genre cultures and to the most detailed and inchoate levels of musical form, style, and sonic substance. It is the mark of serious popular artists and cultural producers that they are aware of these distinctions.

Contemporary North American country music practice and discourse (whether alternative, mainstream, or traditional) presents a compelling example of the fluid, emergent, and complex mappings of styles, sonorities, and social identities. Its significance as a rural and/or working-class cultural practice, one that has always been fragmented and contested but involves a distinctive set of aesthetic and ethical musical values centered on working-class conceptions of craftsmanship and styles of language use, has simultaneously been the basis of country's historical appeal across class lines as roots music. Subjected to one hegemonic regime of nostalgia within working-class culture (and I have not touched on the politics of mainstream country and its traditional critics within working-class culture at all here) and another hegemonic regime in the cosmopolitan universe of alternative culture, with its ironic invocation of authentic roots traditions as alternatives, country presents a field of intra- and interclass cultural practices that can be seen as the terrain of class struggle, class conflict, and class mobility.

At the intersections of working-class and cosmopolitan versions of country music, in places like central Texas, working-class musicians are often ignored and, as in other areas of American culture, often systematically disadvantaged with respect to accessing technologies of self-realization and promotion and the resources needed to engage with those technologies. The living status of working-class country practice creates a problem, however, for the curatorial enterprises of alternative country music making and Americana marketing. Uncharitably, one could say of much alt.country that it exemplifies a canonically postmodern and cosmopolitan cultural practice in its emphasis on the performance of the (consuming) self as a matter of stylistic choice or that it presumes an elitist field of alternative realizations of intention and agency signified by an ironic mode of consumption and disguised commodity fetishism. At its worst, such a cultural practice could be called cynical in its constructions of the cultural authenticities of working-class communities that frequently exclude, marginalize, or parody contemporary voices from within those communities. Even more uncharitably, one might say of alternative country that it draws on embedded associations between nostalgic forms of cultural minstrelsy and a covert nostalgia for regimes of class, race, and gender hegemony embedded in the historical ideologies these forms signify.[23]

Justin's native social milieu brings him into implicit conflict with this covert nostalgia, although his family background might be said to place him in a relatively liminal segment of the rural working-class social structure of central Texas, a fact that must be considered in understanding his ability to channel his talent and ambition into a self-managed professional career that now extends well beyond the local horizons of his community so that his records are available on Amazon.com and popular in Germany and Australia. Born in Brownsville, on the Mexican border, Justin grew up in rural hamlets between the relatively small town of Lockhart and the growing small city of San Marcos. He has always lived in what locals call "a trailer," meaning a premanufactured home, although his current one is large, relatively new, and has room for a serious recording studio at one end. His father is a journeyman electrician from whom Justin acquired both a love of country music and impressive technical skills; his mother is a schoolteacher from whom Justin acquired a passion for learning and a personal distaste for drinking and smoking that is somewhat unusual among nonchurchgoing people in his community.

Justin is Mexican American, or as the locals prefer, Tejano, emphasizing his roots in the Texas-Mexico border region not interior Mexico; but, unlike his parents and like many Tejanos of his generation, he speaks little Spanish and moves comfortably—perhaps more comfortably—in Anglo working-class circles than in ethnically marked Hispanic contexts. Indeed, I have never observed any explicit discussion of his ethnicity among the many white and Tejano working-class fans of his music I have interviewed and with whom I have spent time. Justin speaks little Spanish and rarely listens to Spanish-language music, though this music (primarily conjunto, banda, and norteño) is a constant aural presence in his part of Texas. His earliest memories involve listening to Johnny Cash records; he was playing Johnny Bush and Ray Price songs on the guitar at the age of nine. He was leading a band through the bars of central and southern Texas at fifteen. He is married to a woman of Anglo and Native American heritage whose parents ran a rural tavern where Justin frequently played as a teenager. Elizabeth "Sissy" Treviño has a high-school education and works in an administrative job at a car dealership; she also drives Justin to nearly every job he plays and runs much of the business end of his musical career with exceptional competence and determination. Justin overcame the significant obstacles facing the blind in rural America and was an excellent student in high school. He attended one year of college in San Marcos, intending to major in computer science, but dropped out to pursue music professionally. He earns his share of the family income primarily from live performances in working-class bars and dance halls and largely in a several-hundred-mile radius around San Antonio, usually clearing around $100 to $150 a night for himself after expenses, plus whatever he makes from the sale of his CDs from a table by the bandstand; increasingly he has made an income from the sale of his CDs by retailers (especially Internet retailers) and from his work as a producer in his home recording studio. Despite his success as an alt.country artist, Justin has remained a working-class musician devoted and accountable to his rural, working-class fan base and community and to the proposition that the traditions he carries are living expressions of a specifically working-class and Texan historical claim on country music. But he has become secure enough in his mastery of those traditions to venture, carefully, into the alt.country arena and succeed on his own terms.

Conclusion

To paraphrase Eric Lott, alt.country's relationship to working-class country is one of simultaneous "love and theft,"[24] and following Lott's argument about racialized minstrelsy one is tempted—if not compelled—to see the alt.country phenomenon as expressing deep ambivalence within contemporary popular culture (and especially its youthful leading edge) about class relations and the politics of class identity in the United States. The much discussed "irony" of alternative country depends on the genre's ability to locate the working-class cultural forms to which it indexically refers in the commercial past or the "folkloric" present, but this historicist or folklorizing closure is never perfectly achieved in part because of the liminal relationships between class-cultural communities, the leakiness of class habitus in a society with some degree of class mobility, and the tactical advantages provided to artists and entrepreneurs by the effervescent development of new media and new technologies for the production and marketing of aesthetic commodities (especially the Internet).

This situation creates opportunities, obviously enough, for an ethnomusicologist like myself to work as a musician in working-class settings—indeed, folklore and ethnomusicology have long relied on this taken-for-granted permeability of class habitus in our research methods, at least when we work "at home." Here, however, I call attention to the possibility that this permeability can be exploited by working-class artists, like Justin Treviño, in control of their own aesthetic and entrepreneurial development (and their craft) without "selling out" their commitments to working-class communities or traditions. The crucial, critical task for popular music scholars—and serious fans—is to understand the cultural histories, semiotic codes, and material conditions that bear on the musical enactment of social difference in a relational, dialogic field of discourse. For a properly social critique of popular musical cultures, there is simply no alternative.

Postlude

Justin's career as a recording artist has steadily expanded in the years since *Loud Music and Strong Wine* was released. He has released several subsequent recordings, including *Travelin' Singin' Man* (2001) and *The Scene of the Crying* (2003). Both albums have been picked up for national and international distribution through the Texas Music Group and are widely available in record stores and on major Internet retail sites. Both have been extensively reviewed, almost uniformly in the same glowing terms with which his first two records were greeted. But Justin's working career as a performing musician reflects his continued commitment to his mentors and his working-class audiences. His performance schedule (which can be viewed on justintrevino.com) still consists primarily of gigs at "Opry" shows, dance halls, rodeos, festivals, and taverns across rural southern and central Texas, and many of his dates are with Johnny Bush. He also performs weekly in Austin, however, at Ginny's Little Longhorn Saloon on Burnet Road, a working-class dive that has taken up the mantle of the now closed Henry's. Ginny's is a tiny bar where middle-aged working-class fans and young hipsters (Don Walser's "both kinds of blue-hairs") drink, dance, and trade songs in the kind of atmosphere that has made Austin's music scene very nearly unique for decades and the source of so many invigorating musical trends.

And in a final twist, virtually the only negative comment I have ever seen about a Justin Treviño recording appeared in an otherwise glowing review on the Web site AustinAmericana.com, a guide to the Americana and alt.country scenes in Austin:

> My only quibble with the CD is that it seems to be a little smooth and slick of a production for my tastes. I'm not a raw roots kind of guy, but do enjoy a sound that is a little edgier, a little more "live" sounding. The two fiddles on some selections seem more like an orchestral string section than what I would expect to hear in my local honky-tonk. (Austin Americana Music Guide, n.d.)

It is tempting to let this last full-circle irony speak for itself, although I feel obliged to point out that Justin typically records fiddle tracks with no effects other than a small amount of reverb. The fiddle player on *Travelin' Singin' Man* is Bobby Flores, who has been a member of Ray Price's and Johnny Bush's bands for years. Flores has recorded with most of the legends of Texas country music and is widely regarded as producing simply the finest "tone"—raw sound quality—of any fiddler working in Texas today in both his live and recorded work. Perhaps it should be mentioned, too, that Flores studied classical violin and music theory, along with jazz guitar, at Trinity University, so it is perhaps unsurprising that, when recorded playing the two parts of a classic Texas "twin fiddle" arrangement, Flores' sound might be likened to "an orchestral string section." After all, the tracks were not recorded in a "local honky-tonk" but in a sophisticated digital studio in a trailer in the countryside somewhere south of Austin's city limits.

NOTES

I am grateful to Barbara Ching, Pamela Fox, Steven Feld, colleagues and students at New York University, the University of Chicago, and Columbia University, and several anonymous reviewers for valuable assistance with various versions of this essay. I am especially grateful to Justin and Sissy Treviño for years of close friendship and collaboration. I take the occasion of this essay to pay my respects to the late, great Don Walser by dedicating it to his memory.

1. Justin had released one album prior to *Texas Honky Tonk*. That album was released on cassette only, by a small Texas record company (MCR) when Justin was sixteen. It is no longer available, and Justin considers it juvenilia.

2. This chart, which was phased out in 2002, has recently resurfaced in the industry publication *Radio and Records*, now sponsored by the Nashville-based Americana Music Association. It emerged initially in 1996 to track national radio airplay of recordings that fell into a semicoherent new marketing category that had coalesced out of a disparate and diverse mix of styles: traditional "hard" country, bluegrass, singer-songwriter, "roots" rock, and especially what was becoming codified in the mid- to late 1990s as "alternative country." However, the label Americana appears to be almost exclusively used to describe a radio format. I have rarely heard it used by musicians or fans as a name for an actual style of music, as alternative (or "alt") country is typically used. Some critics do use the term to refer to a "style," but the virtue of the term for many critics is precisely that it obfuscates standard genre boundaries. The Nashville address of the Americana Music Association, a trade organization made up of music industry professionals, is richly ironic since anti-Nashville rhetoric has played a profoundly important role in the emergence of Americana as a cultural and marketing category.

3. In 2001, the Web site of the Americana Music Association described the "target demographic" of Americana format radio as "alternative/college to older pure country listener, disenfranchised mainstream former or current [country music] listener, music intensive, professional, educated, affluent." That description has since been replaced by the following description: "Radio Research's study on Americana radio found the demographic profile of the listener to be predominantly male between the ages of 25–44, having 4+ years of college education, making over $40,000/year, and very active in purchasing CDs and attending live concerts."

4. These Country Gold format stations did not report to the Gavin Americana charts. Had Justin's substantial exposure on such stations been reported, he might well have reached an even higher chart position with *Texas Honky Tonk* and his subsequent albums.

5. Because KCMU was among the first college stations to offer a streaming audio feed over the Internet, its influence was amplified, and Yates has some claim to having invented the Americana label as a radio format.

6. Don Yates, "Justin Trevino: Texas Honkytonk" (record review), *No Depression*

16 (July–August 1998), http://www.nodepression.net/issues/nd16/waxed.html (accessed January 3, 2008).

7. I will use the alt.country label throughout this essay to refer to the alternative country scene of the 1990s. On this scene, see Steve S. Lee and Richard A. Peterson, "Internet-Based Virtual Music Scenes," in *Music Scenes: Local, Translocal, and Virtual,* ed. Andy Bennett and Richard A. Peterson, 187–204 (Nashville: Vanderbilt University Press, 2004).

8. For more on Meyer and Hopkins, see Aaron A. Fox, *Real Country: Music and Language in Working-Class Culture* (Durham: Duke University Press, 2004).

9. I also discuss this genre overlap and distinction in "'Alternative' to What? '*O Brother,*' September 11th, and the Politics of Country Music," in *There's A Star-Spangled Banner Waving Somewhere: Country Music Goes to War,* ed. Charles Wolfe and James E. Akenson, 164–91 (Lexington: University Press of Kentucky, 2005).

10. See Barbara Ching, "Acting Naturally: Cultural Distinction and Critiques of Pure Country," *Arizona Quarterly* 49 (1993): 107–25; Barbara Ching, *Wrong's What I Do Best: Hard Country Music and Contemporary Culture* (New York: Oxford University Press, 2001); Aaron A. Fox, "The Jukebox of History: Narratives of Loss and Desire in the Discourse of Country Music," *Popular Music* 11, no. 1 (1992): 53–72; and Richard A. Peterson, *Creating Country Music: Fabricating Authenticity* (Chicago: University of Chicago Press, 1997).

11. For specific demographics, see Fox, *Real Country,* chap. 2.

12. See Joli Jensen, *The Nashville Sound: Authenticity, Commercialization, and the Nashville Sound* (Nashville: Country Music Foundation and Vanderbilt University Press, 1998).

13. I discuss this at greater length in "'Alternative' to What?" and "Honky-Tonk Music," in *Encyclopedia of Popular Musics of the World,* ed. J. Shepherd et al. (London: Continuum, forthcoming).

14. This scene is the subject of Jan Reid's *The Improbable Rise of Redneck Rock,* 2nd ed. (Austin: University of Texas Press, 2004).

15. See Barry Shank, *Dissonant Identities: The Rock 'n' Roll Scene in Austin, Texas* (Hanover, NH: Wesleyan University Press, 1994).

16. A similar—though more rock-oriented—scene thrived earlier in Los Angeles, transplanting the aura once possessed by the town of Bakersfield into a more convenient locale and producing the country rock megastar Dwight Yoakam.

17. See Reid, *Improbable Rise of Redneck Rock.*

18. Performing as a Top 40 musician in youth-oriented working-class dance halls was a disdained choice for a young musician with aspirations to succeed on the Austin scene. I had no such aspiration but, rather, wished to follow the apprenticeship tradition I was studying ethnographically.

19. It is intriguing to consider that streaming Internet audio, which played an im-

portant role in the rise of alt.country, frequently shares some of the aural properties of AM radio. This was especially the case in the mid- to late 1990s when few Internet listeners had high bandwidth connections. Depending on the bit rate of the encoded signal and the quality and bandwidth of the network over which a signal is carried, Internet radio often sounds much like AM radio: noisy, intermittent, and thin.

20. "Windfall," copyright 1995 by Jay Stuart Farrar, Grain Elevator Music (BMI), Ver Music (BMI), Warner-Tamerlane Music (BMI). All Rights Reserved.

21. Yates, "Justin Trevino."

22. Pierre Bourdieu, *Distinction: A Social Critique of the Judgement of Taste,* trans. Richard Nice (Cambridge: Harvard University Press, 1984).

23. See Barbara Ching, "Going Back to the Old Mainstream: *No Depression,* Robbie Fulks, and Alt.Country's Muddied Waters," in *A Boy Named Sue: Gender and Country Music,* ed. Kristine M. McCusker and Diane Pecknold, 178–95 (Jackson: University Press of Mississippi, 2004).

24. Eric Lott, *Love and Theft: Blackface Minstrelsy and the American Working Class* (New York: Oxford University Press, 1995).

BARBARA CHING

Meeting in the Marketplace: A Taste for Romance in *Songcatcher* and *O Brother, Where Art Thou?*

Scholars have taken to calling the 1927 recording session in Bristol, Tennessee, that resulted in Victor Records impresario Ralph Peer's discovery of the Carter Family and Jimmie Rodgers, "the big bang of country music."[1] It's not surprising, then, that alt.country looks to this defining moment in country music tradition as it enacts its relationship to its roots. Oddly enough, though, the staid Carter Family rather than the "rough and rowdy" Rodgers serves as alt.country music's iconic form of tradition.[2] Uncle Tupelo's 1990 cover of the Carters' "No Depression" can be said to have launched the genre, and, as was recounted in the introduction, a group of Tupelo fans named their Internet discussion space after the song. The founders of *No Depression* magazine, with their title choice, including the long-lived subtitle, the "Journal of Alt.Country, Whatever That Is," further disseminated the foundational link between the Carters and alt.country. Even earlier, California country rockers the Nitty Gritty Dirt Band joined their brand of progressive country to the Carters and their cohorts with their *Will the Circle Be Unbroken* projects. Named after a traditional song popularized by the Carters, the Dirt Band's 1972 triple album featured Earl Scruggs, Merle Travis, Roy Acuff, and Maybelle Carter in solo numbers and group efforts with the long-haired Dirt Band members, culminating in the ensemble track "Will the Circle Be Unbroken," a song about a funeral procession for the singer's dead mother. The album cover, however, implied that the circle remained unbroken thanks to the music on the (round) record: under a round picture of

Robert E. Lee, the caption reads "Music forms a new circle." As I have argued elsewhere, the *Circle* project positioned the Nitty Gritty Dirt Band as the Ralph Peers of the late twentieth century.[3] In 1989, their *Circle II* further solidified the link between contemporary progressive country music and the founding family. This album was dedicated to Maybelle (she died in 1978) and featured Johnny Cash, Rosanne Cash, and Maybelle's daughters. A special verse of the title track even has the whole cast claim that they are singing songs "that Mother Maybelle taught us." On the cover, a photograph of Maybelle replaces the picture of Robert E. Lee, and the caption predicts that "The circle will continue." In 2002, *Circle III* features a rustic image of Maybelle in the cover's circle and has family members still onboard, this time June Carter Cash.

Extending backward and forward in time, the Carter Family offers both a living tradition and a foundational text for alt.country. As Pamela Fox shows in her essay in this volume, the hardscrabble image they offer of life in a remote backwater so readily contrasts with mainstream ease that much alt.country discourse has fetishized and feminized it into a troubling form of rustic abjection. At the same time, Jon Smith persuasively argues that Generation X has developed alt.country as an acquired taste used to distinguish itself from the baby boomer's classic rock. With branches that can be traced to Johnny Cash and his still living and performing children, the Carter legacy remains open to the future. Thus, in this essay I will argue that even the most rustic and remote aspects of that legacy can be imagined as a force for change, an alternative in the true sense of the word. To make this argument, I will focus on two films about the creation of country music, *Songcatcher* (dir. Maggie Greenwald) and *O Brother, Where Art Thou?* (dir. Coen Brothers). In fact, both the Coen Brothers and Maggie Greenwald claim that their films are musicals.[4] Released in December of 2000, both films function in implicit reference (and contrast) to the senses of tradition and authenticity associated with the emergence of both mainstream country music and alt.country. Both films revisit the creation scenario and both cast alt.country stars in small roles. Subsequent soundtracks and sequel projects sparked further creation and collaboration. The *Songcatcher* soundtrack, for example, was subtitled *Music from and Inspired by the Motion Picture.* The "inspired by" songs performed by alt.country luminaries such as Rosanne Cash, Gillian Welch, and Julie Miller linked the film to alt.country rather than contemporary mainstream music. The soundtrack "prequel," *Songcatcher II: The Tra-*

dition That Inspired the Movie, featured archival recordings of Doc Watson, Maybelle Carter, and other traditional Appalachian artists captured during the midcentury folk revival. Likewise, *O Brother*'s soundtrack featured Emmylou Harris, Gillian Welch, Allison Krauss, and traditional stalwarts such as Ralph Stanley, alongside archival recordings such as Harry McClintock's 1928 "Big Rock Candy Mountain" and traditional stalwarts such as Ralph Stanley. Significantly, it achieved best-sellerdom and won the Grammy for album of the year in 2002 without any airplay support from mainstream country radio. Although the film was set in 1930s Mississippi, the follow-up documentary, *Down from the Mountain* (2001), about a reunion concert by the soundtrack performers, situates the music's origins in the trajectory between the Appalachians and Nashville. Most important, the music directors of both films, David Mansfield for *Songcatcher* and T-Bone Burnett for *O Brother,* share an alt.country lineage: both played in Bob Dylan's Rolling Thunder Revue (1975–76) and went on to form the Alpha Band together (1976–79). In short, the music that emerges from both films draws on the alt.country repertoire and displays alt.country's reverence for country music tradition, and their soundtracks drew the attention of new audience members to the music. Moreover, the stories told in both films diverge dramatically from alt.country's agonistic story about its battle with the music industry: in both *O Brother* and *Songcatcher,* the music lives happily ever after in the marketplace.

In discussing these narratives, I will draw particular attention to the interaction of ideas about tradition, musical choices, and narrative to argue that in both films the heroes' and heroines' musical experiences teach them to resist an investment in a pure musical heritage in favor of American diversity *and* entrepreneurship. In both films, musical purists and cultural fundamentalists are linked to troubling forms of racism and patriarchy. Similarly, I focus on the specter of A. P. Carter in the films, the "paterfamilias," as *O Brother*'s Ulysses McGill would say, of the Carter Family, who occasionally performed with sister-in-law Maybelle and wife Sara but whose real role was that of an enterprising songcatcher. A. P.'s songcatching is nearly invisible in alt.country's nostalgic reverence for the family, but through these film narratives, I will explore the desires that motivate songcatchers. It was A. P. who arranged for the initial audition and subsequent contracts with record producer Ralph Peer, and he was also largely responsible for the Carter Family repertoire. A. P. already knew some songs, or at least had access to them through the communal experience of songs that "everybody knows," but he also sought them out through rambling, supposedly disappearing for weeks at a time on song-catching expeditions, often in the company of African American guitar player Lesley Riddle.[5] But what made A. P. especially attractive to Peer was his ability to alter the songs he found, to turn them into something new. Rather than displaying a folklorist's and fundamentalist's reverence for the text, A. P. viewed the texts as sources of inspiration and opportunity, making them eligible for copyright and thus suitable for entry into the marketplace. In these films, the audience can experience the kind of emotions that made Peer's propositions attractive to A. P., who did not want to "see himself as a lifelong dirt farmer."[6] The Carter paterfamilias saw the marketplace as a way to escape his rustic abjection even as his music expressed it, an outcome, I will argue, that also lends the films their happy endings. These films thus both capture and break through the static images of tradition in an alt.country context. Ultimately, I argue that these films contribute to a new discourse of authenticity that validates originality over origins and encourages sympathy, identification, and affection in the audience. They portray a taste for the music as an expression of hope for the country rather than a symbol of superior judgment. Above all, they portray the music, for both its audience and its makers, as a force for progress rather than a static relic from the past.

I am not so much arguing against the critiques put forth in this volume by Pamela Fox and Jon Smith as I am optimistically pointing to a sort of "political unconscious" in these films that creates an imaginary solution to the corruptions of taste in the postmodern marketplace.[7] In *Songcatcher* and *O Brother,* the audience can experience the music as a release from rustic abjection just as the fictive performers do. The desire that emerges from the films is, in a broad sense, the desire for alternatives. The fictional elements of the two films, blended with images of country music history and appearances by alt.country artists, take the shape of romance, a narrative genre defined by Fredric Jameson as a "utopian fantasy which aims at the transfiguration of the world of everyday life in such a way as to restore the conditions of some lost Eden, or to anticipate a future realm from which the . . . imperfections will have been effaced."[8] In positing this utopian element of romance, Jameson draws on Northrop Frye, who breaks the structure of romance into "three main stages . . . the perilous journey . . . the crucial struggle, usually some kind of battle in which the hero or his foe, or both, must die; and the exaltation of the hero."[9] The object of the quest embodies "wealth in its ideal forms: power and wisdom"—not money but, rather, creative power, a triumph of "fertility over the waste land." In addition to a hero and an enemy, romances often feature helping characters such as the faithful companions that accompany Aeneas and Dante on their adventures.[10] The remote and elevated settings also connect these films to the mountaintops and towers of romance.[11] Romance, like alt.country, rides its steed to a place where there's no depression. The narrative structure of these films, then, mirrors both the historical situation and the quest of alt.country fans and artists, expressing the wish for an unmediated relationship with the traditions of country music amid the ubiquity of the commodity form. However, as Jameson has so eloquently argued, the value of genre criticism lies in its ability to reveal the historical specificity of a given example of the form.[12] In these films, that specificity lies not only in their engagement with alt.country, itself steeped in history, but also in their use of irony to muddy the opposition between heroes and villains and to trouble the authenticity of the music that becomes the object of the quests. Thus, in my analysis of these late-twentieth-century narratives, I will draw attention to the nearly unbridgeable differences between the mythic origins of quest romances and the realities of the postmodern marketplace—a sort of metaconflict that, I have argued, structures alt.country itself. Although *O Brother* relies more heavily on irony, I will focus more of my discussion on the less familiar *Songcatcher*.[13]

Songcatcher opens in 1907, twenty years before Peer's discovery of the Carters but at the beginning of an intense interest in the music of Appalachia. Between 1882 and 1898, a Harvard English professor, Francis J. Child, published *The English and Scottish Popular Ballads*, a five-volume collection of ballad lyrics that he believed predated the printing press. While ballad collections had been published before, the scope and purported antiquity of Child's project captured the public imagination; within a decade, folklorists and amateur folk song collectors excitedly reported finding versions of the ballads in the Appalachians. Many enthused about the "purity" of their discoveries due to the supposed isolation of the eighteenth-century British immigrants and their descendants from the corrupting influences of modernization. When the Englishman Cecil Sharp visited the mountains in search of English ballads, he described the people he encountered as "just English peasant folk [who] do not seem to me to have taken on any distinctive American traits."[14] Even during the midcentury folk revival, Kentuckian

Jean Thomas, founder of the American Folk Song Festival, wrote in the liner notes to a 1960 Folkways album featuring highlights from the festival that

> at the close of the Elizabethan era, English, Scotch, and Scotch Irish wearied of the tyranny of their kings and spurred by undaunted courage and love of independence . . . braved the perils of uncharted seas to seek freedom in a new world. Some tarried in the colonies but the braver, bolder, more venturesome of spirit pressed deep into the Appalachians bringing with them—hope in their hearts, song on their lips—the songs their Anglo-Saxon forbears had gathered from the wandering minstrels of Shakespeare's time. These sturdy Anglo-Saxons so loved the mountainous regions of Appalachia that they were content there to live almost untouched by the outside world until a century later. From these sturdy Anglo-Saxons descended the sturdy mountain people of today—who still love to sing the songs of their forbears.[15]

In 1934, *Time* magazine reported that Thomas acted as mistress of festival ceremonies dressed in Elizabethan costume.[16] Paradoxically, as David Whisnant has carefully documented, some found the ballads particularly compelling because they could favorably contrast the ethnic origins of the British Appalachians with the disconcerting influx of non-English-speaking immigrants. Robert Winslow Gordon, the first director of the Library of Congress' Archive of American Folk Song (now the American Folklife Center), advocated the collection of English folk songs for just that reason: "I frankly believe that the whole project of reviving and making known our true American folk stuff is one of the most worthwhile things to be done today. From the point of view of true Americanism. That stuff is the very soul of our past, of pioneers, of the men who made America. It's not modern Hebrew Broadway jazz."[17] While scholars can now document that the music of the Appalachians, like most American music, can be traced to multiple ethnic sources,[18] the origins of American country music continue to be linked to the Child ballads. Bob Dylan, introducing the Carters' "Wildwood Flower" on his *Theme Time Radio Hour,* called the family "the most influential group in country music history" and specifically credited A. P. Carter and the old English ballads for their repertoire: "A. P. collected hundreds of British Appalachian folk songs and recorded them."[19] In fact, several Carter Family numbers can be linked to Child ballads,[20] and even today country singers regularly record key songs such as Child 84, better known as "Barbara Allen."

Songcatchers, a colloquial term for the folklorists and amateurs who went in search of old ballads, can easily be compared to knights in search of a grail; the title of Benjamin Filene's history of early-twentieth-century folk music, *Romancing the Folk: Public Memory and American Roots Music,* for example, draws attention to this tendency. Likewise, Columbia University professor Dorothy Scarborough opened her 1935 memoir, *A Song Catcher in the Southern Mountains,* by explaining that "this book represents the partial results of a summer spent *questing* for folk songs in Virginia and North Carolina."[21] Greenwald's adaptation, recombination, and fictionalization of historical elements all add to the romance plot. Approached by a producer interested in having her direct a film about the early days of the country music industry, she says she was struck by the role of women as both bearers of the ballad tradition and bearers of news about it. She names ballad collector and settlement school founder Olive Dame Campbell in particular: "I set the film in 1907 in honor of Olive Campbell. That was the year that she heard a schoolgirl sing 'Barbara Allen' and recognized it and collected ballads."[22] While Greenwald drew inspiration from the life of Olive Dame Campbell, her additions heighten the quest narrative. In particular, Greenwald stresses the songcatcher's conflict with the patriarchal worlds of academia *and* mountain society that Campbell, in her letters and other records, did not dwell on. Nevertheless, Whisnant provides evidence that the women at settlement schools did indeed find mountain society remarkably patriarchal.[23] Moreover, Greenwald surrounds her heroine, Lily Penleric, with helping characters reminiscent of "real" songcatchers. Lily's friend Alice Kincaid echoes Emma Bell Miles, another historical figure who brought news of mountain music to the mainstream when she published an account of it in *Harper's* in 1904. The well-educated daughter of schoolteachers, she eloped with a feckless mountaineer and supported her family with her paintings, poems, and accounts of life in the highlands.[24] The mountaineer with the most knowledge about ballads, Viney Butler, also embodies a familiar figure in the lore of ballad collecting; Bufwack and Oermann cite several passages of ballad collectors' praise for the "old prophetesses" and grandmothers who shared their vast repository of song. Similarly, Zwonitzer and Hirshberg tell about Carter Family neighbor, Amanda "Aunt Mandy" Groves, an old woman whose "mother lode of songs" frequently lured A. P. to visit her.[25] Greenwald also speculates that *Songcatcher*'s lesbian subplot has a basis in the history of settlement schools given the number of "spinster schoolteachers" who migrated to the mountains in search of worthwhile work and meaningful lives.[26]

Songcatcher's heroine, Lily Penleric, begins the film as the only woman faculty member at a stuffy New England music conservatory, although Greenwald admits in the director's commentary on the DVD that there were no women musicologists in America in 1907. After being refused a promotion to full professor, ostensibly so the conservatory can hire Cyrus Whittle, an English-born expert in balladry, Lily undertakes her "perilous journey," a trip to the mountains. Lugging primitive recording equipment, she hopes to capture pure English folk ballads to serve as incontrovertible evidence of her scholarly prowess. While questing *heroes* inherently have our sympathy, as a *heroine* Lily fulfills the role more awkwardly. Precisely because she carries herself like an unobtainable princess of romance, she must struggle to gain acceptance in Clover, North Carolina, the Blue Ridge community where her sister Elna helps run a settlement school. Inescapably feminized in the male-dominated conservatory yet cold and commanding in Carolina, Lily is an alien or barbarian wherever she goes. No wonder the movie opens with her seated at a piano singing "Barbara Allen" to a classroom full of stiff young men and another lone woman. Once the performance ends, she tells the students that they "must learn to appreciate . . . the simple purity of emotions" contained in this folk song although she does not begin to explain what could possibly be pure or simple about it and her students show no sign of enthusiasm or understanding. Indeed, as Christine Cartwright points out, the tragic deaths related in the song are nearly incomprehensible. "There are no characters other than the lovers; their love does nothing but kill them both; and there is neither motive nor agent of death other than love itself."[27] At this point, all that is clear is that Lily, whose first name associates her with purity (and whose last name implies the sort of mechanical transcribing that she does), *wants* to believe in the purity and simplicity of this music—just as the men who outrank her do.

In fact, "Barbara Allen" serves as an ironic counterpoint to Lily's quest throughout the movie, complicating the normally stark differences between good and evil, pure and impure, male and female, and so on that typically structure a romance. "Barbara Allen" is the first song Lily hears when she arrives—sung by Deladis Slocumb, a young orphan who lives at the school. The first verses tell of sweet William who died for hardhearted Barbara's love and a chastened Barbara who dies in repentance. In the final verses, these two deaths come to represent true love when a rose growing from William's grave entwines with the briar growing from Barbara's.

They buried her in the old churchyard
They buried him in the choir
And from his grave grew a red, red rose
From her grave a green briar
They grew and grew to the steeple top
Till they could grow no higher
And there they twined in a true love's knot
Red rose around green briar

This closing image colors the experiences of many of the mountaineers Lily encounters. One scene even shows two young lovers, Deladis and Fate, the school handyman, tying young branches together to create a "love knot" in order to test the endurance of their regard. But the "true love knots" formed in the Carolina mountains aren't like the eternally entwined one that marks the graves in the song: these knots come undone, and lovers often go their separate ways. In a surprising logic, then, broken love knots may well offer a better, or less sorrowful, outcome for the mountaineers whose lives don't conform to the ancient songs they sing. In this sense, the ballads that Lily seeks may express far more ambivalence than purity of emotion. They may be authentic heirlooms, but ultimately they lead to new stories to sing, songs that offer more emotionally authentic representations and evocations of the lives of their current singers.

Three mountain women assist Lily in her quest for these ballads even as they teach her to confront the paradoxes of Barbara Allen's barbarity. Mountain matriarch and ballad keeper Viney Butler transmits her skepticism about true love knots while two other women, Deladis and Alice Kincaid, triumph over broken love knots. Evoking Emma Bell Miles, Alice, a talented painter from an affluent background, had eloped with a shiftless, ballad-singing mountain man on a family vacation in the region. Abandoned by him, she struggles to feed her children and protect her unborn baby. Because she shares Lily's love of ballads, she convinces Viney to share her wealth of songs. Her suspicion overcome, Viney joyfully sings into Lily's machine although she cannot imagine accepting money for her performances. She also initiates Lily into mountain womanhood by insisting that the songcatcher assist at the difficult birth of Alice's baby. Viney welcomes the baby girl to the world by wishing her a life free of love knots: "Stay single," she says emphatically. Then, spattered with Alice's blood, all three women sing a song that Viney introduces: "I wish I was a single girl again."[28] Significantly, this anti-love song imagines a release from the rustic abjection that Pamela Fox suggests has been engendered into alt.country's nostalgic celebration of tradition. For that matter, the film's emphasis on relations among women and the female heroine in place of the knightly hero of romance further disrupt and discredit the tradition Lily has ostensibly come to preserve.

Viney's grandson, Tom Bledsoe, also plays the role of Lily's aide, reversing and questioning many of the roles that have shaped Lily's quest up to this point. His name (Bledsoe) connects him to the women's blood-stained suffering. Bledsoe has lived outside the mountains, fighting in Cuba, working in coal mines, and returning with hitherto unknown instruments, a banjo and guitar.[29] As the grandson of Viney and a lover of mountain music, he becomes the professor's teacher. Eventually he teaches Lily to play the dulcimer. Initially, however, he suspects Lily's motives and tries to persuade Viney to stop working with her. While she assures him that she intends to "exalt" his grandmother's stock of ballads, Tom insists she will "exploit" them. The difference turns on a syllable and will never be fully resolved—indeed, as I will argue, Lily's quest culminates not in alt.country's aestheticized irony about the marketplace but rather in an embrace of this ambiguity. The unspoken term that negotiates the dispute may be *creativity* because Tom embraces the new at the same time that he defends the old. He plays at community gatherings such as barn dances and funerals but also writes his own songs and, as his instrument collection suggests, he gathers new sounds in addition to old songs. In a key scene, set at the tiny Clover post office, the logical site of important exchanges, Tom plays a banjo duet with Dexter Speaks, a black musician (played by Taj Mahal), thereby introducing an unsettling dose of "impurity" into the music. Lily, Fate, and Deladis happen upon them as they play. While Lily has the composure to compliment the men on their original composition, Deladis gapes in wonder. When Tom asks her if she has never seen a black man before, her subdued response—"Where would I?"—lingers unanswered and uncomfortably in the open air. Although Deladis owes her remarkable ballad repertoire to her grandmother, her unspecified parentage suddenly seems as mysterious as her dark eyes and dark curls. As a further indication of Tom's openness, he, unlike

Lily, is accepting of a lesbian affair between Lily's sister Elna and Harriet, the settlement schoolmistress. As if to heighten Tom's gender disruption, the script casts this disapproval as a masculine trait; when Lily angrily confronts Elna about the affair, Elna retorts, "You sound just like father."

The villains in this story first appear in all the simplicity of the romance plot, but the worst villains are not immediately apparent. Indeed, Lily is constantly forced to reexamine her assumptions about purity and danger. The figure of Cyrus Whittle, whose name so clearly evokes the folk song scholar Cecil Sharp, breaks from Lily's other male colleagues who would chauvinistically deny her the laurels she has earned. Once they get news of Lily's discoveries in the mountains, these patriarchs announce that they are sending Whittle himself to supervise her work. When he arrives in the mountains, however, Whittle, much like Bledsoe, says he intends to assist Lily. Likewise, the McFarland Coal Company and its agent Earl Giddens do not consistently thwart the music and the mountains that nourish it. Nevertheless, the company plans to buy up the land around Clover and mine it. Native to the region, Earl tries to convince his neighbors to sell their land to McFarland. He repeatedly reminds them that they could leave the mountains and get an education if they weren't saddled with failing farms. Inexplicably, he has a degree from the University of North Carolina and claims to prefer Bach to ballads. Although his neighbors unfailingly treat him with hostility, he attends the big barn dance and leads off the final song of the night, a haunting rendition of "O Death." The music thus enfolds him in the community even as his work seems to undermine it. Likewise, he inadvertently unites Lily and Tom when his increasingly aggressive attempts to entice her to join him on the dance floor force Bledsoe to come to her aid. The so-called exploiters and their victims, in short, are drawn to each other through the music they make together. After the evening at the dance, Tom and Lily even begin an affair.

The villainy of the McFarland Coal Company becomes even more tenuous when McFarland himself attends a tea party at the Clover school. Another guest, a withered minister, argues that the church should run the school since a clergyman and his wife "would integrate more normally into the community" than the two women who currently preside there. McFarland and his wife simply ignore him. The party culminates in a fragile standoff when McFarland implicitly rebuffs the minister's chauvinism by offering a substantial donation to the women of the Clover school. He even claims that this gift demonstrates his belief in "progress." Elna and Harriet high-mindedly refuse the money, however, even though the running water that it would have afforded might have saved the school from its fiery end. In contrast, when the conversation turns to Mrs. McFarland's enthusiasm for collecting the native arts, Deladis immediately draws the parallel between Mrs. McFarland's enthusiasm for mountain handicrafts and Lily's songcatching. Rather than rejecting the connection, Lily seizes the opportunity to interest the McFarlands in Alice Kincaid's landscape paintings since this wealthy patroness could help Alice feed her children, and indeed, the McFarlands' patronage eventually allows Alice to support her family on the mountain land she loves.

An ordinary mountain man, Fate Honeycutt (as the name suggests), turns out to be the true enemy of Lily and the music. A petulant adolescent employee of the school, Fate resents the extra work Lily creates. He hears no value in the music so he particularly dislikes hauling heavy recording equipment through the wilderness. In love with Deladis, he also envies the influence Lily has over the girl and the judgment she unsubtly passes on him. As the residents of the schoolhouse gather around the hearth on Lily's first night there, Lily, glancing at Fate as he whittles, asks the women if they aren't afraid of their surroundings. Harriet asks for specifics: what would they be afraid of? Of savagery, Lily replies as she gazes at Fate and his knife. When he stumbles on Elna and Harriet in an embrace, his "savagery" finds an outlet, and it brings Lily to the "crucial struggle" that culminates her quest. Fate joins forces with the most vocally religious men in the community and sets the school on fire. In the church meeting that follows, a new, less unified voice of the community emerges. Viney speaks first, declaring her shame about the destruction of the school and asserting that she has seen "nothing but good" come from the schoolteachers' work. Those who side with Fate, however, cite Scripture, condemning the women as "whores of Babylon." In any case, these men long ago renounced the mountain culture that interests Lily: as part of their religion, they gave up ballad singing. In its place, they inherit the scorched earth of the schoolyard and their exhausted farms while those who side with the settlement school and the songcatcher concomitantly choose to take the music and join the world outside the mountains—even if, like Viney, they choose to finish their days in Clover. She, we learn at the end of the film, will continue to share her songs with songcatchers. Similarly, Alice, now a "single girl" since her husband has been shot by a jealous lover, will support her family as a painter of mountain landscapes. Her images, like the ballads, will take on a life elsewhere.

The presence of alt.country star Iris DeMent lends contemporary resonance to the fate of the ballads.[30] Playing mountain woman Rose Gentry, she and her husband Parley decide to sell their depleted land for an obscenely low price of fifty cents an acre. Giddens persuaded them with the promise of jobs in town and education for their children. Lily witnesses the "bargain," and, although she berates Giddens for his chicanery, the Gentrys seem resigned to the deal. As a final gesture, Parley solemnly takes down his fiddle to accompany Rose as she stoically sings "Saro Jane," a sort of farewell to their life in the mountains and an announcement of another broken love knot. ("Well, my true love she won't have me and it's this I understand / For she wants some free holder and I have no land.") The performance also implies that they are giving the song to Lily for much the same reason that they turned the land over to the coal company: they no longer want it. They need new forms of sustenance. Later, when the churchgoers and the Clover school women have their confrontation, Parley echoes Viney's support of the school (and simultaneously conflates the teachers with the Gidden/McFarland team) when he speaks out in favor of education—especially the education his grandchildren will receive when they leave the mountain—the education that Gidden and Lily already have.[31] The Gentrys, as their name implies, want what the marketplace offers them: freedom from rustic abjection, a place in a changing world, a stake in the future.

As heroes and villains blur, the object of Lily's quest also loses some luster. Likewise, Lily's notions of pure musical heritage, her professional ambitions, and her last remnants of sexual conventions also change. Her relationship with Tom brings admiration for *his* music in spite of the fact that we never hear him sing a traditional ballad. While she braves death by running into the burning schoolhouse to retrieve her manuscripts and recording cylinders, once they are gone, she decides not to begin again (unlike Elna, who chooses to rebuild the school). The folk song collection, she claims, no longer interests her since she has come to love the voices of those who sing them more than she loves the ancestry of the songs. Instead she proposes that she and Tom move to the city (the name Nashville is never uttered) where she will produce recordings of his music and sell them to crowds of new phonograph owners. She also makes it clear that she is not envisioning a typical heterosexual partnership when she scoffs at his concerns about being unable to support her. In other words, they do not plan to "tie the knot." Likewise, Deladis rejects Fate, telling him, "I don't want no part of you. . . . The love knot didn't hold." At this point, Lily declares her love for Deladis. Tom then consents to Lily's plan and invites Deladis to join them in the exodus down the mountain and into commercial music making. She accepts this offer without guidance from any ballads. These three lives will no longer be molded by the broken or deadly love knots that the old ballads tell about.

While Lily originally loved the ballads for the "simple purity" she heard in them, her break with folkloric fundamentalism is complete when she comes face-to-face with the noted ballad collector Cyrus Whittle. As the newly formed family of Tom, Lily, and Deladis move down the mountain, they encounter a jaunty Englishman in a fancy car struggling to make his way up. He asks how to find Lily Penleric and the "recognitions" unfold with Sophoclean speed: Cyrus Whittle learns that Lily's collection has burned and she no longer cares to re-create it even with him as her assistant. She directs him to Viney for help, although it's clear that he lacks the resourcefulness to succeed. Even the shock of his willingness to serve her cannot reignite Lily's faith in pure balladry. Whittle also announces that he will name her as first author on the book he will publish, but Lily is not seriously tempted. Driven out of the academy and the mountain community, Lily Penleric's triumph comes when she *can choose* to leave both. Then she gaily chooses the marketplace and the promise of profiting from new technology yoked to old-style songs. The rejection of ballad collecting is complicated only by Lily's imperious coda: she turns back to forcefully remind Whittle of the correct spelling of her name: "that's Penleric, one N, no K."[32] Her signature, then, remains on these old ballads even as she looks toward transforming them in the future.

As the film ends, the romance plot, too, seems to enter the modern world. Lily keeps moving "down the mountain," thereby leaving the lofty space of romance (which turned into a wasteland) and entering the fertile world of the city where she is no longer a songcatcher but a song producer, a Ralph Peer in love with her version of A. P. Carter. The audience can believe that the trio of Lily, Tom, and Deladis succeed since the closing credits roll with a sound from the future, Emmylou Harris' familiar voice singing a rock-inflected, alt.country version of "Barbara Allen." While Lily once believed she had found "the purest versions in existence," what we hear is far from that, especially since it accompanies a happy ending. As many essays in this collection demonstrate, alt.country's rejection of the marketplace is inevitably complicated by its need for a presence there. This is the dilemma characterized in *Songcatcher* in the unresolvable difference and similarity of exploiting and exalting that bring Tom and Lily together and connect songcatching to song producing. While other forms of alt.country discourse cast the marketplace as the enemy, in *Songcatcher* the marketplace is the utopian space that will allow the voices of the people to be heard outside the mountains, in the spaces where power resides. In an impassioned moment with Tom, Lily insists that this contact is the only way to keep the "mountain ways" alive. In this respect, the alternative that *Songcatcher* imagines for country music and the country that listens to it differs dramatically from alt.country's typical discourse about itself. In this movie, the real enemies are not so much the mediocre musicologists or savage hillbillies or local capitalists that initially menace the music-loving innocents but rather the fundamentalism that enables these men to impose their static visions of the past and future on others. Even Lily's transformation (from the questing hero of a romance into a productive resident in the modern world) hinges on her forsaking the fundamentalism of the old British ballad book. When Whittle plaintively asks, "What on earth could be more important than this collection of songs?," Tom and Lily exchange knowing glances. They'll keep the secret from knaves and fools like Fate and Whittle, but their success in the world requires that they convince many others that the ballads they want to hear are not relics in a song collection but rather part of an ever-expanding collection of voices that *may* be diverse, neither purely black nor white, male nor female, new nor traditional, but *are not* barbarous or alien.

While *O Brother, Where Art Thou?* differs in many ways from *Songcatcher*, particularly in its visual richness and tonal complexity, the film premiered just three weeks after *Songcatcher* with a similarly rootsy soundtrack, musical main characters, a historical setting, and onscreen alt.country stars projecting the music into the present. Like *Songcatcher, O Brother* sends its heroes on a quest for a treasure, this time modeling the romance on Homer's *Odyssey*. Everett Ulysses McGill, a chain gang escapee, has convinced his dim-witted cohorts Delmar and Pete to join him in recovering a heist he claims to have buried before the Tennessee Valley Authority floods his Ithaca, Mississippi, homestead, although he really just needs their help to keep his estranged wife Penny from remarrying. Everett actually has no ill-gotten gains for his partners to uncover; unbeknownst to them, he was convicted for practicing law without a license, ultimately a form of heroism in this film that burlesques many foundational texts. In any case, early in their journey, the quest is given an alternate direction when the three escapees are told by a blind seer that the treasure they find will not be the treasure they are seeking. In fact, they gain their treasure by singing what they call "old-timey" music, particularly the traditional "Man of Constant Sorrow."

What "Barbara Allen" is to *Songcatcher,* "Man of Constant Sorrow" is to *O Brother, Where Art Thou?*, a song that evolves through the film as it touches the lives of most characters although it does not ultimately characterize their lives. Just as *Songcatcher's* heroes forswear fatal love knots, Everett and friends will not endure constant sorrow. Instead, the song is Everett's faithful companion, helping him (and the other Soggy Bottom Boys) to realize a treasure. The song also encompasses the hero's relationship with country music tradition. He has fathered a brood of daughters, the Wharvey Gals, who perform the Carter Family theme song "Keep on the Sunny Side," although in this case they use the song to advance the gubernatorial campaign of the doomed Homer Stokes. While "Man of Constant Sorrow" strikes a cloudy emotional note, it, too, has an important history in the alt.country pantheon. The song was first published by a fiddler, Richard Burnett, in 1913, although he said someone else taught it to him. Cecil Sharp collected a version of it in 1918. Since then, it has been recorded by Ralph Stanley (1959) and Bob Dylan for his first album (*Bob Dylan,* 1962).[33] Although it has no direct association with the Carter Family, it contains the African American gospel tradition the Carters drew upon—in 1928, for example, they recorded "River of Jordan"[34]—and in the film it magically enfolds the birth of the blues. As Everett and his ball and chain mates leave their prison farm, they manage to steal a car. Shortly thereafter, they come to a crossroads where they pick up a young African American who introduces himself as Tommy Johnson. This musician, reminiscent of Robert Johnson, tells them he has just sold his soul to the devil in exchange for guitar-playing prowess and he now intends to earn some money on the bargain. He directs them to a radio station where he has heard that a man will pay them for "singing into a can."

Once there, they discover that recording technology can benefit them more greatly than they expected. The station owner/record producer is blind, so Everett, mistakenly guessing that the man is interested in Negro spirituals, introduces them as Jordan Rivers and the Soggy Bottom Boys.

When asked if they are Negroes, Everett asserts that all but one of them are. When the producer then says he wants "ol-timey material" like that performed on Governor Pappy O'Daniel's radio show, Everett changes the story and Delmar announces that all but one of them are white. They launch into a jolly rendition of "Man of Constant Sorrow," evidently a song so familiar that they can expertly perform it unrehearsed. Significantly, the producer cannot rely on his ears for the truth, and the four men are even able to extract payment for six musicians from him. These escaped con artists evidently sound as authentically old-timey as any of the other acts the producer judges them against—perhaps because their outcast mixture of races and their blend of banal crimes and blasphemy rings true to what traditional southern music *could* sound like.

The scatological connotation of their name (Soggy Bottom Boys) indicates their initial marginality,[35] and it also points to the "treasure they seek" in the soon to be deluged land in Ithaca, Mississippi. Most important, unbeknownst to them, the song becomes a best seller and thus leads to the treasure they get—but not before they meet the requisite obstacles and "crucial struggles" with foes. Some, like the Sirens, emerge directly out of the *Odyssey*, but logically Everett's enemies are the licensed law-enforcing defenders of the status quo, especially Sheriff Cooley (who matches Tommy's description of the devil and whose name and ever-present sunglasses mirror the music-squelching sheriff in *Cool Hand Luke*). As in *Songcatcher*, those who control the culture's fundamental texts oppose the improvisations and creations that spring from other voices. Thus, the Soggy Bottom Boys encounter a violent, oversized, one-eyed Bible salesman and, above all, the diminutive Homer Stokes, Pappy O'Daniel's opponent in the gubernatorial race, employer of the singing Wharvey Gals, Klansman, and namesake of the *Odyssey*'s blind author.

Like the blind record producer, these men advocate racial and cultural purity; unlike him, they have the power, at least initially, to enforce their standards. Meanwhile, in a moment of honor among thieves, Everett, overcome with guilt for lying about the buried treasure, confesses to Delmar and Pete. They are distracted from their anger, however, by their decisive confrontation with the villains: they stumble on a Ku Klux Klan meeting where Tommy is being lynched. They hear Homer declaring that the purpose of the "ceremony" is to "preserve our hallowed culture'n heritage! From intrusions, inclusions, and dilutions!" The Bible salesman stands by his side. The stage directions specify that the Klansmen are "chanting in a high hillbilly wail,"[36] linking the musical component of their cultural heritage not to a valuable form of authenticity but rather to virulent racism. Like *Songcatcher*'s Earl Giddens, the Klansmen join in a rendition of "O Death." In order to arm themselves against these villains and rescue Tommy, the heroes somehow don blackface, infiltrate the ceremony, and rescue Tommy. From there, disguised as old-timers, they crash a fund-raising dinner for Stokes' campaign and entertain the crowd as the Soggy Bottom Boys. The ecstatic crowd can see that the band, as Homer Stokes points out, is "miscegenated." Their manic performance of "Man of Constant Sorrow," however, warms the crowd to integration, so Stokes does not get the approval he was hoping for when he announces that the Soggy Bottom Boys are neither racially nor musically pure: "These boys is not white. . . . Hell, they ain't even ol'-timey." Incumbent Pappy O'Daniel, who up to this point has been losing the gubernatorial campaign to the segregationist Stokes, seizes this turning point to work the room and award the boys a position as his "brain trust." He also pardons them for their crimes and jailbreaks. The song, then, has conferred social status and political power on criminals—and the audience, both within the film and in the theater, applauds this turn of events just as they applaud the song that is neither white nor old-timey. The film even shows radio audiences in their homes smiling at this outcome.

Just as in *Songcatcher*'s presentation of "Barbara Allen," emotional authenticity plays no part in the power of the Soggy Bottom Boys' music. Instead, the success of this record underscores the transformative power generated by the mass dissemination of popular music. Although they are bedeviled with bad luck, living in the poorest state in the union during the Great Depression, and singing under a scatological name, the Soggy Bottom Boys do not experience constant sorrow. Everett Ulysses McGill, their leader, does not even believe in the religious salvation that the song promises and mocks Delmar and Pete's belief that their recent baptism will save them. Instead, McGill truly believes that life in the twentieth century will get ever better thanks to modern developments such as electricity and mass media. The morning after the concert, the men head to Everett's homestead not to find the treasure he promised them but to help him find his wife's wedding ring since she insists on having it before she will (re)marry him. Upon arrival, the "boys" have a frightening encounter with Sheriff Cooley who claims no knowledge of their pardon. While the sudden onrush of the flood spares them from this law enforcement, it makes finding the wedding ring nearly impossible. Nevertheless, Ulysses ebulliently greets the deluge as a man of enlightenment rather than a man of constant sorrow. Even his failed attempt to remarry cannot dim Everett's optimism. Although Everett tries to convince Penny that a ring Tommy found in the flood should suffice, since a ring is "just a symbol," she insists on fundamentalism: no original wedding ring, no wedding. Here the plot breaks its connection to the *Odyssey:* Homer's Ulysses rejoined his Penelope. It also diverges from country music tradition as Everett's daughters, the Carteresque Wharvey Gals, walk away singing only to themselves, leaving the enterprising Ulysses, the A. P. Carter of this singing family, to the treasure he didn't seek: life as a Soggy Bottom Boy. As if to confirm this fate, the blind seer on the railroad car rolls by. Now Everett's treasure, like Lily Penleric's ballads, will be forever under construction in the marketplace. As a member of Pappy O'Daniel's brain trust, Everett will in some sense resume practicing law without a license; at any rate, he need not return to farming, whether at the prison or his flooded homestead. In addition, as a Soggy Bottom Boy, he will not be able to live on constant sorrow alone. Like A. P. Carter working for Ralph Peer, and like Lily Penleric and Tom Bledsoe, Everett will continue to seek treasures, transmuting his cultural heritage into new songs and hence new records.

Visually, the Soggy Bottom Boys' record reinforces this dynamic. It echoes the ludicrous and elusive can of "Dapper Dan" hair pomade that Everett vainly seeks in the same stores where customers ask for copies of the similarly elusive, similarly round, red and black recording of "Man of Constant Sorrow." These commodities, no matter how arbitrary the preference for them (What, after all, can distinguish brand X from Dapper Dan? What distinguishes "authentic" old-timey music from the Soggy Bottom Boys' songs?), are treasures that people seek. For that matter, Penny's lost wedding ring reflects an arbitrary but strongly held desire. Just as Everett will use nothing but Dapper Dan, Penny will accept no substitutes. But Penny's desire locks her into a completely submerged past. Conversely, in the middle of the film, a montage juxtaposes the records and cans of Dapper Dan with yet another circle, the steering wheel of a car, and their very similarity suggests that some meaning, some pattern, and some movement into the future resides in the force of *those* desires. In particular, the presence of alt.diva Gillian Welch, described by the screenplay as a "sad faced woman in a calico dress,"[37] asking for the record in a dusty general store draws the con artistry of this miscegenated "old-timey" music into the present, and perhaps the future, of alt.country. Musical taste in *O Brother* matters, just as it does in *Songcatcher,* because taste allows people to interpret their past, escape it if necessary, and imagine their future. This unbroken circle rolls forward.

Likewise, romance exists and persists to articulate social wishes, rescuing them from the historical forces that repress or distort them. Romance, like alt.country, imagines a transformed society in which wishes may be realized. In these millennium alt.country romances, it is no surprise to see that the stark contrasts between good and evil dissolve just as the object of the quest—folk and old-time music—loses its purity. In fact, the purists, in both *Songcatcher* and *O Brother,* resort to violence in a losing battle to maintain their backward and backward-looking notions of cultural purity. The heroes, on the other hand, look toward a future of making music involving further miscegenation and innovation. Finally, both films transform the object of romance, the grail, into an unfinished product that will *both* sell *and* sing truth to power *because it's the music people want to hear.* By setting the films in imaginary versions of alt.country's past, the filmmakers can evade alt.country's own fundamentalist discourse of purity as well as the elitism of its taste culture.[38] Instead, the films offer their audience an opportunity to respond to *the desire* that moves the music to the marketplace. Rick Rubin's search of Johnny Cash's soul for new and strange versions of old songs created a similar possibility, now perhaps hopelessly frozen over by hip reverence. More recently, Bob Dylan, in his radio shows, pulls surprises from his bag of old songs, also creating brief moments of response that may precede the logic of commodified distinction. It is almost as if songs, once caught, are held in very loose cages, ready to reemerge through the contagious force of another songcatcher's transfiguring desire.

NOTES

1. See Charles K. Wolfe and Ted Olson, eds., *The Bristol Sessions: Writings about the Big Bang of Country Music* (Jefferson, NC: McFarland, 2005).

2. See Curtis Ellison's *Country Music Culture: From Hard Times to Heaven* (Jackson: University Press of Mississippi, 1995) for further discussion of how the contrasting images of the two seem to have established country music's emotional range, pitched between the nostalgic, stoically domestic mountain clan represented by the Carters and the hard-living "singing brakeman" portrayed by Rodgers (35).

3. Barbara Ching, "Country Music," in *The Blackwell Companion to the Literature and Culture of the American South,* ed. Richard Gray and Owen Robinson (Oxford: Blackwell, 2004), 211–13.

4. The Coens make this claim in the liner notes to the soundtrack from *O Brother, Where Art Thou?* (Mercury Records 088 170 069–2, 2000). Jean Oppenheimer reports that Greenwald described *Songcatcher* as a musical in "Elusive Tunes," *American Cinematographer,* December 2000, 77–78.

5. Mark Zwonitzer and Charles Hirshberg, *Will You Miss Me When I'm Gone?: The Carter Family and Their Legacy in American Music* (New York: Simon and Schuster, 2002), 128–33.

6. Ibid., 57.

7. See also Aaron A. Fox's discussion of the "bourgeois and cosmopolitan ideologies of value" at work in alt.country, particularly in the response to the *O Brother* soundtrack, in his "'Alternative' to What? 'O Brother,' September 11th, and the Politics of Country Music," in *There's a Star-Spangled Banner Waving Somewhere: Country Music Goes to War,* ed. C. Wolfe and J. Akenson (Lexington: University Press of Kentucky, 2005),185–88.

8. Fredric Jameson, *The Political Unconscious: Narrative as a Socially Symbolic Act* (Ithaca: Cornell University Press, 1982), 110.

9. Northrop Frye, *Anatomy of Criticism* (Princeton: Princeton University Press, 1957), 110.

10. Ibid., 193.

11. Ibid., 203.

12. Jameson, *Political Unconscious,* 109, 129–34.

13. Much of my discussion of *Songcatcher* as a romance appears in "Happily Ever After in the Marketplace: The Ballads of the Southern Mountains and the Escape from Old Europe," in *Transatlantic Exchanges: The American South in Europe, Europe in the American South,* ed. Richard Gray and Waldemar Zacharasiewicz, 519–32 (Vienna: Verlag der Osterreichischen Akademie der Wissenschaften, 2007). I thank Richard Gray and Waldemar Zacharasiewicz for the invitation to present at the symposium that led to this collection. The participants' responses, suggestions, and questions all helped me develop my argument further, as did the comments of the Austrian Academy's anonymous reviewers. I also wish to acknowledge Elaine Lawless and faculty and students at the University of Missouri whose responses to my first version of the *O Brother* portion of this essay in February 2005 helped me move forward.

14. Cited by David Whisnant in *All That Is Native and Fine: The Politics of Culture in an American Region* (Chapel Hill: University of North Carolina Press, 1983), 116.

15. Jean Thomas, *American Folk Song Festival: Jean Thomas, The Traipsin' Woman!,* Smithsonian Folkways Records FW02358, 1960.

16. http://www.time.com/time/magazine/article/0,9171,747518,00.html (accessed February 2, 2007). The original issue date is June 18, 1934.

17. Cited in an unsigned essay entitled "Appalachian Music" on the Library of Congress website, http://lcweb2.loc.gov/cocoon/ihas/html/dollyparton/country-appalachian.html#ret3 (accessed February 2, 2007). See Benjamin Filene's *Romancing the Folk: Public Memory and American Roots Music* (Chapel Hill: University of North Carolina Press, 2000) for a nuanced defense of Gordon's commitment to documenting African American folk songs as part of the American folk heritage (40–44).

18. See Bill C. Malone's *Country Music, U.S.A.*, 2nd ed. (Austin: University of Texas Press, 1985), 1–29, for a thorough, well-documented discussion of country music's precommercial origins.

19. Broadcast July 12, 2006, XM Radio, station 40.

20. Zwonitzer and Hirshberg, *Will You Miss Me When I'm Gone?*, 24–25.

21. Dorothy Scarborough, *A Song Catcher in the Southern Mountains* (New York: Columbia University Press, 1937), ix, emphasis mine.

22. Howard Feinstein, "Singing Story" (interview with Maggie Greenwald), *Indiewire,* June 14, 2001, http://www.indiewire.com/people/int_Greenwald_Magg_010614.html (accessed July 30, 2006).

23. Whisnant, *All That Is Native and Fine,* 262.

24. See Mary Bufwack and Robert Oermann, *Finding Her Voice: Women in Country Music, 1800–2000* (Nashville: Country Music Foundation Press and Vanderbilt University Press, 2003), for a concise account of Miles' life and work in the mountains (2–22).

25. Ibid., 12; Zwonitzer and Hirshberg, *Will You Miss Me When I'm Gone?*, 119–20.

26. Feinstein, "Singing Story."

27. Christine Cartwright, "'Barbara Allen': Love and Death in an Anglo-American Narrative Folksong," in *Narrative Folksong: New Directions,* ed. Carol L. Edwards and Kathleen Manley (Boulder: Westview, 1985), 245. See also Dave Marsh's "Barbara Allen," in *The Rose and the Briar: Death, Love and Liberty in the American Ballad,* ed. Sean Wilentz and Greil Marcus, 9–17 (New York: Norton, 2005).

28. The Carter's "Single Girl" similarly praises the unmarried life.

29. Actually, banjos were quite common in the mountains, but Greenwald seems to want to emphasize the African connections of the instrument. See Robert Cantwell's *Bluegrass Breakdown: The Making of the Old Southern Sound* (Urbana: University of Illinois Press, 1984), for an extensive discussion of this connection.

30. Traditional and alt.country musicians inform every aspect of the score: Hazel Dickens, a key figure in the midcentury folk revival, sang a verse of "O Death," and North Carolina folksinger and writer Sheila Kay Adams served as musical adviser for the film. See Rod Armstrong's "Catching a Groove with Director Maggie Greenwald" for more on Dickens' role in the film (n.d., http://www.reel.com/reel.asp?node=features/interviews/greenwald (accessed February 3, 2007)).

31. Dwight Yoakam's "Readin', Rightin', Rt. 23" makes a similar statement about

leaving the mountains; it is worth noting that *Songcatcher*'s music director, David Mansfield, played on the record.

32. This ending reconnects Lily's story with Olive Dame Campbell's: "In 1917 . . . she actually brought this small collection to a famous English musicologist, Cecil Sharp. He sensed a great discovery and went into the mountains to collect the ballads. They were going to collect them together, but Olive was pregnant and couldn't travel through the mountains with him. He did indeed publish the definitive book of mountain ballads that he collected over two summers, 1917 and 1918 and he put her name on the book" (Feinstein, "Singing Story").

33. See http://www.bobdylanroots.com/sorrow.html (accessed on February 3, 2007).

34. Zwonitzer and Hirshberg, *Will You Miss Me When I'm Gone?*, 121.

35. As Marian Levy notes, the name also refers to bluegrass founder Bill Monroe's band, the Foggy Mountain Boys (personal correspondence).

36. Ethan Coen and Joel Coen, *O Brother, Where Art Thou?*, (London: Faber and Faber, 2000), 82.

37. Ibid., 46.

38. See my "Going Back to the Old Mainstream: *No Depression*, Robbie Fulks, and Alt.Country's Muddied Waters," in *A Boy Named Sue: Gender and Country Music,* ed. Kristine M. McCusker and Diane Pecknold, 178–95 (Jackson: University Press of Mississippi, 2004), for an extended discussion of the retrograde fundamentalism of much alt.country discourse and taste.

PAMELA FOX

Time as "Revelator": Alt.Country Women's Performance of the Past

While alt.country music remains dominated by male artists, the female proponents of "twang" also contribute in fascinating ways to its complicated rendition of authentic oppositional culture. Alt.country women construct their own imagined relationship with country music history and tradition. And, although they can certainly represent the entire stylistic spectrum on the alt.country roster, a fair number have gravitated toward a different "rawness" than their male counterparts enamored of honky-tonk and its dissolute heroes: "old-time" Appalachian music of country's earliest beginnings. Here I am primarily interested in how this subgenre of alt.country music made by women, with its dark southern gothic tinges, works to enrich our understanding of authenticity's continued presence in alt.country discourse, which at times functions as little more than a reductive insignia for a decidedly hip reconstitution of rusticity. Spatial constraints force me to concentrate on just two examples, both of whom, as first noted by Bill Friskics-Warren, are known for their "breathtakingly austere evocations of rural culture":[1] Gillian Welch and the group Freakwater, fronted by singer-songwriters Catherine Irwin and Janet Bean. Both, in their distinctive revival of traditional Appalachian music, can be said to be reinstating—and perhaps recasting—women's long-standing role as folk culture preservationists through their very work as songwriters and performers.[2] One could go further and suggest that each is appropriating the bluegrass genre for women, boldly mingling, in the Carter Family tradition, prewar feminine parlor and mountain stylings with postwar masculine bluegrass reproductions of such stylings.[3] Yet their similarities are finally not nearly as significant as their differences, which throw into relief the dilemma of "retro" performance posed by alt.country culture overall.

While each has become associated with the signature sound and spirit of the Carter Family, differences in class identity and stage presence also pose some challenging and instructive contrasts. Welch, for instance, early in her career adopted the most extreme visual masquerade of the three—looking, notes *Washington Post* reviewer Richard Harrington, "as though she'd stepped out of one of Dorothea Lange's Depression-era portraits"[4]—yet she is a former student at the University of California, Santa Cruz, who hails from upper-middle-class Hollywood. Louisville-based Freakwater operates on genuine shoestring budgets with the tiny independent label Thrilljockey and, as such, bolsters its musicianship with waitressing and house painting. Irwin and Bean, eschewing vintage costuming, typically opt for flannel shirts and jeans while engaging in esoteric banter for their audiences—along with their punk pasts, they might seem most at home with the college radio crowd. Together the 1930s-style "Orphan Girl" and the more contemporary Freakwater gals prove a dissonant jumble, performing authenticity with quite different missions in mind.

This essay focuses on both acts' representations of an ostensibly authentic "past" via their increasingly self-conscious ruminations on time. Despite these performers' varying efforts to "fix" particular moments of history, identifying with a specific locale and subjectivity via a past musical genre, the referent finally eludes. They and their audiences are left with a distinct sense of *disconnection.* At times, as in much of Freakwater's music, such disconnection is precisely the point. Yet in other work by both artists, it runs the risk of becoming romanticized and ultimately folded back into that earlier sensibility itself. Similarly, their very efforts to preserve an older, arguably feminized, musical form from potential obsolescence can appear to fetishize precisely these obsolete qualities. While both have succumbed to this tendency, Freakwater remains, I argue, much more skeptical of any "revivalist" impulse grounded in notions of authenticity. Dedicated iconoclasts Irwin and Bean offer one of the most intellectual interpretations of the past currently circulating in alt.country performance.

Gillian Welch: Vintage Technology, Vintage Identity

Since her debut in 1996, Welch has achieved enormous critical success, likened by one journalist to a "kind of down-home-storytelling, banjo-wielding Jedi."[5] That success has undoubtedly been bolstered by her associations with the Coen Brothers' sleeper hit film *O Brother, Where Art Thou?*, contributing to its multiplatinum soundtrack as well as showcasing her acting talents in the film itself.[6] But Welch works a distinctive power all her own with the acoustic artistic project she has called "American Primitive."[7] Her initial Web site biography proclaimed her a "neo-traditionalist" who "draws from early sources of American roots music." Exemplified by the appropriately titled *Revival* (1996), but true enough of her later albums as well, her work evokes "a rustic, rich, and bittersweet past with an austere story-telling honesty for the 1990s." In that single sentence, Welch's promotional material proposes a meaningful nexus between the past and the present. But the music as a whole fails to articulate the precise grounds of the connection. Like the quote itself, her songs suggest a continuity of form rather than content: a spare, genuine narrative line. More often, others commenting on her music stress the *timelessness* of her songs' themes. Richard Harrington, reviewing a 1997 Welch performance, admires the "plaintive minimalism" of her style, recapturing "the unvarnished imagery and melodic simplicity of country music's roots, when nothing ever seemed wasted—notes, words or emotions."[8] He goes on to note, however, that "[h]er best songs are like thick pieces of mountain wood whittled into beautiful decoys, only it's not wood but commonplace experience that Welch transforms into something lasting in songs that address such essential concerns as family and community, love and loss, sin and salvation."

Momentarily, I will explore Welch's musical texts in detail to test these claims. Here I want to contextualize such a discussion by examining self-reflexive explanations of her actual sound: how she conceptualizes the production of such (appropriately named) "decoys" through voice, instrumentation, and studio equipment. In published statements, Welch herself refers less to the Carter Family as her musical forebears than the slightly later bluegrass brother duos such as the Stanleys and Delmores, particularly the Blue Sky Boys. "I'm a fool for those two-part harmonies," she confesses; "I think there are some very interesting and unique sensibilities that are embraced by the Appalachian bluegrass and brother teams. The gritty and abrasive qualities and very intense vocals are what I love."[9] This "grittiness" serves as Welch's ultimate marker of authenticity. As she says of her more recent album, *Soul Journey*, "We wanted this record to be anti-manufactured—it's almost anti-professional, really."[10] She is especially fixated on the "impurity" of the vocals in these earlier recordings made possible by the mechanical equipment itself: "The Stanley Brothers made two live records on the Rebel label back in the Fifties that corrupted me forever. These records are just the shit! They're singing into these old tube mics, and every time the vocals get loud there's this great distortion which is all part of the sound. If it was too clean it wouldn't be the same."[11] To achieve this effect herself, she and performance partner David Rawlings deliberately recorded some of *Revival*'s songs in lo-fi. In fact, their producer for that first album, T-Bone Burnett, sought out the equipment used by none other than alt.country icon Hank Williams. Welch explains, "We wanted the record to sound real and tough . . . real and small, with everything mashed together and one thing fighting through another. It gives the songs character. Everything was live, nothing was buried, everything was bleeding into everything else and it sounded great."[12] Her minimalist aesthetic, in other words, consists of a kind of tonal dissonance that has, it seems, a cultural counterpart in the period itself.

But which period? Welch's music, as a whole, approximates this "mashing" and "bleeding" together of styles, genres, and tropes culled from "early" country and folk: 1920s mountain ballads, mid-1950s bluegrass, 1930s gospel; moonshine stillhouses and small-town "barroom girls." As hinted earlier, she celebrates this approach as a form of bricolage, yet in a sense its American Primitive label has a different, reifying effect. The distinctive edges dividing decades, years, and historical moments become blurred. In a fairly recognizable gesture, much like RCA Victor front man Ralph Peer, "song catchers" such as Dorothy Scarborough and the Library of Congress' John and Alan Lomax, Grand Ole Opry founder George Hay, and bluegrass "father" Bill Monroe, Welch appropriates what she finds useful for representing the "past"—seemingly more "authentic" because it is "unvarnished," "live," and thus ostensibly "real"—yet it is produced using vintage recording techniques. Interestingly, she insists that her music is "not a throwback" or "a mood thing" at all, arguing, "I didn't set out to recapture . . . [an earlier era]. . . . It's most natural to me. That's what my voice and writing are most suited for."[13] Not a self-conscious performance or imitation, then, but an unusual, "natural" vehicle for reflecting the *present* world: "To me they're contemporary songs. . . . I just choose to write in a traditional vein."[14] But as her songs themselves demonstrate, Welch has indeed constructed a vintage notion of authentic identity to accompany her older sound. At most, her work functions as an ironic illustration of Raymond Williams' argument that notions of tradition *always* point to ideological conditions in the present.[15] *Time (The Revelator)* (2001), her most acclaimed album to date, attempts most dramatically to break out of such constraints, but it, too, ultimately succumbs to earlier conceptual formulas.

Perhaps more than any other female alt.country artist, Welch gravitates toward "dark" anthems, narratives, and details. And the principal feature of early-twentieth-century rural life recovered in her musical creations is class abjection. Almost all of *Revival*'s songs tell tales of wrenching poverty, deprivation, and disenfranchisement that result in disconnection or displacement. A few, such as "Barroom Girls" and "One More Dollar," glimpse the poignant fates of those who are destined to leave their mountain homes in pursuit of work but are reduced simply to "last night's spangles" or gambling debts. Both options, rigidly gendered, sever their protagonists from their families and, seemingly, their pasts. More frequently, narrators such as "Orphan Girl" and the sharecropper of "Annabelle" have suffered similar fates through no action or fault of their own. Both have lost "ties of kinship" ("Orphan Girl") through the cruel vagaries of a hardscrabble existence: for all of her backbreaking work as a sharecropper, for instance, Annabelle gets a twofold "handful of dust"—a pittance of money and her daughter's death. But both call on their spiritual faith to endure their pain: the former knows that when she's called to "God's Table," she'll meet her earthly and heavenly family, "No more an orphan girl." Annabelle matter-of-factly states, "[W]e cannot have all things to please us," relying on her union with Jesus to explain why.[16] Yet the gospel strains that would seem to conjure a vision of religious community—an old-fashioned evangelist "revival"—in fact underscore a more overwhelming sense of fatalism and alienation.

"Tear My Stillhouse Down" serves as one quintessential example of this dynamic, arguably serving as the set piece for *Revival* as a whole. A rousing number featuring militaristic percussion, the song conveys an old moonshiner's shame over her sinful life. Convinced that her "whiskey machine" serves as Satan's home, she pleads, "When I die, tear my stillhouse down."[17] Interestingly, for this narrator, viable codes of class respectability lie not in permanent visible markers—tombstone, gold-plated sign—but in the complete *erasure* of others that had remained only partially hidden: "Leave no trace of the hiding place / where I made that evil stuff." Producing neither material nor spiritual "profit," her still is the preeminent sign of low-class otherness. In the present, however, it is also a striking sign of obsolescence—the nostalgic figuring of an outdated, and now somewhat mystified, rural culture. In attempting to revive this figure into the present, Welch finally values it precisely *for* its obsolescence: the moonshiner's desire to eradicate the emblem of her shame becomes a vehicle for Welch's own seemingly contrary desire to preserve it. The song thus fetishizes not only the narrator's past—represented by the stillhouse—but also the seeming emptiness of her spiritual request that someone "tear it down." Religion accentuates, rather than combats or relieves, her character's abjection.

Of her four albums, *Time (the Revelator)* is by far the most ambitious and complex (and the first, significantly, produced by Welch herself and her musical partner, guitarist and background vocalist David Rawlings, on their own Acony label). As its title suggests, Welch becomes much more self-conscious about her own artistic vision of time—its symbolic value and uses—so that the album functions as a knowing meditation on *musical* history. The past that is refashioned here has its familiar, if disquieting, moments of jarring dissonance—Steve Miller lyrics jostle up against references to Elvis, John Henry, and Abraham Lincoln to be posed against a present of cell phones and MP3s. If anything, this later work is also positively saturated with earlier spiritual or biblical themes and preoccupations reflecting her own alt.utopia: exodus, emancipation, resurrection, and salvation. Yet with *Time,* Welch focuses as never before to plead for a specific form of *cultural* "revival" located surprisingly not in Mother Maybelle's Appalachian holler but in Graceland: Elvis' own strange version of bricolage. Within this album's own interior narrative, it is 1950s rock and roll that ultimately trumps Lincoln to emerge as the *modern* Great Emancipator.

The album opens with the title track and sets the stage for this text's ensuing exploration of time's "revelatory" power. Though invoking the blues, specifically, with references to both Mississippi John Hurt (via the term *revelator* itself) and snatches of lyrics from Jimmie Rodgers' "California Blues," the song's own arrangement and instrumentation channel a quieter folk tradition. Such a juxtaposition itself issues one challenge to Welch's audience. Does the amalgam work, or has something been lost over the decades? What is the ground bed of authenticity? Form appears to mirror content, as this tune's narrator warns his lover, "[I'm] not what I'm supposed to be." His dissembling act is vulnerable only to the scrutiny of time itself, which eventually reveals whether he's a "traitor."[18] The rest of the album proposes to answer his query, illustrating just how time both unmasks and understands "the imitator."

"April the 14th–Part I" and its companion text, "Ruination Day–Part II," serve as *Time*'s principal anchors, putting all the surrounding songs in conversation with one another. Both, in characteristic Welch mode, compress centuries and decades by orchestrating several national "disasters" happening on the same date in history—Lincoln's assassination, the *Titanic*'s sinking—around the demise of a traveling two-bit, late-twentieth-century band. The songs' narrator haunts the "red-eye zone" of urban nightlife, observing the sad travails of a no-name music act yet still stirred by the mythology of the "rock and roll" life.[19] On "Ruination Day," she resumes her prosaic life even as "the iceberg broke / and the Okies fled / And the Great Emancipator / Took a bullet in the head." The effect is a collapsing of history and a leveling of perspectives: the "great" and "small," high and low, come together, giving this narrator's wistfulness a singular poignancy and urgency devoid of irony. All of these "events" become infused with a kind of grandeur and tragedy. The slow melodic cadence of "April the 14th–Part I" is replaced by a harsher, repetitive chant in "Ruination Day–Part II," lending its multiple instances of "ruination" an even greater sense of fury and power.

Significantly, two other songs are positioned between these companion pieces, serving as a conceptual bridge or kind of "key" that decodes their murkier meanings. The first, "I Want to Sing That Rock and Roll," recorded live at the Ryman Auditorium, eerily re-creates the sound of 1950s and early 1960s folk groups and as such reinscribes Welch's earlier vintage taste. Here, however, the reference point has shifted somewhat to celebrate the introduction of distinctly modern electronic instruments, pointing to a new kind of "salvation" for those longing to be heard above the din: "I wanna sing that rock and roll / I want to 'lectrify my soul."[20] This song revives the prior narrator's desire by returning her to popular music's early roots. Rock's demise in the earlier text experiences a spiritual rebirth as prior allusions to slavery and emancipation are recast in musical terms, positing a more accessible "glory land" where one can imagine clasping the "savior's hand." "Elvis Presley Blues," the next track, conjures up just such a deity—another monumental figure who suffers an untimely and unseemly death. This clever elegy manages to both humanize and lionize the first "king" of rock: a naive "country boy that combed his hair / Put on a shirt his mother made / and went on the air"; a gyrating wonder likened to a dancing girl and "Harlem queen"; a force of nature creating a new religion, shaking it "like a holy roller . . . with his soul at stake."[21] Welch ultimately equates Elvis with folk hero John Henry, the former slave and railroad worker who used sheer strength of will and body to compete against a steam drill, although his victory culminated in his premature death. (Henry makes another cameo appearance in the CD's epic closing track, this time linked to Johnny Cash.) Together, the two songs put another spin on the "April 14th" mosaic, where "ruination" now comes to signify the death of a singular artist who set American popular music on a whole new course, only to be derailed by others' greed and industry corruption.

This second pairing of songs also helps amplify the final two selections, "Everything Is Free" and "I Dream a Highway." For Welch, perhaps the most pernicious emblem of postmodern technology is the MP3, which has sounded a unique death knell for the music community. "Freedom" here resonates with a capitalist ethos run amok—the freedom to exploit songwriters' and performers' creativity. She laments that her body of work will be "given away" yet recognizes that she'll continue to make music "even if it doesn't pay." She ends, though, with a warning: "If there's something that you want to hear / You can sing it yourself."[22] *Time* thus resurrects the battle between humans and technology in numerous guises, rooting for those earlier, now mythic figures—John Henry, Elvis—who reenvisioned, and paid the highest price for, freedom. By the time we reach the fourteen-minute "Highway," it is clear that Welch's music has become the most direct route back to the past she treasures. (Indeed, the album itself was recorded in Nashville's famed RCA Studio B, now ensconced in the Country Music Hall of Fame/Museum.)[23] Cash, the King, Gram Parsons, and Emmylou Harris are all paid (oblique) tribute in this poetic paean to country music history, whose concluding stanza points to a period of bleakness, stasis, and deprivation: "What will sustain us through the winter? / Where did last year's lessons go? / Walk me out into the rain and snow / I dream a highway back to you."[24] The highway metaphor finally suggests a rather linear notion of time where music allows us to move both backward and forward, positioning the past so that it rather mechanistically informs the present. Welch thus may rely less on literal masquerade as her career has burgeoned, but her music still performs a kind of aesthetic "conjuring" that professes implicit faith in an authentic original.

Ironically, Welch downplays the scripted elements of her work, perhaps in part to offset her ill-fitting class background. Instead, she underlines her instinctive pull toward early country material: "I must have a natural inclination toward the stuff. . . . I guess I had the groundwork—the sponge—to absorb it."[25] Most music critics have agreed, echoing Bill Friskics-Warren's sense that "despite the fact that Welch wasn't raised dirt poor in some East Tennessee hollow, her grasp of the emotional and spiritual reach of old-time country music is undeniable."[26] One former band mate from her Santa Cruz years put it more bluntly in a recent interview: "She got a lot of shit when she first started playing, because she wasn't a hillbilly. . . . Like you have to have black lung to write about mining. If she did all the things she writes about, she'd be dead by now."[27] It is not so much Welch's "grasp" of or entitlement to old-time music that I question as it is her use of it and, finally, its effects. She is, undoubtedly, a highly compelling artist and performer, but it is precisely her ease at stepping into this reconstructed world that I find troubling. As will be clear momentarily, when the members of Freakwater take the stage, they almost take pleasure in the disjunction between their late-twentieth-century visual presence and the sound they produce with voice and instrument. They harbor few, if any, illusions about their "natural" relationship with earlier rural culture. And, as suggested earlier, the contemporary trappings of their songs usually work to highlight, rather than erase, the nuanced distinctions between a representational past and present. Welch seems unwilling to take this responsibility for the performative elements of her persona, which is embodied by, but certainly not limited to, her deliberate vintage costuming. Her work as a whole enacts a disquieting version of what Eric Schocket calls "class transvestism."[28]

Freakwater: Deforming the Genre

Although their albums have always garnered enthusiastic critical reviews, Freakwater can scarcely claim to be a household name. Like Welch, they have appeared on numerous alt.country compilation discs and contributed to the soundtrack of a small independent film (*The Slaughter Rule* [2002]), yet they have failed to parlay that exposure into a broader market share for their own artistic efforts.[29] This may be due in part to their exceptionally spare rendering of old-time music (both covers and original tunes), which can seem halting, off-kilter, and *excessively* raw. Some attribute this trait to their very earnestness. As Allison Stewart comments, "Their desire to protect early twentieth-century country and bluegrass tradition . . . is almost palpable. Whatever else Freakwater are, they aren't kidding."[30] It is clear that Catherine Irwin and Janet Bean have unapologetically researched this most rustic of country music genres, situating their work within its rich, if often underappreciated, history. Yet others believe the work isn't traditional enough. Jon Weisberger's *No Depression* review of *End Time* (1999) rehearses his past objections to Freakwater's approach—"flouting, or at least ignoring, important aspects of the traditions created by Sara and Maybelle Carter and Ira and Charlie Louvin," indicated by "wobbling pitches" and "sloppy . . . timing"—and continues to lament their "distinctive habit . . . of mismatching lyric and melodic phrases."[31] Indeed, although they might initially be mistaken for a "country music appreciation society,"[32] their prior work with punk bands and evolving maverick vision quite deliberately *deform* the genre of old-time music.

Compared with Welch's oeuvre, their songs seem remarkably fresh and ultimately contemporary. Although it is their fellow dedicated "revivalist" who accentuates her ties to the present in her publicity materials, and the Freakwater women who appear to delight in being "[s]tubbornly anachronistic,"[33] it is the latter who most successfully articulate the (tenuous) continuities between the 1920s and 1930s and the contemporary moment. They accomplish this in part by pairing older musical styles and arrangements with modern references and stories—a tendency that surfaces here and there in their earlier work but takes a stunningly intricate form in both *Springtime* (1997) and the later *End Time*. As the group's chief songwriter, Irwin also amplifies this effect by associating *both* the past and present with fragmentation, loss, and displacement. Equally important, as Weisberger's critique recognizes (if fails to appreciate), the songs' very form, with their unique, often "disorienting" time shifts, mirrors the lyrical content, highlighting the sense of dislocation and disjunction.

At first glance, the works on *Springtime* seem to conform to a familiar pattern: a predictable roster of grim mountain tunes awash with sin, whiskey, and, most notably, death brought dramatically to life by the ragged vocals of Irwin and Bean and untempered strains of banjo and fiddle. Such "Gothic bluegrass numbers" have become Freakwater's "stock in trade,"[34] so much so that more than a few commentators have chuckled at the "irony" of the album's optimistic title. Without careful study, their individual songs can seem virtually interchangeable, a simulacrum of early country music. Yet rather than simply imitating various stylistic staples of an old-time repertoire, *Springtime* weaves fragmented narrative lines or themes throughout its various songs. "Heaven" and "Flat Hand" eke out the tale of a woman haunted by her child's death or disappearance, while "Lorraine" and "Louisville Lip" allude to specific incidents of racist violence and oppression. These latter two together suggest more pronounced links between what would seem to be a distinctive past and a more modern present, connecting a Klan lynching to the "mythic" story of Louisville's local hero, Muhammad Ali, who allegedly threw his Olympic gold medal into the Ohio River to protest a local restaurant that refused to seat him. Other songs incorporate more urban or contemporary images, such as the car wreck in "Binding Twine" and the Tilt-a-Whirl in "Slowride," while still others settle for modern terms or words (the Pentagon in "One Big Union" and varieties of 1970s Dodge car names—the Swinger and Dart—in "Scamp"). Few, if any, of these signs have an obvious function, meaning, or even presence; they surprise and challenge the listener, who must usually piece together errant details to grasp the reference at all. (Perhaps the most "old-fashioned" song on the album was contributed by a temporary band member, Max Konrad Johnston, who wrote and performed the romance ballad "Harlan.")

Encased within distinctly traditional forms, these tropes do more, I think, than merely update the convention of old-time music as Welch's songs often do, comprising a "catalog of universal woes" where one temporal mode of "disaster" substitutes for another (cf. "April the 14th–Part I" and "Ruination Day–Part II").[35] The songs don't entirely erase the differences between earlier and contemporary decades: "Even one big union," Freakwater laments, "can't help us now." Citing old World War I/labor songs and slogans, they cleverly sing, "Which side are you on has [now] got more angles than the Pentagon."[36] At the same time, rather than compromising or diluting the kind of rustic authenticity associated with this earlier genre, markers of modernity often only serve to enhance it. *Springtime,* like Freakwater's prior albums, clearly reveres the strength and resourcefulness that often underlie a bleak existence—especially those lived by poor or working-class women. Irwin and Bean's voices themselves perfectly illustrate this quality (both live and recorded, with or without amplifying equipment): a stark, rough-hewn power. They extend this power into the present without arguing for an unbroken line or continuum.

Both fragmented and linked together, this song series' structure illustrates its greatest preoccupation: the desires, dangers, and failures of being "bound" to a person, place, or condition through memory. "Twisted Wire," for example, begins with images of shackles and entanglement as its female narrator dreams of her former lover's "bound" hands. The recurring refrain makes such images chillingly concrete, as its "silver hoops of silver wire" emerge as "shackles," which in turn become linked with lies. Reinforcing the analogy between handcuffs and false narratives, the song concludes, "It's in your hands, but not in mine / Twisting wire, twisted lies."[37] "Binding Twine" returns to such imagery by initially introducing tropes of *disconnection:* a "tug of war" over the reality of a past relationship.[38] The female speaker, however, remains seduced by the "simple messages" of remembrance and asks her ex-lover to "bind my memories in twine." In both songs, memory itself becomes just as much a shackle as a comfort or release—relentless, it needs to be contained and/or verified so that it doesn't evolve into another criminal act of deception.

While *End Time* in some ways certainly represented a new kind of artistic venture for this group—tripling the number of participating musicians (including former Waco Brothers' drummer Steve Goulding), adding both electric and percussive instruments to create a much fuller sound, and showcasing Bean's talents as a songwriter as well as a vocalist so that she takes credit for fully half of the original compositions on the album—it continued to mine familiar thematic ground. As with Welch's career progression, Freakwater demonstrated in its most ambitious production to date a near obsession with the workings of time.[39] Richer instrumentation allowed for greater experimentation, so that other, later styles of country music, such as honky-tonk, received more substantial treatment, yet this album privileges personal rather than *musical* history. Here time typically *fails* to serve as a solemn "revelator" in any sphere, any capacity. Just as the romanticized highway trope ultimately crystallizes Welch's understanding of the relationship between past and present, *End Time* finally offers its own much more cynical counterpart: the "cheap watch."

Indulging Irwin's penchant for dark puns, the album kicks off with "Good for Nothing," whose narrator announces "I've been good, and I've been good for nothing."[40] The song as a whole returns to one standard Freakwater emblem: the spring "showers" of its opening lines quickly lead to waters that purport to offer baptismal salvation but instead drown those with true self-knowledge (cf. *Springtime*'s "Washed in the Blood"). An endless round of drinks submerges this speaker, whose fate eerily recalls Welch's *Titanic* disaster: "Many times I've watched my own self drown / Clinging fast to my lucidity / Like a life raft that's slowly sinking down." As with other personas conjured over the course of the album, this one clings fast to her bitter memories of the past, snarling that she'll never "forgive" or "forget." "Cloak of Frogs," a most ironic waltz, revisits such imagery from a different perspective. This narrator turns on her radio to hear a preacher singing "to me, to the fallen," "Take me to the river / Wash me in the water."[41] She is seemingly contrite rather than rebellious, accepting its address; unlike Welch's moonshiner, who seeks to erase all outward "trace" of her sin, this speaker understands that such evidence remains at the core of her personhood, a "mess" that she embodies. At most, it can be "mislabeled" in the semblance of being "born again."

Several other songs written and sung by Janet Bean are much more reflective of her own recent personal experience, which included a divorce from her longtime partner and collaborator in the band Eleventh Dream Day. "My History" and "Written in Gold" offer yet another perspective, then, on the album's central concern with time. Arranged like a mid-1960s country torch song, the first recounts a woman's decision to break with her "history" of a dying marriage. Rather than celebrating her tenth anniversary, she issues her husband divorce papers, attempting to break with her past passivity. Previously protecting herself from the truth—"waiting for it all to drop like a big New Year's ball"—she discovers that such knowledge resonates, rather than "drops," with a singular finality and that in the end it can still fail to teach us much of anything: "I thought that surely the answers would be revealed / We'd know it'd all been for the better . . . But I'm haunted by these words instead."[42] Similarly, in "Written in Gold" the lasting mark of an absent wedding ring illustrates the complex process by which one's personal history stubbornly remains, "tatooing" the body itself with the memory of her marital vows: "Paler skin under a band of gold / . . . Now nail her to the words she swore."[43] The "words" that finally "haunt" both of these female speakers certainly threaten to collapse the past and the present, extinguishing any hope for a new space or identity from which to "begin": "Evermore means something that it never did before."

Yet Irwin's sassy "Cheap Watch" offers another kind of cautionary tale about time's slipperiness, where the danger lies in just such a compression of history. In this saga, distortions of time—a bar sporting year-long Christmas lights, an unreliable timepiece that when wound up makes the hours "fly"—become equated with distortions of human truths. This narrator refuses to take a passive approach to her failed relationship, her "little white teeth wound around what sounds like more cheap lies," and warns that she's going to reveal the truth. And nothing could be made plainer than her own much more accurate and active accounting of time: "One foot on the gas, two feet from Tennessee / The little hand on the twelve-gauge and the big hand swinging free."[44] She revels in severing those familiar "binding ties." Like Bean's rueful heroines, this one momentarily appears to linger over her painful memories as she drinks another beer in that tavern where time appears frozen, but she finally frees herself from its pain.

Freakwater's tenuous membership in the newly chic alt.country club thus derives not only from critics' imposition of rigid authenticity standards but also from the group's own resistance to any collective ethos—its distaste for "binding twine." Irwin is mystified by bluegrass "purists" like Weisberger, protesting that "we don't claim to be playing bluegrass. . . . Anybody who knows anything about it knows that that's not what we're doing and that we couldn't play true bluegrass music if we tried."[45] Yet she's equally frustrated by other alt.country associates, tongue firmly in cheek, who find them too dour. The band's first stint at the increasingly popular South by Southwest Festival to promote *End Time,* for instance, seemed futile: "There doesn't seem to be any point." Concert reviewer and interviewer James Murray comments, "Freakwater know all too well that, in this Society of the Spectacle, only the poseurs taste success and recognition. Those who are real get little or nothing."[46] While the binary he establishes here between the performative and the "real" is undoubtedly problematic, Murray's observation at least recognizes the "spectacular" function of much alt.country, echoed by Bill Friskics-Warren: "In contrast to the trailer-park kitsch of most alt-country bands, Irwin and Bean didn't just woodshed with a clutch of Buck Owens LPs and a Southern Lit reading list and come out making records."[47]

Perhaps most important, Freakwater itself is all too aware of the performativity inherent not only in such "kitsch" but in country music's entire tradition. In a recent interview with Neil DeMause, Irwin and band bassist David Wayne Gay take on the very notion of authenticity to indict none other than their own musical forebears, the Carter Family. Irwin begins, "The whole issue of authenticity is really just a music writer's invention to me. I mean, I don't even know what people mean. Do people think that when they hear 'Under My Thumb' or something?" When challenged by Gay, who goads, "You know what it means. Like, Little Richard vs. Pat Boone doing 'Tutti Frutti'," she notes, "Well, Little Richard wrote that song. But when you hear just a normal person singing a . . . Rolling Stones song, you don't think, 'Did he *really* meet a gin-soaked barroom queen in Memphis?' Is that authentic?"[48] When discussing the reception of their music, she admits, "I feel like we're being accused of something I never even was trying to get away with in the first place. I never pretended that I was riding to Chicago on horseback or something." Gay adds, "Even the Carter Family was part of the folk revival, back when they were doing that, right? They were part of a revival," to which she retorts, "They were part of basically swiping stuff from people who knew less about copyright laws than they did. They were exploiters of the less literate."

As their musical trajectory attests, Freakwater harbors few illusions about revivalism, rejecting the very idea of a natural or authentic rusticity. Their attachment to "dark" material may occasionally flirt with the fetishization of abjection itself (a by-product, perhaps, of an earlier punk sensibility), but they don't make the mistake of *conflating* such a condition with a particular musical or cultural heritage. It seems significant that even the band's name, which turns out to be a term for moonshine whiskey, was in Bean and Irwin's initial estimation their own neologism—a "made-up word they considered meaningless."[49] Appropriately, their devotion to originality may ironically bring them closest to one of country's earliest versions of authenticity.

This essay grows out of a much larger study concerned with the gendering of authenticity in country music discourse and performance, and, while most of my denser theoretical arguments have been jettisoned to foreground close readings of particular works by particular artists, I'd like to close by suggesting that such readings can begin to illuminate a new direction for feminist work on the alt.country genre.[50] Until quite recently, one had to look rather fruitlessly for feminist critical discussions—whether online via numerous alt.country Listservs and fan Web sites or in more scholarly venues. Cheryl Cline heroically launched her own not so quiet war on this music's masculinist practices back in 1997 when she introduced her spin-off 'zine *Country Grrl*, yet few appear to have joined her at the barricades.[51]

Cline's challenge to "air out stuffy old assumptions about women, men, and country music"[52] has been met somewhat by Mary Bufwack and Robert

Oermann's landmark work *Finding Her Voice: The Saga of Women in Country Music*—a popular feminist historical study originally published in 1993 but later supplemented with a substantial chapter titled "Meeting the Millennium: Female Country Triumphs" (now reissued as *Finding Her Voice: Women in Country Music, 1800–2000*).[53] This new chapter concludes with an enthusiastic overview of numerous female alt.country artists, but, as with the study as a whole, it sacrifices in-depth analysis for more comprehensive coverage documenting women's presence in and contributions to country music history. While offering invaluable historical data, the Bufwack and Oermann volume tends to reproduce conventional notions of authenticity promoted by the music industry itself, extending the category to include neglected or underappreciated female performers but stopping short of considering how unstable models of femininity and masculinity, in conjunction with other markers of identity, shape the very definition of country rusticity. Their discussion of Gillian Welch, for instance, finds it "remarkable that she sounds so authentic recreating the ethos of the Dust Bowl because it is so far removed from her upbringing and education"[54] yet fails to probe that disjunction further. (Interestingly, Freakwater receives no notice at all in a virtual compendium of female alt.country artists.)

While pointing to the diversity of musical styles and life histories offered by this panoply of performers, Bufwack and Oermann fashion a disappointingly rigid interpretation of their significance: "The country music business may be controlled by men, but as the style's predominant listeners and prominent performers, women drive its emotional honesty. Even in a musical climate that is increasingly restrictive, the powerful feelings in 'I Hope You Dance' or 'Independence Day' show that female country music remains rooted in real life and real aspirations."[55] Curiously, they defend this claim with a quote from Dolly Parton, which serves as the closing statement of their book: "People don't come to the shows to see you be you," says Dolly, "They come to see you be them and what they want you to be." As Gillian Welch and Freakwater alone demonstrate (not to mention Dolly herself!), that is the most fraught performance of all.

NOTES

1. Bill Friskics-Warren, "Gillian Welch: Orphan Girl of the Hollywood Hills Finds a High Lonesome Musical Home in the Heart of the Appalachians," *No Depression* 1 (summer 1996): 37.

2. It seems hardly coincidental that many alt.country women artists were recruited to perform on the soundtrack for the 2001 film *Songcatcher* (Vanguard Records 79586–2, 2001), including Gillian Welch. For more on that film, see Barbara Ching's essay in this volume.

3. The "parlor" style of singing characteristic of American rural life from the turn of the century through the 1930s was, as its name suggests, almost exclusively domestic—the preferred performance space, both literal and figurative, for women with singing talents and yearnings, typically distinguished from the "assembly" tradition that featured male musicians in public settings such as dances. See Robert Coltman, "Sweethearts of the Hills: Women in Early Country Music," *John Edwards Memorial Foundation Quarterly* (winter 1978): 164–65; Robert K. Oermann, "Mother, Sister, Sweetheart, Pal: Women in Old Time Country Music," *Southern Quarterly* 22, no. 3 (spring 1984): 128–30; and Richard A. Peterson, *Creating Country Music: Fabricating Authenticity* (Chicago: University of Chicago Press, 1997), 138–40.

4. Richard Harrington, "Gillian Welch's Rural Delivery," *Washington Post,* May 5, 1997, D10.

5. Mike Connor, "Roots Seller: How Former Santa Cruz Songstress Gillian Welch Beat the Odds to Become an Americana Sensation," http://www.metroactive.com/cruz/welch-0226.html (accessed September 9, 2003).

6. See "I'll Fly Away" and "Didn't Leave Nobody but the Baby," on *O Brother, Where Art Thou?* Mercury Records 088 170 069–2, 2000.

7. Gillian Welch Web site, "Biography," http://www.geffen.com/almo/gillian/revival.html (accessed April 14, 1997).

8. Harrington, "Gillian Welch's Rural Delivery," D10.

9. Gillian Welch Web site, "Biography."

10. Melanie Haiken, "Gillian Welch: The Orphan Girl Opens Up," *Paste* 5, http://www.pastemagazine.com/action/article?article_id=208 (accessed September 9, 2003).

11. Gillian Welch's Web site, "Biography."

12. Gillian Welch's Web site, "Revival," http://www.geffen.com/almo/gillian/revival.html (accessed April 14, 1997).

13. Joel Bernstein, "Gillian Welch: The Real Retro Artist," *Country Standard Time,* July–August 1998, http://countryst2/gillianwelchFEATURE.html (accessed July 28, 1998). In these comments, Welch in some ways confirms Tamara Livingston's theory of twentieth-century music revivals. Livingston notes "the tendency of revivalist discourse to collapse time and space in service to a new 'authenticity' defined by the belief in the practice's timelessness, unbroken historical continuity, and purity of expression" (which, for Welch, consists of "*impurity*"); Livingston continues, "[M]usic revivalists frequently reject modern technological innovations such as electrical instruments and contemporary popular style influences in favor of

acoustic instruments." "Music Revivals: Toward a General Theory," *Ethnomusicology* 43, no. 1 (winter 1999): 69.

14. Bernstein, "Gillian Welch."

15. See this volume's introductory essay for more on Williams' cultural theory in relation to alt.country music.

16. Words and music in both songs by Gillian Welch, on *Revival,* Almo Records AMSD–80006, 1996.

17. "Tear My Stillhouse Down," words and music by Gillian Welch, on *Revival.*

18. "Revelator," words and music by Gillian Welch and David Rawlings, on *Time (the Revelator),* Acony Records ACNY–0103, 2001.

19. "April the 14th–Part I," words and music by Gillian Welch and David Rawlings, on *Time (the Revelator).*

20. "I Want to Sing That Rock and Roll," words and music by Gillian Welch and David Rawlings, on *Time (the Revelator).*

21. "Elvis Presley Blues," words and music by Gillian Welch and David Rawlings, on *Time (the Revelator).*

22. "Everything Is Free," words and music by Gillian Welch and David Rawlings, on *Time (the Revelator).*

23. George Graham, *The Graham Weekly Album Review,* no. 1251, http://www.georgegraham.com/reviews/welch3.html (accessed September 24, 2003).

24. "I Dream A Highway," words and music by Gillian Welch and David Rawlings, on *Time (the Revelator).*

25. Friskics-Warren, "Gillian Welch," 37.

26. Ibid.

27. Connor, "Roots Seller," 1.

28. Schocket coined this term to refer to narratives produced by middle-class journalists, novelists, and social researchers in the United States between the 1890s and the 1910s (Stephen Crane was the most prominent) who "'dressed down' in order to traverse with their bodies what they saw as a growing gulf between the middle class and the white working and lower classes." "Undercover Explorations of the 'Other Half'; or, the Writer as Class Transvestite," *Representations* 64 (fall 1998): 110. While Welch cannot pretend to immerse herself *literally* in the experiences of her songs' characters as these earlier class "transvestites" did to attempt a more immediate kind of knowledge of the poor, she does suggest a similar affiliation or connection.

29. These alt.country compilation or tribute discs include *Keep on the Sunny side: A Tribute to the Carter Family* (Amoeba, 1991), *Insurgent Country, Vol. 1: For a Life of Sin* (Bloodshot, 1994), and *Exposed Roots: The Best of Alt.Country* (K-Tel, 1998).

30. Allison Stewart, "Spring Forward, Fall Back: Freakwater Does the Two-Step around Fame and Fortune," *No Depression* 13 (January–February 1998): 44.

31. Jon Weisberger, "Foggy Mountain New Grass Breakdown," *No Depression* 23 (September–October 1999): 1, 3.

32. Dan MacIntosh, "Freakwater Doesn't Keep It on the Sunnyside of Life," *Country Standard Time,* March–April 1998, http://www1.usa1.com/~cst.freakwater CONCERT.html (accessed April 21, 1998).

33. Stewart, "Spring Forward, Fall Back," 43.

34. Ibid.

35. Ibid., 46.

36. "One Big Union," words and music by Freakwater, on *Springtime,* Thrilljockey, Thrill 047, 1997.

37. "Twisted Wire," words and music by Sean Garrison, on *Springtime.*

38. "Binding Twine," words and music by Freakwater, on *Springtime.*

39. After the release of *End Time* in 1998, Catherine Irwin and Janet Bean focused on independent music projects; in 2005, they recorded *Thinking of You* as a Freakwater release. I am focusing on *End Time* due to its explicit thematic concern with time.

40. "Good for Nothing," words and music by Freakwater, on *End Time,* Thrilljockey, Thrill 066, 1999.

41. "Cloak of Frogs," words and music by Freakwater, on *End Time.*

42. "My History," words and music by Freakwater, on *End Time.*

43. "Written in Gold," words and music by Freakwater, on *End Time.*

44. "Cheap Watch," words and music by Freakwater, on *End Time.*

45. Bill Friskics-Warren, "Freakwater: Fundamental Things," *Puncture* 45 (1999), http://www.freakwater.net/readingroom.html (accessed August 12, 2003).

46. James Murray, "Freakwater at VZD's in Oklahoma City, March 18, 1999," *100 Year War,* http://www.freakwater.net/readingroom.html (accessed August 12, 2003).

47. Friskics-Warren, "Freakwater."

48. Neil de Mause, "Louisville Lip: An Interview with Catherine Irwin," *Here,* http://www.heremagazine.com.html (accessed August 12, 2003).

49. John Lewis, "Universal Soldiers: Freakwater's Themes for Life," *Option,* 1996. http://www.freakwater.net/readingroom.html (accessed August 12, 2003).

50. See my forthcoming book, *Natural Acts: Gender, Race, and Rusticity in Country Music* (Ann Arbor: University of Michigan Press).

51. However, see Barbara Ching's essay "Going Back to the Old Mainstream: *No Depression* and the Construction of Alt.Country," in *A Boy Named Sue: Gender, Genre, and the Evolution of Country Music,* ed. Kristine McCusker and Diane Pecknold, 178–95 (Jackson: University of Mississippi Press, 2004). Monica Kendrick's "Reel Live Women: A Video Essay," *Journal of Country Music* 21, no. 3 (2000): 32–37, takes a spirited feminist look at more mainstream country female performers, but it does incorporate the Dixie Chicks as part of the "edgier" group bordering on alt.country.

52. See www.steamiron.com/cgrrl/cgrrl-ed1.html.

53. Mary Bufwack and Robert Oermann, "Meeting the Millennium: Female Country Triumphs," in *Finding Her Voice: Women in Country Music, 1800–2000,* 507. (Nashville: Vanderbilt University Press, 2003).

54. Ibid., 503.

55. Ibid., 507. In this quote, they are referring, respectively, to top-selling hits by LeAnn Womack and Martina McBride.

OLIVIA CARTER MATHER

"Regressive Country": The Voice of Gram Parsons

> Gram Parsons [was] the most convincing singer of sad songs I've ever heard.
> —BUD SCOPPA

In 1973, the year he died, Gram Parsons toured as a solo act with Emmylou Harris and his backing band, the Fallen Angels. While in Austin, Texas, Parsons and Harris were interviewed by a disc jockey who asked them what they thought of a new Austin-based style called "progressive country." Harris jokingly replied, "We play regressive country." At the time, Parsons and his band performed rock-influenced renditions of country songs such as "Streets of Baltimore" and "California Cottonfields," and such performances may have indeed sounded "regressive" or noticeably alternative when compared to mainstream country music. For most of his career, Parsons experimented with country sounds in a rock context, making records that introduced a new kind of country-rock hybrid. While in Los Angeles during the late 1960s and early 1970s, Parsons mixed elements from rock, soul, folk, and country (including bluegrass, gospel, the Nashville sound, and the Bakersfield sound), proselytizing among rock musicians for the merits of country. In other words, he was country when and where "country wasn't cool" and accordingly was a forerunner of both alt.country and the more commercially successful "country rock" of artists such as the Eagles and Linda Ronstadt.[1]

During his lifetime, Parsons was relatively unknown and his records sold poorly, even those he made with the internationally successful Byrds. After Parsons' death, Harris championed his songs on her solo recordings, and in 1982 Elvis Costello covered two Parsons songs on his country album *Almost*

Blue. However, it was not until the early 1990s that Parsons' music experienced a rebirth among alt.country artists and aficionados, resulting in compilations, CD reissues, tribute albums, a CD anthology, the first biography, and numerous mentions in the press, especially in the pages of alt.country's leading magazine, *No Depression.*[2] By the 1990s the alt.country community had identified Parsons as one of its progenitors and journalists had documented his influence in the music of contemporary alt.country artists. At least one writer contends that we can distinguish between alternative and mainstream country artists by determining their relationships to Parsons and his music.[3] Emmylou Harris, Dwight Yoakam, Tom Petty, Gillian Welch, the Rolling Stones, and Elvis Costello have counted themselves as Parsons' heirs, even if few of them would consider themselves alt.country musicians.

The most influential release of the Parsons revival was the 1999 tribute CD *Return of the Grievous Angel,* an album of his songs performed by alt.country, pop, and rock artists. The album served to recognize Parsons' legacy in musicians and groups such as Wilco, the Cowboy Junkies, the Mavericks, Whiskeytown, and Lucinda Williams, and it benefited from the cachet of high-profile artists and groups from outside country music such as Beck, the Pretenders, and Sheryl Crow. Interest in Parsons continued through 2004 with the release of the feature-length movie *Grand Theft Parsons,* the documentary *Gram Parsons: Fallen Angel* (which includes interviews with Harris and Parsons family members), and two tribute concerts organized by Parsons' daughter Polly Parsons.[4]

Accompanying Parsons' underground popularity is that which attends other cult figures in pop music history, especially those who die young: a stockpile of myths and legends attesting to the subject's brilliance, in the end another version of the "great man" theory that is just as powerful an idea in the rock press as in Western art music historiography. In the alt.country community, the figure of Parsons looms large not only because his music was inspirational to later country music "outlaws" but because the myths about him are so powerful. Parsons has been constructed as an authentically southern musician whose personal heartache is the genuine source of his musical expression. Such beliefs matter not only because fans, listeners, and critics trust them to interpret his music but because they distract us from taking a closer look at his music and understanding it in cultural context.

The remainder of this essay addresses these issues in two sections. The first reviews Parsons' biography and the myths that pervade much of the writing about him. My purpose is not to present new biographical information but to establish the nature and significance of several key assumptions about Parsons by considering a sample of the journalistic literature. Along the way I will disentangle some of these myths in an attempt to understand the primary ways in which listeners have heard his music. Ultimately myths about his legacy, biography, and musicianship bear significance not simply because they perpetuate untruths but because they shape the discourse around his music.

While the first section deals with myths of authenticity in the literature about Parsons, the second attempts to identify musical markers of that authenticity to understand how listeners might "hear" what they consider to be a genuine expression of emotion. Through a close analysis of two recordings ("Hot Burrito #1" and "A Song for You") I discuss how particular elements of the music can, within a certain context, communicate emotional vulnerability. I focus mainly on Parsons' singing since in numerous written accounts of the music, Parsons' voice comes through as the most meaningful musical manifestation of his mythologized self. Parsons' singing was not always "in tune," and, though commentators have acclaimed his ability to move listeners' emotions, they must admit, if rarely, that Parsons' singing often suffered from common problems of execution. For example, in 2004 at the West Coast premiere of his documentary *Gram Parsons: Fallen Angel* at a Los Angeles film festival, German director Gandulf Hennig explained to a live audience what attracted him to Parsons' music: "The singing was so soulful, it was so authentic, even when it was out of tune." Due to its irregularities, Parsons' singing may have missed the mark by some country standards, and, in fact, his music has not been widely received in mainstream country circles. I argue that Parsons' problems with vocal execution do not disqualify his recordings as "country" but point to an alternative set of priorities—priorities that favor other facets of country singing. Emmylou Harris' remark that Parsons' country style was "regressive" indicates that he understood the difference between his music and mainstream country. While some traditional country fans might criticize his singing, his position as an outsider gave him the freedom to sing country on his terms.

Much of the second section relies on technical explanations of singing techniques, chord progressions, melodic contour, and song structure. The analysis is not intended to disconnect the music from its context or to alienate readers who do not regularly engage music with this terminology. Rather,

I mean to tie claims about Parsons' music to actual sounds. Although the evaluations of all listeners are subjective, they usually ground their opinions in the lyrics and music they hear. If we are to begin to understand why Parsons' music has such appeal for the alt.country community, then we must investigate how the music works, and this requires the examination of key musical details. In my analysis, I aim to flesh out some of the ways in which Parsons' music, and his voice in particular, performed the sense of interiority and authenticity that writers highlight.

The Importance of Biography

Parsons claimed country as his musical roots, but his first efforts were in rock and folk. In the mid-1960s, he fronted the Shilos, a regional touring group that emulated popular folk acts such as the Journeymen and the Kingston Trio. It wasn't until his enrollment at Harvard in the fall of 1966 that Parsons showed serious interest in country music. At this time Parsons was "reintroduced" to country, he said, through Buck Owens and crossover acts such as Ray Charles.[5] He founded the International Submarine Band, and in 1967 the band recorded one album, *Safe at Home,* which is often dubbed the first in country rock.[6] *Safe at Home*'s song list included Parsons originals and several covers, including songs by Merle Haggard and Johnny Cash.

Parsons then joined the Byrds and convinced the band to record in Nashville with country session players. The resulting *Sweetheart of the Rodeo* of 1968 was a musical left turn for the group and their lowest-selling album to that point, but it was a showcase for hired sideman Parsons.[7] They covered country songs such as "I am a Pilgrim" (Merle Travis) and "You're Still on My Mind" (George Jones), but the only Byrd to make the final cut as a contributing songwriter was Parsons ("Hickory Wind," "One Hundred Years from Now"). That same year, Parsons and bassist Chris Hillman left the Byrds to form the Flying Burrito Brothers, a group devoted to playing a mix of genres with country at the center, what Parsons called "cosmic American music." The band wrote country songs, covered country songs, performed at country clubs, and employed a pedal steel guitarist as a full member.[8]

After two albums with the Burritos, Parsons moved on to a solo career, recording two albums with Emmylou Harris and Elvis Presley's backing band in 1972 and 1973. Harris joined Parsons on male-female duets such as

"That's All It Took" (previously performed by George Jones and Melba Montgomery) and "brother duets" such as "Love Hurts" (originally performed by the Everly Brothers). In 1973, soon after completing the sessions for *Grievous Angel,* Parsons died of a drug overdose at the age of twenty-six in Joshua Tree, California. Three days after his death, his road manager, Phil Kaufman, stole Parsons' body from the Los Angeles International Airport and drove it back to Joshua Tree National Park. There he immolated it in accordance with a pact he supposedly made with Parsons that whoever died first among the two would not have a traditional funeral but would be burned in the desert.[9]

Like other tragic rock star deaths, Parsons' demise by overdose fueled myths about him and encouraged exaggeration of his contributions. What is at stake for today's advocates of Parsons' music is that which is important to many musical communities, though possibly more self-conscious in folk and neotraditionalist movements: sincerity and authenticity. Writers locate authenticity primarily in his biography, specifically his southern background and personal experience with tragedy. As in the cases of numerous deceased rock musicians, narrators embellish important parts of the story. For example, in the liner notes for *Return of the Grievous Angel,* music critic Bud Scoppa addresses insiders with a one-sentence summary of the musician's life and work.

> If you're reading this, chances are I don't have to tell you that Gram Parsons was the subversive Harvard-educated hillbilly who invented country-rock in the mid-Sixties with the prototypical International Submarine Band before perfecting it with the Byrds, the Flying Burrito Brothers, and on a pair of extraordinary solo albums before fatally overdosing in 1973 at a mere 26.

Scoppa is correct about Parsons' death and rock résumé, of course, but his evaluation of Parsons as the "subversive Harvard-educated hillbilly who invented country-rock" is misleading, if widely believed.[10] These kinds of biographical understandings (or misunderstandings) matter because they ground debates around commercialism concerning not only Parsons' music but also country rock and alt.country more broadly. This essay does not debunk the myths in order to establish the "real story" of Gram Parsons. Instead, I would like to illustrate how these stories function and frame the music, in particular the idea that Parsons created country rock and his "hillbilly" background necessitated his singing country music.[11]

In reality, Parsons did not single-handedly "invent" country rock but rather made his contributions within the context of the growing country rock scene in Los Angeles. A cursory comparison of Parsons' career with Chris Hillman's reveals the impossibility of Parsons being solely responsible for the style. When Parsons was playing in folk groups in high school, Hillman was a serious mandolin player with a number of bluegrass bands; by the time Parsons was a college freshman, Hillman had joined the Byrds as their bass player and helped them rise to international notoriety with "Mr. Tambourine Man" and "Turn! Turn! Turn!" Parsons' entrance into the Byrds certainly tipped the scales in favor of country beginning in 1968; it was no coincidence that he joined just before they recorded *Sweetheart of the Rodeo.* Yet the project would not have worked without some interest on the part of the pre-Parsons Byrds, especially Hillman.[12] Hillman also worked with Parsons in forming the Burritos and cowriting most of the band's original songs. Even if we were to credit Hillman equally, we could not ignore the non-Byrds who experimented in country before or at the same time as the Burritos: Ritchie Furay, the Grateful Dead, Michael Nesmith, Linda Ronstadt, and others.[13]

For many fans, critics, and biographers, Parsons' role in the beginnings of country rock matters little because his personal life evokes what we often want to believe about the personal lives of musicians, especially country ones. Listeners have come to expect that country singers, especially "hard country" performers, have lived through the tough life experiences described in their songs. This idea permeates our understandings of singers such as Hank Williams Sr. and George Jones.[14] Parsons is perhaps a better candidate for the title "father of country rock" than Bob Dylan or anyone else from the country rock scene because his background lends itself to an interpretation of his life as stereotypically "southern gothic," which then imparts a sense of authenticity to his music and lyrics. Much of Parsons' upbringing was truly tragic: his father committed suicide when Parsons was twelve, and his mother died of complications from alcoholism when he was a teenager. That he came from a southern, wealthy, dysfunctional family reminiscent of a Faulknerian narrative suggests that Parsons was all the more qualified to lead the movement that he did. The presumption is that he knew the heartache behind country while having the means to live in rock star excess. His death from a drug overdose didn't hurt the myth, either—historians and fans have since wondered "what might have been" and retroactively read personal tragedy into his songs.

The characterization of Parsons as a hillbilly is one of the most powerful myths about him since it provides another essentializing link between him and country music.[15] The flip side of this myth is that Parsons was not a hillbilly at all but a southern gentleman par excellence, complete with good manners, charm, and a syrupy drawl.[16] In any case his regional credentials qualified him as the exemplar of country within the Los Angeles rock scene, whether dressed in sequined glitz or fashionable working-class chic. It was assumed that Parsons' music would be quintessentially southern, that he naturally knew how to write country, and that as a longhair in the rock scene he was the natural spokesperson for this music among his peers. In truth, Parsons lived his childhood and adolescence in Georgia and Florida but in a wealthy family that generally didn't listen to or play country music. Most country musicians do not have the kind of privileged upbringing that Parsons had, and in this way his life goes against the stereotype of the country singer. Other than gigging, it appears that Parsons never worked a day in his life, choosing instead to live off his large inheritance. But what counts to mythmakers is that he was intensely southern regardless of his musical background.

Even while he was alive, critical reception of Parsons' work hinged on his background, as in Stanley Booth's review of the Burritos' 1969 album *The Gilded Palace of Sin*. This was Parsons's most lengthy *Rolling Stone* review, and it is the earliest substantial appraisal of his music in regional terms. Booth begins with a discourse on the inherent southernness of Waycross, Georgia, Parsons' hometown, painting the area around it as puritan, backward, and extremely isolated: "Culture exists there only in the anthropological sense." That Booth spends more than one-third of the article detailing the landscape, economy, and culture of Waycross shows how important place and origins are to his assessment of Parsons' music. Booth wants to prove beyond doubt that Parsons is truly southern and then contrast the region's conservatism with Parsons' image, noting his long hair and countercultural style of dress. He reads almost every track on *The Gilded Palace of Sin* in light of regional issues or as representations of a small-town boy lost in the big city, practically ignoring the contributions of Hillman and other group members. For him, all of Parsons' music is about the juxtaposition between a traditional, rural South and "the hostility of the modern world."[17]

It was not only the rock press that mythologized Parsons. His own boasting about his musical experimentation enhanced his reputation as well.[18] He told stories about his attempts to build bridges between hippies and working-class Angelenos by singing at country bars in Los Angeles.

> It took me two years to win the Palomino Club's talent contest. . . . Every Thursday I would religiously drive out there and wait my turn, and for two years I was beaten by yodeling grandmothers and the same guy singing "El Paso" every week. . . . When things were tough at the Palomino I started to go out to the tougher ones. I heard about the Aces, out in the City of Industry. . . . So I started going out there every weekend. The first couple of times I nearly got killed; there I was in my satin bell-bottoms and the people couldn't believe it. I got up onstage and sang, and when I got off a guy said to me, "I want you to meet my five brothers. We were gonna kick your ass but you can sing real good so we'll buy you a drink instead." Thank God I'd got on that stage.[19]

Parsons even took credit for the country forays of some of rock's biggest superstars, creating an image of himself as a visionary. Speaking of the Rolling Stones, he said, "I think they've done a few country-sounding things since I got to know them."[20] Parsons' visual style, in the form of the Nudie suit, was another expression of his artistic confidence. Associated with country stars such as Porter Wagoner and Gene Autry, Nudie Cohen's custom-made sequined cowboy suits were the highest mark of country glamour. On Parsons and his bandmates they looked comedic, as if the Burritos were making fun of hyped country style. Parsons' take on the Nudie suit was a countercultural one: his suit features cannabis leaves, pills, nude women on the lapels, and a cross on the back of the jacket.[21]

What makes the myths about Parsons so powerful is not just that they rely on existing stereotypes but that those stereotypes frequently contradict one another. The figure of Parsons embodies the rural and the urban, the South and the nation, the religious and the libertine, and multiple class identities. Competing aspects of his story do not cancel each other out but give him credibility with several groups, making him an effective apologist for country music. They anchor him deeply on each side of "country" and "rock," granting him legitimacy and supposedly proving his genius for negotiating clashing values. The fact that the aura of myth surrounds an individual rather than a group, scene, label, or song is no small part of how the myth works: its indwelling of one person allows followers to be satisfied in its resolution and to use it to make sense of shifting identities. Many in the rock scene disliked country because of its association with conservative politics, but Parsons' persona provided a safe introduction to country music, the South, and white working-class culture.

Parsons' Voice

In a discussion of Billie Holiday and Bing Crosby, David Brackett explains how their performances are seen through the lens of the singers' personal lives and, in the case of Holiday, in light of her suffering. He argues, "What seems to be taken for granted in many discussions of Holiday's (and Crosby's and many other musicians') music is an unmediated connection between biography and musical meaning."[22] Critics locate sincerity in the voice, interpreting its idiosyncrasies, state of health, and even failures as representative of the singers themselves. In his work on Karen Carpenter, Mitchell Morris makes a comparable point: that Carpenter's struggles with anorexia provided a frame through which much of her musical work has been interpreted and that likely contributes to her posthumous popularity. In an atmosphere in which listeners have observed the public suffering of a musician, her songs become "metaphors for the nature of the singer herself."[23]

In evaluations of Parsons' music, his singing similarly serves as a point of intersection for his biography, the sad lyrics of his songs, and the genre of country itself. With a voice that has been described as "frail," "mournful," and "tortured," Parsons delivered lines on lost loves, despair, and heartache. The most commonly cited example is "Hot Burrito #1," also known as "I'm Your Toy," from his first album with the Burritos, a song composed by Parsons and Burritos' bassist Chris Etheridge. Hailed as "perhaps the best song Parsons . . . [had] yet written," this recording has come to stand for the intensity of emotion behind his music. Critic Allan Jones says of "Hot Burrito #1": "It's a song that can cut you in two. Beautiful pain. . . . It can freeze your heart, that song."[24] In a 1973 review, Scoppa states that he "can't think of a performance on record any more moving than Gram's on his 'Hot Burrito #1'," and in the opinion of Chris Hillman, "The best vocal Gram ever did was 'Hot Burrito #1' and '[Hot Burrito] #2'."[25]

To what musical details do these comments refer? How did Parsons express "pain," and what characteristics of his voice made it sound "frail," "mournful," and "tortured"? When writers praise Parsons' exhibition of personal struggle, they point to moments when his voice cracks or shakes. By certain standards of singing, Parsons' "expression" might be heard as a musical weakness or a kind of vocal failure; he frequently sounds out of tune and out of control. How are we to interpret such "mistakes"? We could simply brand him incompetent as a country singer, but this would not explain the deep investment listeners hold in his recordings. On the other hand, it might be possible to see Parsons' songs as ironic performances of failure, that he played the part of a rejected or otherwise downtrodden "regressive" country subject. This reading would require some evidence of self-consciousness in musical moments of failure, something not consistently found in Parsons' later recordings. While a few of Parsons' songs, like his adoption of country showbiz attire, exaggerate aspects of country performance, it appears that he took his recorded vocal performances quite seriously. We must therefore evaluate this music in a way that incorporates his mistakes into a larger aesthetic.

In an article on Miles Davis, Robert Walser discusses the problem of Davis' technical "mistakes," asking, "How are we to account for such glaring defects in the performances of someone who is indisputably one of the most important musicians in the history of jazz?"[26] He goes on to show that Davis' cracked notes and other idiosyncrasies are the result of Davis' experimentation with trumpet technique, that as Davis pushed the boundaries of acceptable performance practice he risked failure. His failure in the eyes of jazz critics and advocates of classical trumpet playing was a sign that Davis was operating under a different set of standards, one that valued variation in sound quality and a creative, nontraditional use of the instrument. Considering Parsons' influence on at least two generations of alt.country musicians, an adaptation of Walser's question is helpful: how are we to account for such glaring defects in the performances of someone who is indisputably one of the most important musicians in the history of alt.country?

Walser's answer for Davis points to at least one possible explanation for Parsons' blemishes: in his later work, Parsons challenged himself stylistically on his chosen instrument, his voice. The songs of Parsons' solo albums vary widely in their vocal requirements. He turns from sensitive duet singing with Harris ("Hearts on Fire") to pop crooning ("Brass Buttons") to bluegrass ("Cash on the Barrelhead"), entailing a range of types of voice placement, intensity of vibrato, dynamics, and timbre (sound quality). Because vocal style is one of the most recognizable markers of genre, his choices were all the more important in marking his "cosmic American music" as country, rock, and folk. Parsons' existence between country and rock, a liminal space, put him in new and unknown vocal territory for him.

Parsons' recordings present his version of country music. They display the musical characteristics he finds important in the style—intimacy, close attention to words, and an enjoyment in harmony singing—at the expense of parameters such as tight control over pitch. His purpose in singing country was not to execute every note, rhythm, and ornament with technical correctness but to showcase dynamic contrast, smooth legato lines, idiomatic diction, and country harmony singing. Like Dylan's singing, Parsons' work established an alternative mode of country vocal expression, giving permission to alt.country musicians to sing country even if their voices don't conform to the Nashville sound. Parsons' work, much like that of alt.country's, is a rock musician's reading of the country style, an intercultural translation that resorts the list of country's musical priorities to conform to his concerns.

The moments when Parsons struggles are like what George Lipsitz calls "creative mistakes." Lipsitz recounts how Ronnie Spector of the Ronettes enjoyed performing Hank Williams' songs as a child and that her trademark "whoa-oh-oh-ohs" came from her attempts to imitate Williams' country yodeling. In some views, Spector "got it wrong"; her voice sounds very little like the singer she was trying to mimic, but her "misunderstanding" proved fruitful.

> From one perspective, her rendition of the song might seem ignorant or incompetent, but from another viewpoint it can also be interpreted as an uninterrogated and perhaps unexpected form of intelligence and competence—finding a song that turned cultural contradictions into a creative expression of cultural hybridity.[27]

Similarly, Parsons' renditions of country songs, while problematic by some standards, are likewise seen by others as "creative expression[s] of cultural hybridity."

A close reading of Parsons' recording of "Hot Burrito #1" illustrates the way he negotiated his inadequacies as a singer to make the recording for some listeners the "best vocal Gram ever did." I do not argue that the song succeeded in spite of the vocalist's failures or, the opposite, that his mistakes alone account for a kind of authenticity with which listeners can identify. Instead, I hope to show how Parsons' vocals work with the lyrics and music of the song to construct an abject singing subject. Parsons' mistakes are honest ones, not calculated, planned, or exaggerated. They are the by-products of his particular voice at a particular time in his career and the result of his attempts to sing in a dramatic, dynamic, and challenging style. I will first explain how the lyrics and chord structure of the song construct a feeling of hopelessness and then describe his delivery in select portions of the song.[28]

"Hot Burrito #1" is structured into three verses (all with similar melody and harmony) and a bridge with a second melody and harmonic pattern. Aside from a brief introduction and outro at the end, the song progresses as follows: verse 1, verse 2, bridge, verse 3, bridge, verse 3. Musically, "Hot Burrito #1" creates an impression of melancholy and romantic hopelessness that spotlights the feeling of loss in the lyrics. It accomplishes this mainly through downward chromatic motion and by constantly thwarting a lasting resolution on the "home key" of F major. The trend of descending chromaticism starts at the beginning of the song in the four-measure introduction before Parsons' first entrance. At its most basic, the harmonic pattern of the first three measures is centered on D minor. As the band arrives at each new measure of D minor, the bass guitar's notes move down by one-half step (D–C♯–C), resolving on G in the fourth measure with the rest of the ensemble. The introduction sets a precedent for the rest of the piece: though not the only aspect of the song's harmony, descending chromatic motion appears in all three verses and the guitar solo section.

However, the bass guitar and voice lines often work in opposition to the descending motive. For example, during the bridge the bass and lead guitars directly challenge the insistence of descent with, perhaps predictably, ascending chromaticism. They temporarily break out of the doom of the verses in what is one of the most exciting moments of the song. The bridge begins with two measures of instrumental music in which the bass guitar changes notes every two beats (twice as fast as in the verses), climbing from C-sharp to D to E-flat. This stark shift in harmonic rhythm and direction leads the listener to believe that something important is about to happen, and it is at this point that the subject remembers when he had more control in a relationship: "Once upon a time, you let me feel you deep inside."

The rising tension in the bridge also sets up a melodic breakthrough for the vocal line. Until this point, the vocal melody's highest pitch is an E-flat (almost always reached by half-step movement from below), but here Parsons breaches an E-natural via a whole step from the D below. He does this most dramatically on the last word of the bridge, "cried," reaching a new level of emotional and musical intensity in imitation of the sound of crying. This outburst lasts only momentarily; it succumbs to F major and the next verse's descending line. Even with the continual return to F, the song never feels truly resolved until the end when the band remains on F major. All other arrivals on the tonic are fleeting and unstable; every time we land at "home," we never stay because chromatic motion takes over. That a piece of music would migrate to minor key areas from an initial statement of a major tonic is normal in Western popular music, but this song's almost constant movement toward instability and its method of doing so through chromatic voice leading is uncommon in rock.

The harmonic motion of "Hot Burrito #1" is a demonstration of the singing subject's constant longing. Even though the song finally terminates on F major, it is not the singer but the band that must complete the task, and it does so in a repeat of part of the ascending motive from the bridge for a "big finish" ending. The lyrics argue for the rights of the subject to a relationship with the beloved, but the music tells us that this desire will never be satisfied. His only resistance against the trap of the harmony is his breakthrough to E-natural in the bridge (his highest pitch) and his appeal to past emotional intimacy. That Parsons is unable to execute his part without vocal problems makes his pleading even more meaningful; he is trapped in nostalgia and suffering, and we know that he will ultimately fail in his attempt to escape the cycle.

Parsons' vocal struggles are about control, specifically control over pitch, vibrato, and timbre, all of which are demonstrated in the first verse. His first entrance, on the word "You," is too low (it is "flat"), and he scoops up to land on middle C. He also phonates the start of this word with vocal fry but so quickly clears his tone that the beginning of the entrance sounds like a shake, and in combination with the inaccurate intonation it sounds as if Parsons is nervous.[29] In line 2, on the opening words "But that won't," he again begins the phrase under pitch before he finds his mooring. At the end of the phrase, he inflects "night" with a fast, shallow vibrato that he uses throughout the rest of the song, especially noticeable on final words of phrases (i.e., "now," "arms," "then," "time"). The word "night" stands out even more because Parsons delivers it with a nasal tone and a southern accent. On his entrance to the final line of the verse ("To do"), his voice cracks a little and he scoops up to the pitch. The final word of the verse, "now," sticks out like "night" did in line 2 due to Parsons' vibrato, high degree of nasality, and accent, sounding more like his accented version of "night" than a standard English pronunciation of "now."

Throughout the recording, Parsons continues to have pitch problems (the second time he sings the phrase "but I don't want no one but you to love me" he is sharp) and to lose control of his vocal tone to cracks and vocal fry. His voice is so shaky that it frequently sounds as if it is constantly on the verge of cracking or breaking completely. In some instances, these "failures" are the result of his attempts to be expressive. For example, his voice drops into a vocal fry on the line "I'm your toy, I'm your old boy" because he is singing more softly than usual. He doesn't have the breath support or the vocal agility to sing this quietly without his voice dropping out, thus giving the impression that his voice is tired.

Parsons' difficulties manifest themselves to a greater extent on his solo albums *GP* and *Grievous Angel.* As in the case of "Hot Burrito #1," writers have lauded the emotional content of these albums. Says Jones:

> Both "GP" and "Grievous Angel" need no analysis. There are no words to describe the sense of desperation, and the haunting quality of these last works. They just need to be listened to. . . . Within the perspective of Parsons' death the pain of some of the songs like "Kiss the Children" and "A Song for You" on the first album become too real. You just have to try and understand the pain, as Parsons says, because it takes so long to explain. . . . "Love Hurts" is a statement of pure pain. You can feel your nerve endings singing along to it. It's the same with "Brass Buttons," one of Gram's most tortured love songs.[30]

We hear Parsons' instability intimately on the solo albums since his voice seems to have been miked closely and is mixed so as to sound much louder than the band and backing vocals, even when he's singing softly.

"A Song for You" from *GP* further demonstrates Parsons' difficulties in performance. In the first line, "Oh my land is like a wild goose," he sings characteristically out of tune (slightly sharp) and out of tempo with the band. He rushes the beginning of the phrase, corrects himself by the words "like a," but then rushes his melisma on "wild" and his arrival on "goose." Phrases like this one give the impression that at this time in his career Parsons was not comfortable with slow grooves because of his poor control over tone and pitch in general. (Without strong breath support, Parsons might not have been able to execute rhythms properly or match the groove of the other musicians.) Specifically, it is his treatment of a certain kind of melisma (as on "wild" and "goose" in the example) that exposes him as a different kind of country singer. These three-note melismas encompass the interval of a third and are characteristic of country singing.[31] Singers use them to ornament syllables that they want to emphasize but in such a way that it will not affect a listener's basic understanding of the melody. Parsons' inability to "nail" his melismas gives away his status as a country outsider: even casual country fans would know that he was not a "real" country singer from Nashville.

As in his work with the Burritos, Parsons sang duets on his solo albums but this time with a female partner, Emmylou Harris. Harris' parts are usually mixed as supporting vocals, sounding much farther back in the sonic field than Parsons' tracks. Harris fails to match pitch with the band (e.g., on "loose" in the first verse of "A Song for You"), but her tone and volume are consistent, so she sounds like a secure foil to Parsons. This is partly due to Parsons' distance from the microphone. Especially on ballads, Parsons recorded close to the microphone, and these tracks were then given the most prominent place in the mix with the rest of the band, in effect broadcasting the details of his voice and its production. The risk of this recording technique is that, while it increased the level of intimacy, it exposed Parsons' voice as if putting it under a microscope. Close miking also captures subtle dynamic shifts, and on several tracks his voice suddenly becomes louder or softer, as if he is either rapidly moving toward and away from the microphone or singing with uneven bursts of air. Due to what sounds like inconsistent breath support in "A Song for You," several notes "pop" out of the texture, especially in verse 2 (on the words "to sing a song to" and the first instance of "sails") and his lower range in general. As Mitchell Morris argues, this kind of "close-up" of the singer's voice works much like a filmic close-up of an actor's face onscreen; the gesture itself signals to the audience that we are now witnessing a new level of interiority. And, as Morris shows in his discussion of Karen Carpenter, close miking creates a maternal and nurturing sonic environment that leads listeners to believe that they have access to a special kind of emotional intimacy. This use of technology was a perfect match for Carpenter's voice because it focused in on the intricacies of her diction, breath, and beginnings of notes, all of which sounded simultaneously natural and professional. In other words, the microscoping of close miking allowed listeners to hear most clearly those vocal strengths of Carpenter's voice that listeners most wanted to hear.[32] At first glance, close miking would seem to be a disadvantage for Parsons since it broadcast his mistakes and difficulties, but it highlighted his attention to words and diction, his wide dynamics, and his nuanced changes in overall feeling.

The breaks, cracks, and strain in Parsons' voice in recordings such as "Hot Burrito #1" and "A Song for You," which by other standards might disqualify him as an effective singer, work to represent the subject's misery in a spectacle of despair. It is precisely this vocal sensibility, along with knowledge of his biography, that has led many to believe that Parsons had to sing country. In one of the few scholarly articles about him, Michael Grimshaw argues for such a necessary connection between Parsons' personal life and his singerly persona. For Grimshaw, it is his imperfections that signal authenticity.

> Parsons did not possess a voice of great range or depth—nor can it be said of perfect pitch. But what it did have was a soft aching fragility, a tender sorrow and the nasal purity of a man singing because this was the only way to express the hurt, suffering, and sorrow—and occasionally the joy he encountered in a short life. As such, he sang country music because it is music that speaks of need and salvation, of dislocation and grace, of the attempt to try and follow the will of God—and of the grudging reconciliation with failure.[33]

The history of Parsons' voice tells a different story, one of construction and development, not one of essence and natural country talent. It reveals that he learned to sing country in his twenties just as he learned to sing folk as a teenager. It also shows that the instrument we take to be the most direct conduit of the self and its identity is often the result of musical education and context. As recorded through 1966, Parsons' singing style was markedly unlike the "world-weary honey crackle" he adopted in the late 1960s.[34] The Parsons recorded in 1965 and the one recorded on his solo albums of the 1970s sound like two different singers. As the lead singer of the Shilos, he imitated folk and pop singers with open vowels, vibrato, resonance through both chest and head cavities, and even occasional crooning.[35] His clear diction and accent demonstrate little if any of the slurred delivery of rock and roll singers of the time or the southern accents and nasal tone of country artists. If anything, Parsons' singing accent in the early 1960s shows a proclivity toward a British one: in his "November Nights," recorded in 1966, Parsons sings the word "hand" of the chorus more like the sound of *a* in *father* than the sound of *a* in *cat*.[36] Also notable is Parsons' control on these early recordings. He consistently sang in tune, and his voice was well supported by his breath. In general, his voice sounds stronger, fuller, and more capable of wide changes in dynamics. His good intonation was no fluke; a live recording of the Shilos from the period shows that the group could perform its songs live as well as it could in the studio.[37] Parsons' interest in folk is remarkable because it required singing techniques and a style strikingly different from what he would adopt two years after leaving the Shilos. It also shows that the singing style of his country period was learned, not something directly absorbed from his southern upbringing.

The belief in Gram Parsons' necessary connection to country and the relevance of his songs to his life story has combined with the anticommercial ideology of alt.country to establish his posthumous persona. The similarity of his image to others in rock suggests that his legend is no more remarkable than that of other rock heroes. However, the manner in which he and his devotees have constructed his myth has made scholarly evaluation of his music difficult, complicating his accomplishments and discouraging contextual explanations of his music. His myth embodies the fears and concerns of a variety of roots projects but especially that of alt.country. It is integral to alt.country's supposed heritage in "cosmic American music," its critiques of country rock, and its commitment to sincerity in the form of neotraditionalism. Aside from his constructed persona, Parsons' greatest influence on alt.country was his "regressive" version of country music. His willingness to take technical risks produced recordings that validated the desires of "outsiders" to sing country music on their own terms.

NOTES

Opening epigraph: Bud Scoppa, liner notes, Various artists, *Return of the Grievous Angel: A Tribute to Gram Parsons,* Almo Sounds AMSD–80024, 1999.

1. As Bill Malone notes, "Although many young musicians experimented with country forms, no one converted the enterprise into a mission until Gram Parsons appeared." *Country Music, U.S.A.*, 3rd ed. (Austin: University of Texas Press, 2002),

387. Parsons and Harris can be heard recounting the interview at the end of track 6 ("Cry One More Time") on Gram Parsons and the Fallen Angels, *Live 1973*, 1994.

2. Ben Fong-Torres, *Hickory Wind: The Life and Times of Gram Parsons*, 2nd ed. (New York: Pocket Books, 1991). A second biography was published in 2002, Jason Walker, *Gram Parsons: God's Own Singer* (London: Helter Skelter, 2002). A third, released in October of 2007, is the most detailed account of Parsons' life: David N. Meyer, *Twenty Thousand Roads: The Ballad of Gram Parsons and His Cosmic American Music* (New York: Villard, 2007). Recent tribute albums include Various artists, *Return of the Grievous Angel: A Tribute to Gram Parsons*, Almo Sounds, 1999; Various artists, *Conmemorativo: A Tribute to Gram Parsons*, 1993; Jeff and Janet, *Jesus Built a Ship to Sing a Song To*, Kokopop 3, 1993; and the Coal Porters, *The Gram Parsons Tribute Concert*, Prima SID010, 1998.

3. Peter Blackstock, "Personal Parsonage: *Return of the Grievous Angel—A Tribute to Gram Parsons*," *No Depression* 22 (July–August) 1999, http://www.nodepression.net/archive/nd22/depts/waxed.html (accessed September 2004).

4. The concerts, titled "Return to Sin City: A Tribute to Gram Parsons," were held on July 9 and 10, 2004, at the Santa Barbara Bowl in Santa Barbara and the Universal Amphitheatre in Los Angeles, respectively. They featured Keith Richard and Norah Jones and spoke to Parsons' continuing influence on the alt.country scene with performances by Jay Farrar, Jim James, and Raul Malo. The concert is available on DVD. Polly Parsons also cowrote a biography of Gram, *Grievous Angel: An Intimate Biography of Gram Parsons* (New York: Thunder's Mouth Press, 2005).

5. Fong-Torres, *Hickory Wind*, 62.

6. Rick Kienzle, liner notes to Various artists, *Heroes of Country Music, Vol. 5: Legends of Country Rock*, 1996.

7. Bud Scoppa, *The Byrds* (New York: Scholastic Book Services, 1971), 85.

8. The Flying Burrito Brothers had a special affinity for songs with connections to the Bakersfield sound ("Sing Me Back Home," "Tonight the Bottle Let Me Down," and "White Line Fever" by Merle Haggard; "Together Again" by Buck Owens; and "Dim Lights, Thick Smoke [and Loud, Loud Music]" by Joe and Rose Lee Maphis).

9. Fong-Torres, *Hickory Wind*, 191.

10. In contrast, the author of the most recent Parsons biography, David N. Meyer, is one of the few writers who speaks critically of the Parsons mythology. However, his evaluation of the musician's significance succumbs to exaggeration: "[I]t can be argued that Parsons exerted greater influence on our national musical taste than any other single musician" (*Conmemorativo*, in David N. Meyer, *Twenty Thousand Roads: The Ballad of Gram Parsons and His Cosmic American Music* xx–xxi. [New York: Villard, 2007]).

11. My discussion of Scoppa's writing is not intended to single him out; others imply, if not explicitly claim, that Parsons is the *fons et origo* of country rock. See Holly George-Warren, "A Long Lost Soul for a Long Time," *No Depression* 22 (July–

August 1999), http://www.nodepression.net/archive/nd22/features/parsons.html (accessed September 2004); Ted Grimshaw, "Redneck Religion and Shitkickin' Saviours? Gram Parsons, Theology, and Country Music," *Popular Music* 21, no. 1 (2002): 93–106; Fong-Torres, *Hickory Wind;* and Walker, *Gram Parsons.* See also Jimmy Cornelison: "Perhaps it was Parsons, more than any other single force which brought country music out of its closet existence into the mainstream of American society." "Gram Parsons' Music Continues to Live On," *Music City News,* August 1983, 12. In this case, the writer not only gives Parsons too much credit but gives country music too little.

12. The Byrds touched on country music as early as 1965 when they recorded "Satisfied Mind," a tune made popular by Porter Wagoner, for their *Turn! Turn! Turn!* album.

13. John Einarson's *Desperadoes: The Roots of Country Rock* (New York: Cooper's Square, 2001), is an exception to the "great man" trend in country rock historiography.

14. See Barbara Ching, *Wrong's What I Do Best: Hard Country Music and Contemporary Culture* (Oxford: Oxford University Press, 2001).

15. Descriptions of Parsons as a hillbilly or country boy also indicate an assumption that all people from the South are from the mountains or rural areas. Neither was the case in Parsons' life.

16. Judith Sims, "Ex-Byrd Gram Solos: He's No Longer in a Hurry," *Rolling Stone,* March 1, 1973, 14.

17. Stanley Booth, "Records: *The Gilded Palace of Sin,*" *Rolling Stone,* May 15, 1969, 15. Booth wasn't the only critic who saw Parsons' music as a direct result of his background. *Melody Maker* writer Lorraine Alterman says, "Growing up in Georgia is what put Gram's roots solidly in country music." "Parsons Knows . . . ," *Melody Maker,* April 7, 1973, 33.

18. Parsons was known for embellishing his background, and many of these untruths have made it into print. Though untrue, Parsons bragged that his father had been an itinerant country singer. He also told friends that his family home had been used in *Gone With the Wind,* and Sims prints a claim that Parsons sang country on the radio as a child, which none of his biographers have been able to substantiate (Cornelison, "Gram Parsons' Music Continues to Live On"; Fong-Torres, *Hickory Wind,* 7). In this way, Parsons fits into a tradition of extreme self-consciousness about life experience and authenticity in country music discussed by Pamela Fox in "Recycled 'Trash': Gender and Authenticity in Country Music Autobiography," *American Quarterly* 50, no. 2 (June 1998): 234–66.

19. Sims, "Ex-Byrd Gram Solos." Parsons' ventures to clubs like the Palomino (in the San Fernando Valley) and Aces (in the City of Industry, over forty miles east of downtown Los Angeles) point to the cultural significance of the layout of greater Los Angeles. The places where Parsons and his friends lived were countercultural spaces

(Hollywood, Topanga Canyon, Laurel Canyon) while the San Fernando Valley and City of Industry were conservative, suburban, and largely populated by middle- and working-class Californians, many of whom had been part of the Okie migration. See Peter La Chapelle, *Proud to Be an Okie: Cultural Politics, Country Music, and Migration to Southern California* (Berkeley: University of California Press, 2007). For Parsons' project to succeed, he had to go to places where country fans lived because hippies and "rednecks" rarely occupied the same physical spaces.

20. Alterman, "Parsons Knows . . . ," 33. There is a bit of truth to this claim. According to Keith Richard, Parsons taught him about country substyles: "We used to sit around at the piano for ages, trying to figure out little licks, and he'd show me the different ways Nashville will play it from Bakersfield" (Fong-Torres, *Hickory Wind,* 130).

21. Peter Doggett points out that the Burritos weren't the only Los Angeles rock musicians to wear Nudie suits: Michael Nesmith ordered one the same month. See *Are You Ready for the Country: Elvis, Dylan, Parsons, and the Roots of Country Rock* (New York: Penguin, 2000), 71.

22. David Brackett, *Interpreting Popular Music* (Berkeley: University of California Press, 2000), 38.

23. Mitchell Morris, "The Voice of Karen Carpenter," in *The Persistence of Sentiment: Essays on Display and Feeling in '70s Pop* (Berkeley: University of California Press, forthcoming).

24. Allan Jones, "Country Parsons," *Melody Maker,* July 27, 1974, 30.

25. Bud Scoppa, "Records: *GP,*" *Rolling Stone,* March 1, 1973, 69; George-Warren, "A Long Lost Soul for a Long Time." Jones applies the theme of pain to the rest of Parsons' work as well. About the Burritos' version of "Wild Horses" he says, "He sounds so wasted on that song it's not true. It's as if he's pulling himself up by his own hair, through his own desolation. There's none of Jagger's devastated elegance. Every word is dragged out torn at the edges. This is pain with a capital P—and a capital AIN for that matter." The "pain trope" is still a common one for Parsons writers; Meyer identifies it as the most significant aspect of "Luxury Liner," Parsons' first composition of his country period (*Twenty Thousand Roads,* 170–72). About Parsons in general, Meyer states, "Nobody so embraced the core of pure country: a straightforward presentation of the singer's emotional pain" (172).

26. Robert Walser, "Out of Notes: Signification, Interpretation, and the Problem of Miles Davis," *Musical Quarterly* 77, no. 2 (summer 1993): 343.

27. George Lipsitz, *Dangerous Crossroads: Popular Music, Postmodernism, and the Poetics of Place* (London: Verso, 1994), 160.

28. Scholarship in popular music often evaluates singing, but few authors explain how individual singers' voices make meaning, and there is currently no established method in musicology for this type of work. A few scholars have begun to lay the groundwork for voice studies. See Richard Middleton, "Rock Singing," in *The Cam-*

bridge Companion to Singing, ed. John Potter, 28–41 (Cambridge: Cambridge University Press, 2000); Morris, "The Voice of Karen Carpenter"; John Potter, *Vocal Authority: Singing Style and Ideology* (Cambridge: Cambridge University Press, 1998); and Richard Rischar, "A Vision of Love: An Etiquette of Vocal Ornamentation in African-American Popular Ballads of the Early 1990s," *American Music* 22, no. 3 (2004): 407–43.

29. Vocal fry is a sound made with loose vocal chords, producing a rough sound low in pitch relative to the range of a singer's conventional singing voice. Its timbre is virtually never used in classical singing but is intentionally employed by pop and rock singers. It can, however, indicate that the singer's breath support is weak or that the singer is tired.

30. Jones, "Country Parsons."

31. See Rischar, "A Vision of Love"; and Sammie Ann Wickes, "A Belated Salute to the 'Old Way' of 'Snaking' the Voice on Its (ca.) 345th Birthday," *Popular Music* 8, no. 1 (1989): 59–96.

32. Morris, "The Voice of Karen Carpenter," 210.

33. Grimshaw, "Redneck Religion and Shitkickin' Saviours?," 98.

34. George-Warren, "A Long Lost Soul for a Long Time."

35. See the album *Gram Parsons: The Early Years, 1963–1965*, and note 37.

36. Gram Parsons, *Another Side of This Life: The Lost Recordings of Gram Parsons, 1965–1966*, Sundazed, 2000.

37. My thanks go to an original Shilos member, Paul Surratt, for allowing me to listen to a recently discovered and unreleased live recording of the Shilos at the Derry Down club in Winter Haven, Florida. Surratt also told me that all ten of the songs the Shilos recorded that were later released as *Gram Parsons: The Early Years, 1963–1965*, were recorded in one hour with no overdubbing. Most of the tracks show that the band was well rehearsed and had carefully planned its arrangements in advance of the session.

AARON SMITHERS

Old Time Punk

Designations that categorize music genres—country, punk rock, alt.country ("whatever that is")—and their perceived boundaries generally function as a marketing tool and fuel for debate. Critics and fans toss these labels off like syntactical grocery lists, while musicians claim to avoid them and the music industry attempts to sell them. Neither genres, however, nor the labels that name them, are as stable or enduring as we would like them to be. S. Renee Dechert, in her discussion of Uncle Tupelo, demonstrates how genres are constantly "evolving and changing to reflect shifts in cultural values and norms, each new discourse in dialogue with its predecessors,"[1] yet musicians, scholars, and music enthusiasts alike continue to affix a genre- based designation to each musical selection or repertoire we hear in an effort to place it within a strict category. How else would we know where to find our music in the local record store or online music distributor?

As a means of distinguishing the alt.country movement from modern commercial country music, media critics, fans, labels, and performers often cite roots in punk attitudes and performance styles as well as a reverence for and devotion to traditional country. Dave Goodman's description of Uncle Tupelo in *Modern Twang*, for example, has been repeated often enough to become alt.country mythology: a "Black Flag type punk band, . . . that combined these elements with a long tradition of country music" and spawned a movement.[2] Early alt.country poster boy Ryan Adams scarcely gave an interview in which he did not attempt to separate himself from country music by declaring that his musical roots were in punk rock. This characterization of alt.country as a punk-traditional country hybrid, however, is too simplistic to account for the diversity and history of the music shaded beneath branches of the alt.country family tree. To refer only to punk and traditional country roots ignores the musical significance of the country rock movement of the 1970s; furthermore, it denies the impact, influence, and diversity of countless other American underground rock bands of the 1980s, including performers who relentlessly strove to create regional, grassroots support systems for their music, paving the way for the independent music industry's growth in the 1990s.[3] I propose that Uncle Tupelo and other performers who participated in the growth of the "No Depression" wave of music that came to be called alt.country were more likely influenced by country rock and their own regional underground scenes than the often difficult, ultra-aggressive hardcore that is Black Flag.[4]

This is not to deny that characteristics of punk are recognizable within the music of many bands labeled alt.country, but they are by no means clearly detectable in the music of all or even most of these bands. Many alt.country performers also demonstrate little or no sonic affinity with traditional country music. Why, then, does the punk-traditional-alt.country connection continue to be made? The answer lies in the continual construction and recognition of the notion of authenticity.[5] Performers and fans of punk rock create strong divisions between "authentic" punk and "commercial" rock, just as certain groups of performers and fans of country music distinguish between authentic traditional country and modern commercial country.[6] Therefore, alt.country performers must construct a paradoxical identity that connects them to country music's past and yet separates them from that genre's most popular present formations found on commercial country radio and Country Music Television. Establishing roots in punk bridges the temporal gap between what the alt.country movement views as the current sacrilegious state of country present and the holy state of country past.[7]

This bridge allows industry performers to define musicians as sincere by associating them with punk and country music made prior to 1980 that, though commercial, is nevertheless viewed by alt.country proponents as more authentic than the commercial country music produced today. The industry can then market the music to alt.country fans that, like punk fans, hold the concept of authenticity as one of their core principles.[8] Even Kelly Willis, a skilled alt.country songwriter and gifted singer whose music barely even rocks, has been drawn into the absurdity of this stance, claiming to be ignored by the industry because of her punk attitude.[9] Like Willis, Adams and Uncle Tupelo are talented performers who stand strong on their musical merits, but, as Mark Rubin, the bassist of the Bad Livers, Rubenchyk's Orkestyr, Pine Top Syncopators, and many more bands, acerbically notes, "It's easier to sell a scene than a quality."[10]

Various correlations link alt.country, classic punk, and old-time country. Scholars make note of the similarities between the do-it-yourself (DIY) aesthetic of punk and country music's populist leanings.[11] Alt.country and punk musicians personally relate to the anti-establishment philosophy of musicians such as Woody Guthrie.[12] They also identify with many country music stars that have suffered from alcohol and drug abuse, especially Hank Williams because he lived so hard and died so young.[13] Musical connections are made on the basis of the perceived simplicity of the styles; many songs in all three idioms involve only a few chords, and most musicians in these genres are self-taught.[14] Philosophical connections are made on the basis of a shared blue-collar foundation of the music and a devotion to independent channels of music production and consumption.[15] The raw sound of performances and recordings, often with low production values (whether an intentional aesthetic choice or a financial one), also contributes to such stylistic comparisons.[16] But these generalizations are overused—they do not apply to countless musicians who perform within these idioms. That is not to deny that these connections exist. However, to understand the alt.country music formation more accurately we must fragment the genre as it is typically defined and look for *specific* musical and cultural signifiers that delineate the traditional country-punk relationship. In order to locate these signifiers in the alt.country spectrum, we must focus our gaze on specific bands and their music as it was created within particular contexts. Rather than attempting to define the alt.country scene as a whole, this essay examines four bands, their histories, and their music as it was produced within their local and regional scenes.

According to Will Straw, a musical scene is "that cultural space in which a range of musical practices coexist, interacting with each other within a variety of processes of differentiation, and according to widely varying trajectories of change and cross-fertilization."[17] Scenes are not consistent in character over time but fluctuate according to the particular cultural activities and the context of those activities. Alt.country has been consistently and frustratingly elusive because, as a genre, it has been defined as a hybrid of forms—punk and country—and its participants openly acknowledge and celebrate its fluidity. Because the concept of scene "designates particular clusters of social and cultural activity without specifying the nature of the boundaries which circumscribe them,"[18] it directly reflects alt.country's need for constant redefinition as an "alternative" without ever concretely specifying what it is an alternative to other than the equally elusive "mainstream."

With such a seemingly indefinable frame, using the concept of scene as a theoretical base for analysis appears imprudent. Nevertheless, scenes provide an accurate model of the constant variability of cultural production. Under scrutiny, scenes may elude distinct, recognizable boundaries because individuals involved in the production of scenes—including performers, journalists, and fans—are constantly drawing and redrawing these boundaries (though sometimes unintentionally). Described in the personal narratives of individual participants and demonstrated through practices of production and consumption, these boundaries are dependent on the desires and goals of the individual; they may not be the same. According to Peterson and Beal, Goodman, and Molinaro, the most common factors used to designate the boundaries of the alt.country scene are genre and the combining of forms to create hybrid genres, the perceived authenticity of performance, and the independent channels of music production and consumption. As argued earlier, the discourse connecting punk and country is indeed an important element of alt.country as a generic construct. Yet many of those bands I identify as representative of this hybridity equally utilize a hillbilly performance idiom.

It is the wails, hollers, and hoots amid the scratches and hiss of hillbilly and country music recorded in the 1920s, 1930s, and 1940s that inspire some musicians identified with some of the alt.country scene. They have put down their electric guitars and turned off their amplifiers to pick up banjos, fiddles, mandolins, and even tubas to perform the music of Dock Boggs and Iggy Pop side by side. In the music of bands such as the Bad Livers, the Meat Purveyors, Split Lip Rayfield, and Zero Skills, Inc.—all with members who performed and participated in punk rock bands and now perform mostly on acoustic instruments, often employing traditional styles—the relationship between punk and country is located on the surface of their presentation within their historical and social contexts, not only in the text of their promotions.

Austin, Texas, with its vibrant music community, is home to three of these groups; it is a city with a history of country music outside the mainstream. The oldest and most prominent band in the set is the Bad Livers, who exemplify the ways in which all the musicians in this discussion reflect an affinity between punk and traditional music in song choice, instrumentation, lyrical content, physical appearance, performance style, and approach to the production and distribution of their music. Formed in 1989 by banjo player and songwriter extraordinaire Danny Barnes, bass and tuba player Mark Rubin, and the eclectic fiddle, accordion, and mbira player Ralph White, the Bad Livers developed a unique approach to playing old-time and bluegrass music. Barnes and Rubin both grew up attending underground shows, in Austin and Norman, Oklahoma, respectively, and took an early interest in performing music before they met in Dallas in a band called Killbilly, a rock band that included some bluegrass numbers as part of its repertoire. Having a shared respect for each other's musical talents and tastes, they formed the Bad Livers with the like-minded White.[19]

From the start, the Bad Livers exposed their punk connections. On an early, twelve-inch, 45 rpm extended play (EP) record pressed on yellow vinyl, the band's photo shows that the large Rubin has visible tattoos while his upright bass displays stickers depicting the Misfits, Motorhead, and Black Flag. Barnes wears ripped jeans, a T-shirt with the sleeves cut off, and the long hair of a metalhead while White sports a T-shirt advertising the pummeling and often offensive Chicago-based noise-rock band Big Black fronted by the revered audio engineer Steve Albini. Their first single was released as a 45 rpm record pressed on green vinyl with sleeve art featuring a cartoon of a crazed farmer on a hot-rod tractor, possibly a reference to similar artwork from the 1982 album *Junkyard* by the seminal Australian art-punk band Birthday Party. Produced by the Butthole Surfers' Paul Leary, the Bad Livers seven-inch vinyl record featured a cover of punk rock legend Iggy Pop's "Lust for Life."

At the same time, however, the Bad Livers are not always pleased that their early career began "dangerously close to a novelty punk-bluegrass fusion."[20] Rubin points out that the punk covers are what reviewers and many listeners focused on while at the same time the nascent trio

> played Mississippi Fred McDowall and [Thelonious] Monk, and we'd also play stuff from our collective memory, like Rocky Erickson. Then people from the punk scene started seeing what was happening, and journalists, being a lazy bunch, they'd fasten on to the one Motorhead or Stooges song, not

> the Art Tatum or Charlie Poole or Son House. It's true that we were drawn to punk, but more because of our anarchic disposition and the punk DIY ethic, but to call us a country-punk group is just lazy.[21]

In this way, the Bad Livers, as well as the other bands profiled in this essay that followed in their wake, reflect an ideological connection to punk through their eclecticism. Molinaro traces this trend in alt.country to post-punk, suggesting punk's second wave demonstrated "that 'punk' was not a sound but the idea behind any number of styles."[22] According to Danny Barnes, "That's what I was getting at with reconciling yourself unto punk rock, where you had that punk rock experience. . . . It doesn't necessarily have to be at a punk rock show."[23] So the Bad Livers made the music they wanted to make. They looked like punks because "all of [their] friends were in punk rock bands. Our peer group, they had punk rock bands," and they played punk songs because "that's what we listened to in the car."[24] The result is what Barnes describes as the Bad Livers' "own form. It's a sound and a culmination of sounds that doesn't really exist in any other band."[25] He relates their music to punk because it "is a culmination of forms—plus some sort of fly-by-the-seat-of-the-pants creativity thrown in."[26]

Perhaps as a reaction against early attempts to categorize their music as "slam-grass" or shtick, the Bad Livers also recorded a cassette consisting entirely of traditional gospel tunes entitled *Dust on the Bible.* Danny Barnes says, "I made it as a gift to my family for Christmas. I was practicing making a record. I was gonna do an acoustic gospel record of songs that really meant a lot to me emotionally."[27] This recording held true to the DIY aesthetic of punk rock. The band members recorded it in their living room and originally released it solely on cassette with a cover illustration depicting an open Bible and a skull and featuring graffiti-style lettering. The subsequent CD release on Chicago's now defunct Quarterstick Records discarded this image in favor of an unlabeled photograph of what appears to be the Holly Springs Primitive Baptist Church, located three miles south of Bremen, Georgia. It remains their best-selling record to date, selling well at the folk and bluegrass festivals that were among the fifteen hundred shows they performed over the next seven years.[28]

The Bad Livers' full-length records also demonstrate the band's multifaceted personality. The first, *Delusions of Banjer,* again produced by Paul Leary, includes traditional songs such as "Country Blues," learned from a

Dock Boggs recording, and standards such as Don Reno's "I Know You're Married" but also "Pee Pee the Sailor" by the Butthole Surfers and originals performed in a progressive old-time style. Danny Barnes' lyrics often address the troubles of modern life while reflecting on the traditions of the context from which he takes his music. It is important to note that the lyrics do not bespeak a romantic longing for the past, as has often been suggested of alt.country, but rather reflect and critique, presenting poignant and often grotesquely humorous images of rural life. "Shit Creek" offers an example. The narrator poses a question, both existential and literal—"What can I do just to find my peace of mind?"—before locating himself in the metaphorical "Shit Creek" where Barnes and Ruben explain in harmony, "The shit stays about a foot deep." The song concludes with a modulation, the fiddle melody smoothes, the tone shifts from dark to light. The final verse beckons the listener into the narrator's world: "Won't you please come to Shit Creek now and then? It's so damn good to have a damn good friend." While there is probably no way out of "Shit Creek," at least music, and the bonds formed through music, can provide a respite from the trials of being poor (and hopefully from the smell).

The instrumentation includes banjo, guitar, bass, and fiddle, and the harmonies are high and lonesome, but the music is progressive, combining elements of blues, rock, jazz, and classic old-time that fit together perfectly within the Bad Livers' sound, which they not only maintained but expanded on their second, self-produced release, *Horses in the Mines.* Recorded entirely at home, the album exhibits Barnes' experimental tendencies on selected tracks, which feature distorted vocals and environmental sounds, including a dog barking and a television droning in the background—sounds sure to alienate some traditional bluegrass fans. Barnes continued to move in an experimental direction on subsequent Bad Livers' recordings as well as solo projects.[29]

Delusions of Banjer, Horses in the Mines, and *The Golden Years* EP, a recording from KUT Austin 90.5 FM that features a live version of "Lust for Life," were released on Chicago's Quarterstick record label. Quarterstick was a division of indie rock stalwart Touch and Go, a label that primarily released records by hard rock and postpunk bands, including the Dead Kennedys, Jesus Lizard, and Butthole Surfers. For their third full-length LP, *Hogs on the Highway,* the Bad Livers maintained their distinctive style while working with noted country music producer Lloyd Maines—who would later produce his daughter Natalie's country band, the Dixie Chicks—and moving over to roots-based Sugar Hill records. Remaining at Sugar Hill for two more releases, *Industry and Thrift* (1998) and *Blood and Mood* (2000), the Bad Livers again demonstrated, this time through label representation, their ability to negotiate and move comfortably within both the punk and traditional music milieus.

The Meat Purveyors, known as the Texas Meat Purveyors before they were threatened with a lawsuit by a meat distributor of the same name, also hail from Austin, and it is no surprise that they list the Bad Livers as an inspiration.[30] Importantly, however, they also cite Austin cowpunk bands the Hickoids and Joan of Arkansas and include covers of obscure Austin musicians on their recordings and in their performances. Reflecting a variety of influences, from punk to rock to the Grateful Dead, the Meat Purveyors play bluegrass. In 1996, guitarist and songwriter Bill Anderson joined with vocalist Jo Walston, bassist Cherylin DiMond, former "deadhead" mandolinist Peter Stiles,[31] and fiddler Darcie Deville, who sits in on recordings and occasional performances. Banjo player Nora Floyd left the band early on and was not replaced. Their decision not to replace a key instrument in the traditional bluegrass ensemble reflects their oppositional stance to purists. Like the Bad Livers and many alt.country artists in general, the Meat Purveyors are uncomfortable with attempts to categorize their music and avoid the alt.country tag.[32] But, unlike the Bad Livers, whose leader, Barnes, said, "I have way too much respect for bluegrass music to say that we have anything to do with it,"[33] the Meat Purveyors accept that their music is at its core bluegrass.[34]

From a traditionalist's perspective, however, the Meat Purveyors have violated many of what Rubin has described as "certain little hoops that you have to jump through in order to be a bluegrass band."[35] In addition to lacking a banjo, the Meat Purveyors' performance style demonstrates a decidedly punk edge. Most songs follow a straightforward three-chord structure with only short solos or breaks. Unlike the Bad Livers, whose penchant for musical styles outside of rock and country, such as jazz and conjunto, is reflected in their music, the Meat Purveyors do not stray from this territory. Anderson is the primary songwriter, and the band's first release, *Sweet in the Pants*, includes a rollicking version of a song entitled "My Biggest Mistake," originally recorded by Anderson's former blues-based punk band, Poison 13. The guitar is extremely prominent in the mix, mostly chorded rather than flatpicked, and Walston offers a forceful vocal delivery of the rather monotonous melody. The song describes twenty-one days and nights spent after the narrator has killed her lover. A twisted take on the traditional murder ballad, the singer drinks and smokes worriedly, not out of remorse but concern for not having buried the victim deeply enough, singing, "My biggest mistake was when I left you in a shallow grave."

Signed early in their career to Bloodshot records, the self-proclaimed home of "insurgent country," the Meat Purveyors released three albums that follow a similar format as those of the Bad Livers, mixing traditional songs ("Willow Garden," "Working on a Building"), country and bluegrass standards ("Lady Muleskinner," "Why Baby Why," "Can't You Hear Me Calling?"), rock covers ("S.O.S," "What Goes On," "Round and Round"), and original tunes. Importantly, the Meat Purveyors also include tracks by local underground rock bands, including "Dempsey Nash" by Austin musician and producer Brian Beattie of the 1980s alternative rock band Glass Eye, as well as "We Kill Evil" and "Go Out Smoking," favorites by the local rock group Pocket Fishermen. Lyrically, however, the Meat Purveyors explore slightly different territory than do the Bad Livers, emphasizing doomed relationships, drugs, and excessive drinking, lifestyle characteristics associated with both the punk and hardcore country aesthetics to which the Meat Purveyors adhere.

Unlike the Bad Livers, who perform comfortably in both bluegrass circles and rock venues, the Meat Purveyors eschew folk festivals as performance spaces. They strictly prefer rock clubs and not just because of the non-family-oriented nature of their lyrics. To quote Anderson, "It never feels good to play before the sun goes down. I can't come up with stage patter until I've had a couple of drinks. I don't want to get drunk at two in the afternoon."[36] Stiles agrees: "When you actually have daylight and a sober audience, it gets really bizarre."[37] By choice, then, the Meat Purveyors exemplify the punk-country juncture. They perform their music on traditional country instruments, but they incorporate a variety of songs in idioms ranging from traditional to rock into their repertoire. Additionally, they opt for venues that are outside the country music network but within the punk milieu.[38]

Split Lip Rayfield, Bloodshot records label mates of the Meat Purveyors, exhibit many of the same characteristics. Based in Wichita, Kansas, Kirk Rundstrom, on guitar, and Roy Wayne Gottsine, on mandolin, performed together in a band called Scroat Belly, whose music was often described as "thrashgrass." Scroat Belly was essentially a heavy metal rock band that incorporated country-sounding guitar solos into its music, and its members wrote lyrics reflecting the darker side of rural life, most often about heavy drinking, as demonstrated by the song titles "Drinkin' and Flailin'," "Drinkin' Around," and "Booze Won't Let Me Down." Wanting to perform similar music using acoustic instruments, in 1996 Rundstrom joined with banjo player David Lawrence, soon to be replaced by a reluctant Eric Mardis,[39] and Jeff Eaton, who constructed an upright bass instrument from the gas tank of an old Ford truck, dubbed the "Stitchgiver." Gottsine would rejoin his former bandmates on mandolin for their second release, *In the Mud*.[40]

The members of Split Lip Rayfield attack their instruments with an aggressive fury. While performing fewer rock covers than the Meat Purveyors, they also include a mix of traditional music such as "Little Liza Jane," country standards with a proclivity for trucking songs such as "Long Haul Weekend" and "Pinball Machine," and originals with nontraditional lyrics. One original, "Cutie Pie," typical of Split Lip Rayfield's music, avoids following a standard bluegrass song structure in which virtuosic solos are interspersed within the verse-chorus progression. Rather, once the band starts, it plows through a song with a feel more characteristic of speed metal, revealing its performance history. This is not the result of limited playing skills—Rundstrom, Mardis, Eaton, and Gottsine can pick with the best of them—but rather a matter of choice. Split Lip Rayfield also avoids the typical bluegrass circuit, preferring to follow the course of underground rock bands performing at small venues that typically feature rock-oriented music.[41]

Available on its self-titled debut album, "Cutie Pie" reflects Split Lip Rayfield's typical lyrical approach. Seemingly sung from the perspective of a male from rural Kansas, the subject matter of the verses runs from religion (suggesting that "Everybody pray to Jesus, 'cause it's free") to sex (she lifts her skirt for his pleasure) to the physical strength of the female love interest (she beats him up) to the male narrator's explanation of traditional gender roles (she cooks and cleans and takes responsibility for paying the bills while he goes out), all of which eventually results in his being alone (the narrator is left high and dry).

The song is humorous with the tongue held firmly in cheek. Like many of the Bad Livers' and the Meat Purveyors' lyrics, Split Lip Rayfield's song texts neither celebrate rural life nor long for the past but matter-of-factly, and often humorously, comment on life in its environment. While the singers of the songs may not be as deprived and depraved as the characters in the songs, these caricatures reflect very real feelings of anger, resentment, sadness, and alienation and the struggle of contending with modern life. Rather than resorting to punk's aggressive confrontational posture, these artists use humor in their songs to critique the economic oppression over which they and their audience have little control. Former band member David Lawrence commented on Split Lip Rayfield's early songs, "Humor is always in place. A lot of bad stuff has happened and the best thing you can do is try and make something funny out of it."[42] Humor also distances the songs from country music that fetishizes a romanticized rural, working-class way of life, both past and present, allowing for a psychological connection to narratives of struggle but with a wink and a nod. As a reflection of its members' Kansas upbringing, Split Lip Rayfield's original songs are decidedly more rural in their subject matter than the Meat Purveyors' or the Bad Livers'.

The final example takes us back to Austin. Zero Skills, Inc. arguably exhibits the most distinctly punk-oriented character among the bands discussed here, as indicated by the extremely lo-fi production of their recordings, their outward presentation, and their DIY aesthetic. This final attribute, however, could be the result of the inaccessible nature of their music and their abusive lifestyles, hinted at in the group's self-description: "The burr in yer skivvies, the seeds in yer shwag, the relapse in yer rehab. Yer a mud flap girl, and it's a Peterbilt world. Keep the bugs off yer glass and the bears off yer ass. 10–4."[43]

It was often difficult to name members and instrumentation of Zero Skills, Inc., accurately as they seemed to rotate according to who showed up for performances and who was able to play. Key members, however, were part of Austin's 1980s cowpunk scene, which included like-minded bands such as the Hickoids. According to their Web pages, the band currently consists of MariaM on drums and rubber chicken; KevinS on electric queso guit; MikeA on Plan 9 banjo, space fiddle, and welding; BrianP on underwater guit; and SkotS on purpleglow artifact doublebass. Members often appeared unkempt and unshaven in old, torn clothing, a mixture of western-wear shirts, cowboy hats, and spiked jewelry and chains typical of punk fashion. I have seen the acoustic bass in poor condition with holes in the body patched with what appeared to be duct tape and cardboard from Lone Star beer twelve-packs.

Their recordings, *Tractor Down* and *Drunker'n Hell* from 1996; 2001's holiday album *Christmassacre;* and *Cornstalked Her, Tracktor Down, Andy Kilter* from 2005, were initially self-released homemade tapes and CD-rs (although *Christmassacre* was pressed as an LP) and were available only occasionally at local record stores and performances. More recently, recordings have been made available by a Portland, Oregon, record label, Southeast Outlaw, and *Cornstalked Her* was released on Pecan Crazy Records based in San Marcos, Texas.

Like the Bad Livers' more experimental moments, and more like early avant-garde postpunk music than hardcore, Zero Skills, Inc. often includes extraneous noise in its music, including field recordings and sounds from unrecognizable instruments. Instruments are also played through effects pedals to alter their sound, for example, running a banjo through a distortion pedal or a phase effect to produce feedback and psychedelic sonic alterations. Its repertoire on *Drunker n' Hell* includes twisted hillbilly originals reflecting on daily life, avant-noise-acoustic pieces, and covers of songs such as the Butthole Surfers' "Texas Ranger Man," a song about wanting to be intimate with a law enforcement officer's daughter. Yet the band also performs country classics such as "Convoy," though not without the addition of citizens band (CB) radio static and noise in the background, as well as curse words.

"Big Trash Day" includes the sound of microwave popcorn popping over the introduction's lovely acoustic guitar melody. Lyrically, the song is reminiscent of "Shit Creek," describing home life under poor economic conditions. In the second verse, the narrator intones, "When the food stamps come, gonna buy some food, go out back and have a barbecue." Like the field recordings mixed into the song, the lyrics invite the listener into Zero Skills, Inc.'s world, to sit under "the shade of a hackberry, homemade shack" and, importantly, listen to the banjo and fiddle music that they play at home. The song continues to reflect on the occasional antagonism between punks and their neighborhood environments. Passersby deride the residents as slackers, freaks, and hippies. Rather than shout back, they respond with exhibitionism and vandalism. A neighbor sees them "fornicating" and flees. The landlord threatens eviction and they respond with a "Microwave oven through the front window" and "a hole in the wall," gleeful that the landlord will have to deal with the repairs and bear the financial responsibility.

Throughout the song, a languid fiddle weaves in and out of the banjo, guitar, and gutbucket bass, sawing harder and deeper as the song progresses. In the final verse, the fiddle's double-stops accent the singer's drawling howl, ending the loping tune with an assertive and confrontational tonality. Employing a similar technique to greater effect on "Ruby Ridge," Zero Skills, Inc. concludes a mournful ballad about the controversial events involving the family of Randy Weaver and federal agents in Idaho in 1992 with the sound of someone beating sheet metal to drown out the acoustic melody. Like music from the postpunk underground, Zero Skills, Inc.'s songs often deconstruct style, melody, and genre, disappearing into noise, clatter, reverb, and distortion.

Zero Skills, Inc., during the late 1990s and early 2000s, performed mostly at parties, occasionally gigged at a punk rock pizza restaurant in Austin known as The Parlor, and more rarely played local rock venues or special events. As the name indicates, their band members take a humorous approach to their limited musical abilities, which seem to matter little to them anyway. They obviously do not perform with the desire of commercial success but, rather, reflecting a punk rock attitude for the pleasure of making music their own way for anyone who cares to listen.

The music industry persists in maintaining the myth of a punk-country relationship across the entire alt.country spectrum in order to fabricate an aura of authenticity while the popular press continues to overgeneralize the unique characteristics of these musical styles and specific musicians. I have offered select musical examples primarily from one geographical region that do offer a factual base for this myth, but these musicians, performing with hillbilly instrumentation in aggressive styles with roots in rock, are largely underground, flying beneath the radar of even the alt.country movement. I propose that only by approaching alt.country through a scene-based analysis can we come to understand the movement as a whole.

NOTES

1. S. Renee Dechert, "'Oh, What a Life a Mess Can Be': Uncle Tupelo, Bakhtin, and the Dialogue of Alternative Country Music," in *Country Music Annual, 2001*, ed. Charles K. Wolfe and James E. Akenson, 70–91 (Lexington: University of Kentucky Press, 2001). Also see Mikhail M. Bakhtin, "Discourse in the Novel," in *The Dialogic Imagination*, 301–55 (Austin: University of Texas Press, 1981). Genre has long been a defining concept of folklore studies. Bakhtin's theory of genres as constantly in dialogue with one another, past and future, as employed by Dechert, has also been influential in folklore theory as folklorists have increasingly come to embrace the idea

of generic categories as porous and evolving. See Trudier Harris, "Genre," *Journal of American Folklore* 108, no. 430 (autumn 1995): 509–27.

2. David Goodman's description has since been repeated in the commercial press as well as in essays on "alternative country." See the entry for Uncle Tupelo in his *Modern Twang: An Alternative Country Music Guide and Directory* (Nashville: Dowling, 1999), 309; and Richard A. Peterson and Bruce Beal, "Discographic Essay: Alternative Country—Origins, Music, Worldview, Fans, and Taste in Genre Formation," *Popular Music and Society* 25, nos. 1–2 (2001): 233–49, http://people.vanderbilt.edu/~steve.s.lee/country.htm (accessed July 5, 2007).

3. For discussions of this process, see Michael Azerrad, *Our Band Could Be Your Life: Scenes from the American Indie Underground, 1981–1991* (Boston: Little Brown, 2001); and Holly Kruse, *Site and Sound: Understanding Independent Music Scenes* (New York: Peter Lang, 2003).

4. This idea was approached in John Molinaro's thesis, "Urbane Cowboys: Alt Country in the '90s," master's thesis, Department of English, University of Virginia, 1998, http://www.lib.virginia.edu/etd/theses/ArtsSci/English/1998/Molinaro/front.html (accessed July 5, 2007). Molinaro acknowledges the importance of bands such as the Replacements and Husker Du on Uncle Tupelo's sound and references Freakwater's roots in the Chicago rock scene.

5. For a discussion of the construction of authenticity, see oft-cited Richard A. Peterson, *Creating Country Music: Fabricating Authenticity* (Chicago: University of Chicago Press, 1997), 205–33. For a history and critique of authenticity in relation to folklore, see Regina Bendix, *In Search of Authenticity: The Formation of Folklore Studies* (Madison: University of Wisconsin Press, 1997).

6. For case studies of these distinctions in both the country and punk scenes in Austin, see Barry Shank, *Dissonant Identities: The Rock 'n' Roll Scene in Austin, Texas* (Hanover, NH: Wesleyan University Press, 1994). Shank and his consultants use the term *sincerity* rather than *authenticity* as the basis for value, but the idea resonates with Peterson, Bendix, and this essay.

7. Molinaro developed the metaphor of a "bridge" in "Urbane Cowboys." He suggests that alt.country is the bridge between punk and the country music of the 1920s and 1930s, drawing connections between the socioeconomic climate of the 1980s and the Great Depression.

8. Writing about the Bad Livers, Grant Alden states, "It's natural for aging punks, who respond to the shared aesthetic demand for absolute honesty even if the standards of virtuosity are different." Grant Alden, "Deconstruction Blues," *No Depression* 8 (March–April 1997): 7, http://www.nodepression.net/issues/nd08/badlivers.html (accessed July 5, 2007). The Meat Purveyors' Joe Walston notes, "I think what gets people with a punk pedigree more interested in country music is going way back and listening to the really, really old stuff, because that was when it was really, really good." Christopher Gray, "Driving and Cranking," *Austin Chronicle*, August 2, 1999,

6, http://weeklywire.com/ww/08–02–99/austin_music_feature1.html (accessed July 5, 2007).

9. Kelly Willis says, "I did want that punk kind of attitude. But because of that, the industry would look at us as not really serious." Chris Wodskou, "The End of No Depression," *Exclaim!* June 1, 1999, 4, http://www.exclaim.ca/articles/multiarticlesub.aspx?csid1=1&csid2=779&‹d1=747 (accessed July 5, 2007).

10. Ibid.

11. See Peterson, *Creating Country Music;* and S. Renee Dechert and George H. Lewis, "The Drive-By Truckers and the Redneck Underground: A Subcultural Analysis," in *Country Music Annual, 2002,* ed. Charles Wolfe and James E. Akenson, 130–50 (Lexington: University of Kentucky Press, 2002).

12. According to Peterson and Beal, in a survey of alt.country fans the third highest rated release of 1998 was *Mermaid Avenue* (Elektra), a CD of Woody Guthrie covers by Billy Bragg, a British singer-songwriter with punk leanings, along with Wilco. It was successful enough to spawn a second disc in 2000, *Mermaid Avenue, Vol. 2.* See Peterson and Beal, "Discographic Essay," 3.

13. Molinaro, citing Richard Peterson, notes, "Nearly all country artists have cited Hank Williams" ("Urbane Cowboys," 1). See Phil Irwin, writing as Thee Whiskey Rebel, whose essay comments on the substance abuse of many classic country musicians: "Hank did for country what Elvis did for rock and roll . . . or what Jimi Hendrix did for guitar. A country singer's singer. If you don't like Hank Williams, go f*** your mother you turdball." Thee Whiskey Rebel, "Country Western Music: 'The Next Level' beyond Punk Rock," *Traitor Baitor,* n.d., 8, http://home.conectiv.net/~whiskyreb/country.html (accessed March 10, 2003).

14. Shank, Kruse, and Azerrad provide excellent ethnographies of underground rock musicians, including how they learned their instruments and approach performing music. Molinaro uses Peterson's "hard core vs. soft shell" country criteria to describe the untrained and raw nature of much alt.country music.

15. Dechert, "Oh, What a Life a Mess Can Be," 78; Molinaro, "Urbane Cowboys," 2.

16. Molinaro traces the lo-fi aesthetic to the indie rock of the 1990s. The Meat Purveyors' Peter Stiles and Jo Walston have declared Bill Monroe's vocals to be "Totally raw and crazy. Totally Punk Rock" (Gray, "Driving and Cranking," 6).

17. This work includes a theory of music scenes. See Will Straw, "Communities and Scenes in Popular Music," in *The Subcultures Reader,* ed. K. Gelder and S. Thornton, 504 (London: Routledge, 2004).

18. Will Straw, "Cultural Scenes," *Loisir et société/Society and Leisure* 27, no. 2 (1997): 412.

19. For extensive biographical information about the Bad Livers, see Mark Rubin's "Biography" of the band online at http://badlivers.com/bio.html (accessed July 5, 2007). Goodman's *Modern Twang* entry is also an excellent summary. For an in-

sightful interview with Barnes, see Raoul Hernandez, "Complete Freedom," *Austin Chronicle,* November 5, 1999, http://www.austinchronicle.com/gyrobase/Issue/story?oid=oid:74552 (accessed July 5, 2007). For an interview with Mark Rubin, see Andy Langer, "Mark Rubin: Against the Grain," *Austin Chronicle,* November 5, 1999, http://www.austinchronicle.com/gyrobase/Issue/story?oid=oid:74553 (accessed July 5, 2007).

20. Alden, "Deconstruction Blues," 3.

21. Wodskou, "The End of No Depression," 3.

22. Molinaro, "Roots," 3.

23. Hernandez, "Complete Freedom," 3.

24. Ibid.

25. Tim Stegall, "Phantom Power and Spiritual Benefits," *Austin Chronicle,* Feb. 13, 1997, 2, http://www.auschron.com/issues/vol16/issue24/music.badlivers.html (accessed July 5, 2007).

26. Ibid.

27. Hernandez, "Complete Freedom," 10.

28. Ibid. According to Barnes, "We sold thousands of those things. Thousands of them. We made more money off that cassette than anything we've ever done."

29. Ibid., 15. For examples, see the Bad Livers' final album, *Blood and Mood* (Sugar Hill, 2000), and Danny Barnes' solo release, *Danny Barnes and His Oft Mended Raiment* (self-released, 2006).

30. Michael Corcoran, "Meat Purveyors Serve Up Slices of Bluegrass Heaven," *Austin 360,* July 29, 2004, http://www.austin360.com/search/content/music/xl/04-july/music_07–29–04.html (accessed July 5, 2007).

31. Bloodshot Records, "The Meat Purveyors," http://www.bloodshotrecords.com/artists/themeatpurveyors/ (accessed July 5, 2007).

32. Corcoran, "Meat Purveyors Serve Up Slices of Bluegrass Heaven."

33. Alden, "Deconstruction Blues," 4.

34. Mandolin player Stiles states, "I think it's absurd not to call it bluegrass. I mean, we always add a disclaimer so that the traditional people don't get totally freaked out when they see it, but it's still bluegrass to me." Gray, "Driving and Cranking," 2.

35. Alden, "Deconstruction Blues," 4.

36. Gray, "Driving and Cranking," 7.

37. Ibid.

38. Ibid.

39. Apparently Mardis always wanted to play guitar and idolized classic rock and metal guitar heroes. For a history of Split Lip Rayfield, see Jeff Beaudoin, "Without Compromise: Split Lip Rayfield Ain't over Yet," *Wichita City Paper,* December 7, 2006, http://www.wichitacitypaper.com/articles/article.23.shtml (accessed July 5, 2007).

40. Guitarist and founder of Split Lip Rayfield, Kirk Rundstrom, died of compli-

cations from cancer on February 22, 2007. See Rachel LeClear, "Can't Stand Losing Him: Kirk Rundstrom Loses his Battle with Cancer at 38," Lawrence.com, February 27, 2007, http://www.lawrence.com/news/2007/feb/22/kirkrundstrom/ (accessed July 5, 2007).

41. Later in their careers they began to play events more associated with traditional and acoustic music, including the Telluride Bluegrass Festival. Whether this was the result of a loosening of conservative festival organizers and attendees or a softening of Split Lip Rayfield's style was debated. See Beaudoin, "Without Compromise."

42. Ibid.

43. Zero Skills, Inc., *The Austin Chronicle Musicians Register* (2002), http://www.austinchronicle.com/gyrobase/MusiciansRegister/BandProfile?oid=oid:484884 (accessed July 5, 2007).

STEVIE SIMKIN

"The Burden Is Passed On": Son Volt, Tradition, and Authenticity

"Searching for a truer sound"
—"WINDFALL"

Authenticity is a term with a vexed history in the analysis of all kinds of popular music from folk and country to rock, rap, and hip-hop. Although its definitions and applications are legion, there are a number of distinct connotations that have commonly circulated in discussions of the alt.country genre, where the term is often invoked in attempts to define the "essence" of the form. This study considers alt.country authenticity and tradition via a close study of a particular artist. Jay Farrar is, *pace* his own objections to the title, routinely acknowledged as a founding father of the alt.country movement, particularly on account of his work in Uncle Tupelo (1988–94) and the first incarnation of Son Volt, the band that emerged following his split from Jeff Tweedy (who went on to form Wilco). In both band incarnations,[1] as well as his solo efforts,[2] Farrar's work has remained central to the definition and ongoing redefinitions of the genre.

In terms of geography, as well as musical roots and lyrical preoccupations, the alt.country genre and its "authenticity" are often defined by the genre's shifting position on the urban-rural axis. Indeed, the movement's aesthetic has been shaped and defined in large part by a collision of the rural (country and folk music traditions) and the urban (punk and alternative rock). According to Raymond Williams' analysis of the tension between the country and the city, capitalism is always at the heart of the matter,[3] and study of Farrar's lyrics, from *No Depression* (1990) to *The Search* (2007), reveals an abiding preoccupation with the plight of the victims of a cruelly single-minded economic system. Gerald Creed and Barbara Ching have suggested that "the rural/urban distinction underlines many of the power relations that shape the experiences of people in nearly every culture,"[4] and the tension between country and city has certainly been a recurring theme in popular music ever since Johnny B. Goode left Louisiana for the great Golden West. A native of Belleville, Illinois, not far from the Missouri border, Farrar is highly conscious of his family's roots in rural Missouri, a geographical happenstance that is highly significant: while Austin, Texas, is a representative focal point for some strands of alt.country, rust belt localities such as Belleville (Uncle Tupelo) have been equally important, as have such urban centers as Minneapolis (the Jayhawks) and Raleigh, North Carolina (Whiskeytown).

Farrar's music, attitude toward the record industry, and lyrical preoccupations all resonate with Williams' discussion of the way in which certain generalizations have clustered around the country—"peace, innocence, and simple virtue"—and the city—"learning, communication, light." However, in Farrar's negotiations of the complex tensions between the two, Williams' list of "hostile associations" has become increasingly pertinent, particularly the "noise, worldliness and ambition" associated with the urban.[5] As I will show, Farrar's lyrics often set the urban (destructive, artificial, transient) against the rural (creative, authentic, permanent), although the divisions are rarely clear-cut. In his ballad "Methamphetamine"—written, I would suggest, with Gram Parsons' "Hickory Wind" at the back of his mind—the singer muses on the days when he "Had a good job in a back-up band, / Playing guitar in Branson. / Two shows a night brought the money to chase down sin."[6] Branson, Missouri's very own little Las Vegas corresponds to Parsons' sorry state of "riches and pleasures" ("Hickory Wind") or even to "Sin City" itself, and, like the wind that calls that singer home from a "far away city," so Farrar's lonely, recovering addict pleads, "Would you take me back, North Carolina, / Would you take me back, Arkansas: / Blissful days still there to remember. / Methamphetamine was the final straw." The song has its musical roots deep in country tradition, and its lyrics, both in form (first-person narrative-reflective) and content (the perils of sin city, the redemptive salve of the call to the rural home), lay claim to a well-defined sense of authenticity. At the same time, "Methamphetamine" is a good example of the way in which the binary between the urban and the rural that Williams critiques as historically oversimplified is often rendered both more complex and more telling in Farrar's work.

If authenticity is less an objectively measurable property than it is a token of cultural capital, as I will suggest, then any attempt to trace its transactions must also take account of Farrar's own preoccupation with it in various forms: in the commitment of the rock artist to an authentic vision versus the pop singer's sellout commercialism, in "organic" instrumentation and recording methods and techniques, in his awareness of his own position in relation to musical tradition, and in the aforementioned focus on the relation between the artificial urban and the "real" rural. From a wider consideration of alt.country's authenticity, this study will develop a close analysis of Farrar's own relationship, conscious and unconscious, to the twisted roots of a putatively authentic American musical tradition.

"Working in the halls of shame"
—"SLATE"

Keir Keightley notes how rock has historically dissociated itself from mass market pop music by its insistence on a talismanic authenticity: "Pop is understood as popular music that isn't (or doesn't have to be, or can't possibly be) 'taken seriously.' Rock, in contrast, is mainstream music that is (or ought to be, or must be) taken seriously."[7] According to this conceptualization, rock views itself as superior to the realm of pop, which is a mass medium primarily pursuing commercial ends. Of course, the economic reality is that rock music fairly swiftly lost or gave away its countercultural status and was itself co-opted by processes of mainstream absorption and commodification. If any traces remain, untainted by commercial pressures, then they have been found historically in the "alternative" or "underground" scenes that have consistently tried to hold the fine and shifting line between a commitment to authentic artistic vision, on the one hand, and the demands of the market on the other. In this context, the distinction between major and independent record labels is significant: indeed, the gulf between these two wings of the music industry has been crucial in the birth and growth of the alt.country scene, as it has with most brands of alternative or underground rock music, and Farrar himself has a particularly interesting history with regard to the vagaries of the music business.

Rock history is littered with the debris of head-on collisions between artistic vision and the demands of major label executives: most notorious, perhaps, was David Geffen's decision to sue Neil Young for submitting supposedly uncharacteristic and uncommercial material in the mid-1980s.[8] As this volume's introductory essay notes, alt.country "indie" labels such as Bloodshot, Outpost, and Yep Roc have staked out hard-fought ground, taking pride in the associated overtones of craft (as opposed to manufacture) and a homegrown ethic that maintains close links among label, artists, and fans. The received wisdom dictates that a major label (urban conglomerate) sees the record music industry's primary purpose as not to indulge the whims of its artists but to shift units. Independent labels (with "cottage industry" associations) have traditionally been cherished for the relative artistic freedom and autonomy they allow their signings. For the independents—as is so often the case with music that can be identified as part of an underground scene—the relationship between a band and its fan base is crucial: the label is close enough to the ground to realize that the band's followers' extreme dedication and commitment means there is very seldom any difference between what the audiences demand and what the artist wants to give them.

A rejection of a particular brand of commercial pop is central to the agendas of most bands that have been tagged with the alt.country label.[9] While the independent context for their work often allows the bands freedom to swim against the mainstream, the genre bears its own industrial scars, usually from major labels: Wilco took a royalty cut to release *Being There* (1996) as a double CD and was let go by Reprise when the company rejected the first version of *Yankee Hotel Foxtrot* in 2001. A number of artists in the genre have made the shift from major to independent, and if these moves are usually involuntary—more often than not the artists are dropped after disappointing sales—it is also true that they have often found greater creative freedom and satisfaction in smaller stables. Both Todd Snider and Kelly Willis left MCA after three albums: Snider moved to John Prine's Oh Boy label, and Willis released an EP via A&M before financing her next album herself (appropriately titled *What I Deserve*) and selling it to Rykodisc (1999). Oh Boy's slogan reads, "Serving fine, fresh and real music since 1981," and Ryko, though a bigger label, is admired for its commitment to its artists and for its servicing of niche markets (although it finally succumbed to the majors when it was acquired by Warner Music Group in March 2006).

Authenticity, then, is often defined by a commitment to artistic vision, set against the pressures of the marketplace, and Farrar has been preoccupied with this tension at least since Uncle Tupelo began to make waves beyond its immediate touring circuit. The reference to working in the "halls of shame" in "Slate" (from Uncle Tupelo's swan song *Anodyne* [1993]), is often perceived as an indicator of Farrar's discomfort over the band's signing to a major label, Sire. The song's rueful line "Gambled once and won / Never made a dollar" also indicates that he feared the worst. Some of Farrar's associates suggest that his decision to break up the band in December 1993 (although it limped through one final tour in spring 1994) was due in part to a growing sense of unease in the face of a commercial breakthrough: a major label record deal, wider circles of touring, and even a TV appearance on Conan O'Brien's show (performing Tweedy's "The Long Cut" on February 21, 1994).

While Tweedy can at times be circumspect (and sometimes gloriously unabashed) about such matters, Jay Farrar's own lifelong suspicion about commercialization has lingered. Indeed, the management of his solo years would suggest that his rejection of commerce is far more than a token commitment to the alternative strand in popular music. It has become something of a cliché that, in a head-to-head contest between the first post-Tupelo offerings, Jeff Tweedy's band Wilco's *AM* (1994), and Son Volt's *Trace* (1995), the latter came off as the more mature and confident torchbearer for the alt.country movement. However, since the first flash of post-Tupelo activity, Farrar's position in the marketplace has gradually downsized. Meanwhile, Tweedy has moved away from the genre and simultaneously (and not coincidentally) graduated to much greater commercial success with *Yankee Hotel Foxtrot* (2002) having notched up 590,000 sales in the United States at the time of writing.[10] In a recent interview for *Harp* magazine, Farrar suggests that he and Tweedy were working in Uncle Tupelo with different motivations: "He probably had more of an unconditional ambition, and I was more ambivalent about it."[11] In the same interview, he remarks that around the time Wilco was making headlines over wrangles with its label about the release of *Yankee Hotel Foxtrot,* the label "refused to put out my first solo album as well, during that same shakeup at Warner Brothers. . . . I just didn't make a story out of it."[12]

It may be that for Farrar Son Volt offered one way out of the trap of commercialism. If so, it is ironic that "Drown," the first single from Son Volt's debut album, quickly attracted the attention of alternative format radio stations. A video also went into rotation on VH–1, providing the band with a minor hit on both college and mainstream rock radio—the only one Son Volt's first incarnation would score in their four years of recording. Farrar admitted that the success took him by surprise. A few years (and no more hits) later, one interviewer suggested that the inclusion of a more up-front rocker such as "Straightface" on *Wide Swing Tremolo* (1998) had perhaps been included at Warner's prompting. Farrar was dismissive, insisting, "The record company had nothing to do with it."[13] Whatever the case might have been, Warner Brothers let artist and band go at some point between the semiretirement of Son Volt and the completion of Farrar's first solo effort, *Sebastopol,* which was released through the independent label Artemis Records in 2001. Asked at that time about his sojourn with Warner Brothers, Farrar classified it good-humoredly as a "learning experience" that he wouldn't care to repeat.[14] Before his next release (*Terroir Blues* in 2003), Farrar would, as he put it himself, "restructure" his relationship with record labels by setting up his own company and releasing the album via Artemis.[15]

Farrar's very practical and, in theory at least, confrontational solution to the record label dilemma was to found his originally named Act/Resist but rechristened Transmit Sound shortly thereafter.[16] In a 2003 interview, he remarked, "It is easy to get pretty cynical about new music being thrown at you because so much is kind of generated by corporate record labels and spewed out."[17] In the *Dallas Music Guide,* Farrar asserted, "Good music comes from the grassroots level, especially when times are really bad at the top,"[18] and elsewhere he is quite unequivocal about the political subtext of his label's name: "I've always had a feeling that all musicians should do it [put out records on their own] if they can. It's looking at it from a social revolt perspective."[19] The deployment of the term *grassroots* is crucial, implying the investment of power in the individual rather than the corporation, valuing independence and autonomy; it also carries connotations of the rural and homegrown. The same sentiments fed into his songs around the time Act/Resist was founded, Farrar's famed lyrical obscurity giving way at times to a more overt and confrontational style. In "6 String Belief," he declaims:

Palates will ebb and masses will flow.
Killed by consolidation,
Killed by saturation,
The underground will correct
With reaction rebellion.

The closing lines rail at "corruption in the system" and declare that "a grassroots insurrection / Will bring them down, will bring them down." Against "consolidation" and "saturation," Farrar clings to the "rock 'n' roll around my head alive and kicking . . . like a six string belief." The live rendition on *Stone, Steel and Bright Lights* (2004) is performed solo acoustic and sounds slightly unfinished.[20] In the version recorded for *Okemah and the Melody of Riot* (2005), thick layers of electric guitar replace the acoustic strum, and the muscular chords and propulsive rhythm track hammer the message home.

A mention of the controversy surrounding a planned and aborted Son Volt reunion in 2004 offers a fitting conclusion to this part of the investigation. According to Farrar, following a reunion to record "Sometimes" for the Alejandro Escovedo benefit album *Por Vida,* a decision was made to reunite the band to make a new album. What happened next is worth reciting in Farrar's own words from Jane Ganahl's *Harp* interview.

> On the first day of pre-production for the recording, major new demands that had not been talked about or agreed upon were made that could have and should have been discussed months ago. Despite that setback I still wanted to see it all work out. I called them all and told them come on, let's set up and play music, we can rise above these differences and work it out as we go. But they refused to show up and they seemed to only want to communicate through their lawyer. It was a devastating thing to go through.[21]

This is the fullest account I have read of the controversy. Other interviews with Farrar all tend to emphasize the sense of a conflict between artistry ("let's set up and play music") and commerce (the others' insistence on communicating through a lawyer). Whether Farrar's decision to retain the band name with a completely new lineup was a symptom of the same commitment to art (the determination to retain a band identity that has always been essentially "Farrar plus others" in any case) or a recognition of the importance of a recognizable brand (for commercial reasons), it is impossible to say. The truth probably lies somewhere between the two. It is certainly the case that, in the way Farrar himself narrates it, the story is scripted as a cautionary tale, another installment in the struggle to defend an authentic commitment to making music for the sake of it against the shadowy men in suits.

"The sound of a hundred dollar guitar"
—"CATCHING ON"

"There's something wrong when Garth Brooks lists one of his main inspirations as Journey," Jeff Tweedy noted ruefully in 1993,[22] and no one epitomized mainstream country in the 1990s better than Brooks, who was listed as Billboard's Top Country *and* Top Pop Album Artist in 1990, 1991, and 1993 (the years that span most of Uncle Tupelo's recording career). With a clean-cut Stetson-crowned image, boosted by commercial radio airplay and TV music channel coverage, Brooks and those who have followed in his wake are supposedly propelled by *commercial* rather than "real" *artistic* success. Their touring format—based around arenas and featuring the kind of spectacular lightshow and pyrotechnics associated with mainstream rock bands—removes them still further from roots music tradition. However, almost as important is the fact that the music itself is perceived as profoundly lacking in raw immediacy and sincerity, qualities Keir Keightley identifies as essential to romantic authenticity in his distinction between the romantic and modernist traditions in rock. The romantic, Keightley suggests, maintains a "belief in a core or essential rock sound" (as opposed to modernism's "openness"), prioritizes "liveness" over "recorded-ness," and has a tendency to hide rather than celebrate musical technology.[23] The Nashville sound of the early 1990s onward is decidedly "unromantic" in this sense, instead perceived as homogeneous, pitch tweaked, click-track perfect, and pro-tooled into sterility.

Tweedy's distaste for Garth Brooks' citation of Journey probably has as much to do with the smooth, sterile surfaces of Journey's (and Brooks') music as it does with the fact that Garth's confession of Adult Oriented Rock inspiration represents a betrayal of country music as a genre. Alt.country has, almost without exception, embraced a commitment to traditional instrumentation and "live" recording techniques, epitomized by an early milestone of the genre, the Cowboy Junkies' *Trinity Session* album (1987), which was recorded in one night with one microphone. For many alt.country artists and bands, digital trickery and even, in many cases, overdubs are considered indicators of the *inauthentic.* Uncle Tupelo, for much of its career, consisted of three musicians—guitar, bass, drums. In the studio, this necessitated overdubbing layers of guitar and vocal harmony. Later the band members recruited additional musicians for recording and touring, allowing them to add fiddle, pedal steel, banjo, and other embellishments and making full live recording possible on *March 16–20, 1992,* and *Anodyne.*[24] *March*'s title is a neat statement about authenticity in itself, bearing something of a "field recording" aura about it. In the past Farrar has declared a commitment to the use of analog tape in the recording process,[25] and both *Trace* and *Straightaways* (1997) were largely recorded live in the studio. Farrar notes the use of overdubbing only for "some of the solos and background vocals" on *Trace.*[26]

Related to a preoccupation with traditional recording techniques is a focus on vintage equipment. Farrar notes that one of the reasons Son Volt chose to record *Trace* where it did was "because the owner had a lot of vintage amplifiers," one of which, a Webster Chicago from the 1940s, was featured in the cover art of the album (fig. 6).[27] *Anodyne* features a rough black-and-white shot of rows of acoustic and electric guitars leaning against a small stage with miked drums partially captured in the foreground and electrical cables snaking away into a blur of light in the background (fig. 7). A more overt musical celebration of this kind of instrumentation crops up on *Okemah and the Melody of Riot,* a tribute to the power of rock and roll and a Luddite celebration of analog technology; "Gramophone," with its loping, Crazy Horse riff, sounds like a defiant affirmation of faith on Farrar's part. "Three generations can't be wrong, / Roll around, roll around with their favorite songs," it begins, continuing with an unashamedly traditionalist recommitment to the "Vinyl disc with power to hypnotize, / Visions of blues and jump and jive." The nostalgic tone recalls Aaron A. Fox's fascinating account of conversations in a Texas bar, where fond recollections of outmoded technology—early live radio, phonograph machines, and the regular family gatherings around them—dilate into a wider celebration of sociability and community set against commodity and urban social alienation.[28] It is the same kind of nostalgia that hovers around "Windfall," where picking up a country radio station's "truer sound" of the pedal steel "sounds like 1963 / But for now sounds like heaven."

This brand of authenticity—live recording techniques and a limited range of instrumentation that endorses electricity but draws the line at electronics—can be understood as an attempt to connect to a mythologized lineage that extends via Elvis and Sam Phillips at Sun Studios all the way back to the hyperromantic image of blues artists being recorded directly to lacquer master discs. However, it could also be argued that an unwavering com-

Fig. 6. Cover of Son Volt's *Trace* (Warner Brothers, 1995).

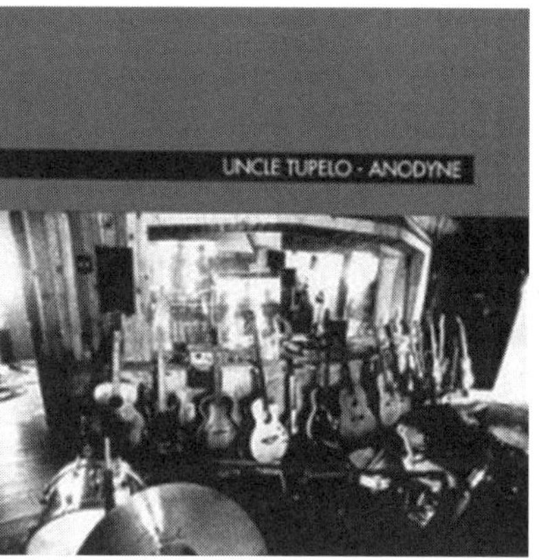

Fig. 7. Cover of Uncle Tupelo's *Anodyne* (Sire/Warner, 1993).

mitment to such a narrow construction of authenticity can be limiting. The critical reception afforded the first three Son Volt releases illustrates the point: *Straightaways* was widely (though not universally) perceived as a disappointing follow-up to *Trace,* the most frequent criticisms being that it broke no new ground or that its songs sounded like they could have been outtakes from the *Trace* sessions. Farrar was unapologetic and was the first to admit that *Straightaways* was indeed more or less an extension of their first album. Press kits and interviews emphasized its aim to capture the sound the band had developed through heavy touring: *Trace* had, after all, been cut before Son Volt's dynamic had been road tested; Mike Heidorn jokingly referred to it as "our first date."[29]

On the other hand, critics generally recognized that the final release by the first Son Volt incarnation, *Wide Swing Tremolo,* featured a broader musical palette with more varied pace, style, and rhythm; the same message was emphasized in the marketing of the album. Experiments included the use of a mountain dulcimer played with a steel slide bar on "Dead Man's Clothes," miked up and with some contact pickup added: organ and chamberlain ("Carry You Down"), treated vocals ("Straightface," "Dead Man's Clothes"), and even a drum loop (on analog tape) for the album's closing track "Blind Hope." Along with the twelve full songs, the album also featured two instrumental fragments that helped to create a sense of shift from the traditional honed and shaped songs that make up *Trace* and *Straightaways*.[30] Furthermore, the live-in-the-studio feel of the first two albums was replaced with a more layered style of production. However, while *Tremolo* may have represented a perceptible shift in terms of production and instrumentation, closer inspection reveals again a nagging sense of reiteration: "Strands" recalls *Straightaways*' "Left a Slide," for instance, and "Hanging Blue Side" is reminiscent of "Windfall" in terms of its melody, rhythm, and instrumentation. "Right on Through" is very much in the tradition of *Trace*'s "Live Free." In this regard, *Wide Swing Tremolo* can be understood as a logical conclusion to the first stage of Son Volt's career arc, its tradition-innovation crisis perhaps indicative of some of the intractable problems of a genre so deeply entrenched in a romantic sense of authenticity.

Since 2000, Farrar has moved between solo and band work, indulging in other side projects, including a soundtrack (*The Slaughter Rule*, 2003) and a collaboration with Anders Parker, *Death Songs for the Living*, under the band name Gob Iron (2006). Although there were certainly some personal family reasons for the hiatus in Son Volt's activity when it finished the tour supporting *Tremolo*, there also seem to have been creative reasons why Farrar decided to step out of the Son Volt frame: the solo status allowed him to establish a new direction for his writing. His solo releases *Sebastopol* and *Terroir Blues* can even be interpreted as steps along a path leading away from romantic preoccupations toward what Keightley defines as the modernist: "celebrating technology," an emphasis on "recorded-ness" rather than "liveness," and "experimentation and progress" rather than "tradition and continuity with the past."[31] Farrar talked in interviews of the songs on *Sebastopol* being "built one part at a time"—the antithesis of the live-in-the-studio approach[32]—and half-jokingly referred to it two years later as "the synth period."[33] While *Terroir Blues* continued some of that experimentation, it was at the same time much more firmly grounded than *Sebastopol* in the acoustic guitar, slide guitar, and pedal steel; Farrar described *Terroir*'s style as "going back to familiar instrumentation but trying out some different forms as well."[34] The title of the album, too—*terroir*—translates from the French as "soil," another commitment to "authentic" roots.

In the wake of the troubled resurrection of Son Volt, discussed earlier, Farrar eased back into the live-in-the-studio approach that had marked all his band-oriented projects up to that point, using very few overdubs.[35] He made it clear in interviews around this time that the album was made up of songs he had accumulated, "more up-tempo melodic songs that lend themselves more to being electrified."[36] Musically, *Okemah and the Melody of Riot* was generally more straightforward than Farrar's solo work; although "Medication" and the two-takes closer, "The World Waits for You," were reminiscent of his recent experiments with odd tunings and tape loops, for the most part *Okemah* is made up of harder-edged material, harking back to the rockers on *Trace* and *Tremolo* in particular. It seems that the ghost of electricity had finally caught up with Farrar, and the plugged-in style and attitude eschewed the quieter side of the country-rock divide the band's first incarnation had straddled. The revamped Son Volt's second release, *The Search,* followed in March 2007 and was billed as a more varied collection of songs. Stylistically, it ranged from material more country oriented than anything on *Okemah* ("Methamphetamine," "Highways and Cigarettes") to guitar drones evoking Led Zeppelin ("Automatic Society") and some atonal riffs reminiscent of alternative rock ("Satellite"). Even the four-square rocker "The Picture" was given a makeover and embellished with a soulful horn section. On a few other songs, such as "Underground Dream" and "Adrenaline and Heresy"—and notably on the additional tracks released on iTunes and later on a limited vinyl edition, *On Chant and Strum*—Derry Deborja's keyboards and some treated vocals recalled the more varied textures of *Sebastopol.*

> "It's just me and Jay, playing our guitars along with it all"
> —"D. BOON"

The antipathy felt by alt.country proponents toward contemporary country pop, and their own commitment to authenticity in their recording methods, is part of a much wider divergence between the mainstream and the alternative or insurgent. Actual, perceived, and rhetorical oppositions between the two are historical and cyclical: the birth of the "Nashville sound" in the late 1950s and early 1960s, for example, was seen by many "hard country" artists and fans as an unacceptable sellout to the mainstream.[37] Specific historical detail is pertinent, also, in a consideration of the genesis of alt.country. Uncle Tupelo emerged around the time that alternative rock was itself being absorbed by the industry and spat out again as a marketing term. The alternative scene—or what was known at the time as college rock—was in a direct line of descent from punk. It is worth remembering that a large sector of alt.country territory—in terms of both performers and audiences—resides not in the country but in the city, and punk itself is very much an urban cultural phenomenon. Rooted on one side of the Atlantic in New York City (New York Dolls, the Ramones) and Detroit (MC5, the Stooges) and on the other in London (Sex Pistols, the Clash, the Damned), the next incarnation of this (anti)aesthetic was Generation X. Marooned in Reagan's America, hardcore bands such as Black Flag, Bad Brains, and the Dead Kennedys raged against a society in which the gap between the affluent and the underclass had widened into an unbridgeable chasm.

There are certainly parallels to be drawn between the alternative rock emerging at this time and the country-punk blend (or oscillation) in the nascent Uncle Tupelo sound:[38] bands such as Husker Dü, the Pixies, and Throwing Muses were building their songs around slow/fast structures and quiet/loud dynamics. The rhythmic switches heard on *No Depression* soon became a hallmark of the Tupelo sound and were featured on most of the songs that made the cut for *Still Feel Gone:* Tweedy's "Nothing," "Watch Me Fall," and "D. Boon"; Farrar's "Punch Drunk," "Postcard," and "Discarded."[39] The album was launched in 1991, a couple of weeks before Nirvana's hit *Nevermind* and three weeks after Pearl Jam unleashed its own commercial monster, *Ten.* Tweedy readily acknowledged the debts owed by the first two albums to the alternative scene of the late 1980s: "I think you can really hear a young band trying to decide whether or not it wants to be Dinosaur Jr., or Husker Dü, or whatever band you want to think of from the time."[40] It seems that the choice of Paul Kolderie and Sean Slade for production duties on *No Depression* had a lot to do with the band's admiration of their work on Dinosaur Jr.'s *Bug.*[41] Tweedy's "D. Boon," recorded for *Still Feel Gone,* was a tribute to the Minutemen's front man, and the influence of any number of alternative and punk bands can be traced in the harder edges of Uncle Tupelo's first two albums, although they differ from most by virtue of the fact that neither album ever loses its melodic core. The members of Uncle Tupelo could never have been mistaken for Nirvana wannabes, even when they were regularly splicing "Smells Like Teen Spirit" with the Monkees' "Steppin' Stone" onstage in the first half of 1992. In this context, the collision of two forms commonly perceived as antithetical—punk and country music—might be seen instead as a genuine new alternative at a time when, all of a sudden, one could hardly turn around without sighting another collective of dirty clothes, dirtier-sounding guitars, and soul-baring, howled vocals. Even if the deliberate hybridization of the genres is something that both Jeff Tweedy and Jay Farrar would deny ("It wasn't like we were ever intentionally trying to merge punk and country or anything. . . . That's just what came out"),[42] there is no doubt that what emerged was something with few precedents and no guarantee of real marketability.

Perhaps nothing is more revealing of a band's influences than a consideration of the peers and predecessors that it chooses to honor or desecrate in its choice of cover versions. Farrar's earliest bands, the Plebes and the Primitives/Primatives (the band's name appeared in both forms at different times), mostly featured Farrar's brother Wade on lead vocals, and they were essentially a garage rock band, covering all kinds of tunes, both familiar and recherché, from the 1960s.[43] A typical set list from the summer of 1986 included the Standells' "Dirty Water" and Them's "Gloria" alongside older chestnuts such as Bo Diddley's "Diddy Wah Diddy" (covered by the surf group the Astronauts as well as Captain Beefheart and others), and Skip James' "I'm So Glad." The latter was probably sourced from one of the *Nuggets* collections of 1960s cult classics first issued in 1972 and re-released in the mid-1980s on CD, which included a version by the group Five Americans.

The changes in Uncle Tupelo's cover repertoire charts a journey from the garage rock of the 1960s, via punk, toward country, and on to a distinctive sound of its own. Contemporary underground music was central to early Tupelo set lists: the punk band X's "Surprise Surprise" and the Soft Boys' "I Wanna Destroy You" were familiar inclusions around 1990–91, as well as the Clash's rockabilly "Brand New Cadillac" (originally written and performed by 1950s rocker Vince Taylor), a high-energy take on Gang of Four's "I Found That Essence Rare" that lacked the original's funkiness, and the Minutemen's "I Felt Like a Gringo." In June 1991, the writer Chris King noted an apparently spontaneous and quite possibly unrehearsed bash at "Anarchy in the UK."[44] The Softboy's "Destroy You" was featured in electric mode, more venomous than Robyn Hitchcock's version, as the B-side of the single release of "Gun" in 1991, while the following year, on a tour promoting the *March* album, it resurfaced as a slow, acoustic, Jeff and Jay harmony ballad.

A consideration of Son Volt's cover repertoire, by contrast, leans heavily toward country and country rock (discussed in detail later) but also sees the return of the garage rock influence, suggesting that it may have previously been more reflective of Farrar's predilections than Tweedy's. Highlights include a towering, thrashing rendition of Cheap Trick's "Downed" (1996) and a set of *Nuggets* selections: the Creation's "Making Time" (1999), the Del-Vetts' "Last Time Around" (1998), and the Flamin' Groovies' "Shake Some Action" (1996). The Kinks' "This Is Where I Belong" (1997) rubbed shoulders with more mainstream 1970s rock such as "Born to Be Wild" (Steppenwolf, 1997), "Tumbling Dice" (Rolling Stones, 1999), and "Heard It on the X" (ZZ Top, 1999).[45] Garage rock would also leave its mark on a number of Farrar's originals composed for the band such as "Drown," "Catching On" (both from *Trace*), and the blistered-lip, fuzz-harp rocker "Straightface" (*Wide Swing Tremolo*).

If, as some popular music histories claim, alt.country is the music of a generation of musicians (roughly speaking, 1960s born) that grew up on punk and alternative rock while at the same time being drawn to country, folk, and bluegrass music, often via the enthusiasm of the previous generation, then the collision of the two styles begins to seem less curious if no less insurgent. The extent to which Farrar, Tweedy, and Heidorn were aware of the significance of their emerging style is moot. What is not in doubt is that, even while that style drew freely on urban *and* rural musical traditions, it was no less "rooted." As early as 1988, Tweedy was making it clear that "To us [Uncle Tupelo] . . . hard-core punk is also folk music. We draw a close parallel between the two. We'll play both in the same set if we get a chance."[46] In this regard, although the punk element might have had a modernist and distinctly urban slant ("the shock of the new"), it seems to have been more important to these musicians for its romantic elements: roots, populism, sincerity, and directness, characteristics that reveal its kinship with the folk traditions that are otherwise at odds with the music of alienated city life. At the same time, for Farrar, the acoustic *March* album was an important statement, a marker that "we weren't part of the pack of bands that was coalescing into this grunge-rock phenomenon."[47] For all its hybridity, Uncle Tupelo's music was tapping deeply into structures of feeling (to adopt Raymond Williams' term) that were authentic to both the experience (contemporary urban alienation) and heritage (rural folk and country) of its two songwriters. This is one instance when the cultural token of authenticity seems to be far less clear-cut in its lineage. The simple binary of the "authentic" rural and the "artificial" urban is revealed as more complex and multivalent.

> "Sounds like 1963, but for now, sounds like heaven"
>
> —"WINDFALL"

In a 1999 interview, Farrar explicitly acknowledged this dual lineage in a fascinating remark about musical tradition and hybridity: "I don't think the

Rolling Stones ever envisioned punk rock, but they made it possible. . . . Merle Haggard never envisioned Uncle Tupelo, but he made that possible, too."[48] What Farrar is suggesting here is something akin to the notion of "affordances," a concept that has its roots in psychology but has subsequently been applied in a variety of different contexts, which refers to the fact that physical objects in an environment offer a range of possibilities to the person using them.[49] This helpfully puts the emphasis on circumstance and potential rather than deliberation and intention and illuminates other pockets of alt.country development such as the Hollywood club circuit that saw Dwight Yoakam, X, the Knitters, and the Blasters comfortably sharing the same scene in the early 1980s. David Goodman characterizes the alt.country sound as "an alternation between or a joining of grinding punk, country rock, and acoustic country,"[50] and many of Uncle Tupelo's country covers embody this schizophrenic quality, particularly in the band's early years. Versions of two Johnny Cash favorites in particular, "Cocaine Blues" and "Orange Blossom Special," alternated country blues style pick and strum with pummeling guitar, juddering rhythm, and rudimentary soloing, as did their take on Leadbelly's "John Hardy," another regular in their set list around 1989.[51] Correspondingly, Black Flag's "Gimmie, Gimmie, Gimmie," mentioned earlier, all hammering guitar and scowling, howled lyric, was often reinvented with an almost parodic Johnny Cash "boom-chicka-boom" rhythm and a softly imploring vocal tone.

In the spring of 1990, the Louvin Brothers' "Atomic Power" (later recorded for the *March* album) made its first appearance on Uncle Tupelo's set list, and it quickly became a regular feature. By the end of 1992 and into 1993, the band was opening its shows with a set of acoustic songs that included "Satan, Your Kingdom Must Come Down" and "Moonshiner" alongside some of the material Farrar had penned in their shadows, including "Criminals" and "Grindstone." Farrar and Tweedy's growing appreciation of traditional folk and country also found a more direct outlet in the occasional, more or less spontaneous shows staged from the end of 1991 onward under the moniker Coffee Creek, which featured almost exclusively classic country material originally recorded by artists such as Merle Haggard, George Jones, Charley Pride, the Flying Burrito Brothers, Neil Young, and Buck Owens. By the time they cut *March 16–20, 1992,* and *Anodyne,* the country influence was even more overt: around this time, Farrar name checks "Ernest Tubb, Lefty Frizzell, Buck Owens . . . Hank Williams [and] Merle

Haggard."[52] Farrar's childhood home environment has repeatedly been characterized by his associates as one saturated with music. Uncle Tupelo's drummer, Mike Heidorn, has suggested that there were more "folky" instruments in Farrar's house because his parents hailed from the Ozark-Missouri area.[53] Farrar himself frequently cites the influence of his mother's tastes (Woody Guthrie, Leadbelly, the Dillards, Del Reeves), as well as his father's (Jimmie Rogers and Hank Williams).[54] In the liner notes to the *Uncle Tupelo 89/93: An Anthology* CD, he notes dryly that he "grew up in a family environment where an appreciation of folk music was advocated on a near daily basis," and in a British interview in January 2004 he admitted that the elements of country music in Uncle Tupelo represents "a period of time . . . when we were acknowledging the music of our parents and coming to terms with that."[55]

It is significant that members of Son Volt tended to avoid use of the word *country* when interviewers asked them to describe their style, opting instead for the less loaded term *traditional.* However, the most common description of the band remained the catch-all *country rock* with some of the more discerning writers acknowledging that the band's material, at least on CD, was divided fairly cleanly into either the rock or the country category. In this sense, Son Volt did represent an evolution from the hybrid style that epitomized Uncle Tupelo: the slow/fast, quiet/loud aesthetic was replaced with a listening experience sequenced to set the country sway and lilt of "Windfall" against the steady rock groove of "Live Free" and the steel and fiddle of "Tear-Stained Eye" against the guttural twin guitar roar of "Route."

The country-rock classification opens up another line of tradition that is crucial for an accurate assessment of Farrar's commitment to his roots. Around 1990, the *Nuggets*-style material took a back seat in the Tupelo set lists, giving way to raw-edged versions of Bob Dylan's "Maggie's Farm," "A Hard Rain's A-Gonna Fall," and "Knockin' on Heaven's Door," as well as renditions of Neil Young's early compositions "Mr. Soul," "Cinnamon Girl," "Down by the River," and the later "Everybody Knows This Is Nowhere." Farrar would return to Neil Young's songbook when on tour with Canyon and, later, the new Son Volt, frequently encoring with extended renditions of "Like a Hurricane" (2003), "Cortez the Killer" (2005), and a buzzing "Pocahontas" (2007). Son Volt has also covered "Let's Go Downtown" (1996) and a couple of Dylan songs in concert, notably "Going, Going, Gone" (1995) and "Obviously 5 Believers" (1997).

As Peter Doggett has noted, Dylan and Young are the two singer-songwriters in the canonized rock tradition that have made the most notable forays into country territory.[56] Neil Young's influence is discernible in some of Uncle Tupelo's original material, particularly in Farrar's grinding, churning guitar riff on "Looking for a Way Out" and the guitar solo on "Postcard" (*Still Feel Gone*). The Byrds and related artists (Gram Parsons, the Flying Burrito Brothers), who are often credited with kicking off the country rock movement, have made notable appearances in the Son Volt repertoire. Mike Heidorn recalls listening to the Byrds with Jay Farrar as far back as the mid-1980s,[57] and Farrar notes that, despite his family's roots in traditional music, his own avenue into country came initially via the Byrds and the Burritos,[58] and that *The Gilded Palace of Sin* (1969) was "a real pivotal album when I first heard it."[59] Though not a Byrds original, "Tulsa County" is most familiar from their version,[60] and a studio version was included on Son Volt's *Switchback* promo EP (1997), which was rounded up for the *Retrospective, 1995–2000,* collection in 2005. "A Song for You" had a number of live outings in 1996, and in April 1997 Roger McGuinn joined the band for a rendition of "5D" at the Irving Plaza in New York City. Uncle Tupelo contributed a version of Gram Parsons' "Blue Eyes" to the 1993 Parsons tribute *Commemorativo,* and, for Farrar, the Byrds' significance abides: when asked to contribute to a regular column in the music magazine *Uncut,* he chose the Byrds' *Fifth Dimension* as "a record that changed . . . [my] life."[61] In 2004, Farrar took part in a Parsons tribute concert, offering faithful versions of "Drug Store Truck Drivin' Man" and "Devil in Disguise," and during the band's 2007 tour "You're Still on my Mind" was played in a version very close to the Byrds' *Sweetheart of the Rodeo* rendition (Gram Parsons having picked it out of the repertoire of his beloved George Jones).

In fact, it is a defining feature of Son Volt's country covers that they are performed faithfully, not yielding an inch to anything arch or camp: the musicians' respect and reverence for the material is unmistakable and unshakable. On what may always remain their definitive anthem, "Windfall," Farrar sings of "Switching it over to AM / Searching for a truer sound." Farrar tagged this reference to a particular Louisiana station "that does a truck-driving show from midnight to 6, and plays a lot of older country songs."[62] On early tours, the band included numbers such as "She's More to Be Pitied" by the Stanley Brothers, "Apartment #9" by Johnny Paycheck (both 1996), and Merle Haggard's "Sing Me Back Home" (1995) and "Is Anybody Goin' to

San Antone?" (1996). Interestingly, Farrar connected the latter to tradition via the country pop crossover artist Charley Pride rather than the renegade country rocker Doug Sahm.[63]

Perhaps nothing provides a clearer testimony of Farrar's respect for the country and country rock traditions than his preoccupation with the pedal steel guitar. "I love the instrument a lot; it's beautiful," he noted in an interview with the *Music Monitor*,[64] reserving plaudits for Eric Heywood's contributions to *Trace*. The pedal steel is so central to the traditional country sound that it has sadly taken on the contours of cliché for those who are ignorant of the genre: its keening tone, characteristic pitch bends, and portamenti lend it a quality that might be described by some as profoundly emotional and by others as lachrymose. However, the instrument also has a track record of being used in more adventurous ways by country rock bands: Clarence White's highly amplified Stringbender guitar, with its ability to mimic the sound of pedal steel, was probably the most important defining characteristic of the Byrds' sound around 1969–70, perfectly captured on instrumentals such as "Nashville West" and "White's Lightning" (*Untitled*, 1970) and throughout the archival release *Live at the Fillmore* (recorded in 1969). Sneaky Pete Kleinow achieved a similar effect with his overamplified pedal steel in the Flying Burrito Brothers' live shows. In Son Volt's music, Heywood's steel graduated from its original position among Farrar's more country-oriented material (harmonizing with Dave Boquist's fiddle on "Windfall," shimmering below the rhythm section on "Tear-Stained Eye") to a more central position on the rockers. On *Straightaways*, Heywood not only provides the emotional core of a song such as "Left a Slide" (tellingly, Farrar has never attempted to perform the song live since Heywood stopped touring with him), but he pulls alongside Boquist's electric lead on the rock-oriented "Cemetery Savior." In concert, the centrality of the steel was even more obvious, with some intricate interplay between Boquist and Heywood. For a time on a tour in 1997, the rocking minor hit "Drown" was even reworked to allow the steel to carry the tune's signature riff.

One more aspect of Farrar's approach to his musical roots bears some scrutiny: Despite the fact that he plays down his own significance, the maps and genealogies of the alt.country movement, while they may occasionally question the notion of Uncle Tupelo as the sole progenitor, more often routinely acknowledge the seminal status of the band. Son Volt's debut tends to retain its "classic" status in those accounts, and, although the band's new releases no longer command the attention that their first releases did, Farrar's work is still routinely assessed in light of his late 1990s legacy. This complicates the genealogies: if the alt.country genre that Uncle Tupelo helped to instigate is defined in part by its commitment to "hard" country and folk, then—nearly twenty years after Farrar, Tweedy, and drummer Mike Heidorn played their first shows—we have reached a point where the two songwriters in that collective are routinely assessed in the shadows of their younger selves.

As one might expect, there has been a natural shift away from Farrar's back catalogue as the band's original repertoire has expanded, and his attitude toward demands for old songs at live appearances seems a little ambivalent, denying a sense of owing the fans anything but confessing that he tries to find "the songs that still mean something to me, that I can maintain a connection to."[65] Meantime, some concertgoers have persisted with calls for Tupelo standards such as "I Got Drunk," "Moonshiner," and "Whiskey Bottle." The latter is an interesting case in point. It was requested the night of Son Volt's official debut at 7th Street Entry, Minneapolis, on June 16, 1995, and remained unplayed, only to be performed the following night ("probably because nobody scream[ed] for it," noted Peter Blackstock).[66] Although it was performed periodically early in Son Volt's touring history, it was later dropped from the set, while songs such as "Still Be Around" and "Chickamauga" remained. It was requested repeatedly and finally explicitly, if politely, refused during the band's London debut (Dingwalls, November 5, 1997). Nearly five years later, Farrar would finally break it out for the first time as a solo artist, using it as an encore at London's Borderline club (August 16, 2002). It then resurfaced periodically, as did "Punch Drunk." In both cases, the songs were shorn of the originals' angry riffs and redrawn with melancholic, regretful, acoustic lines.

Such performance choices are thought provoking. Farrar's revisitations of his twenty-something hard-drinking songs as a thirty-something family man no doubt have something to do with this. The revamped acoustic "Punch Drunk" and "Whiskey Bottle" may also be seen as part of the turn toward a more meditative approach evident when the direct, confrontational industrial angst of "Sauget Wind" is juxtaposed with the creeping menace of "Ten Second News" with its beach "known for cancer" and the doom-laden line "There's a cough in the water / And it's running into town." Both songs deal with the environmental impact of industrialization, but the second is at the same time less direct and more haunting. In much of his work since the dissolution of Uncle Tupelo, Farrar has oscillated between angry showdowns with the encroaching city—its urban sprawl, technology, and championing of commercial interests at every turn—and the vanishing, precious refuge of the country. It is this preoccupation that forms the final part of my investigation.

> "In this city of artificial stars"
> —"BANDAGES AND SCARS"

Descriptions of Son Volt's music repeatedly invoke terms such as *simple* and *organic* and cite qualities such as "honesty and conviction."[67] As I have argued, much of this can be attributed to roots-oriented choices in recording and instrumentation and the band's country-folk-blues musical influences. However, as I suggested in my opening consideration of the song "Methamphetamine," Farrar's lyrics, particularly post-Tupelo, focus with growing concentration on the positive cultural connotations of the rural and, even more intensely, on the negative overtones of the urban. On *Trace,* some of this is voiced in tenderness, as in the prayerful "may the wind take your troubles away" ("Windfall"), and the equally reverential observation on the enduring, inescapable cycle of nature, where "When we're all passed over, / The rhythm of the river, / It will remain" ("Live Free"). However, the dominant tone of *Trace* is much darker than these lyrics suggest. A number of songs mine more deeply a vein of social critique that Farrar had already opened up in his previous band. The early Uncle Tupelo albums were in keeping with Goodman's definition of the alt.country genre's preoccupations: "a focus on the darker side of small town life, and a heightened social/political consciousness."[68] Farrar's contributions in particular can be matched quite readily to the songs of alienation, disillusionment, and despair in the face of Reaganomics that dominated the grunge scene around the same time. The opening lines of Uncle Tupelo's debut growl about "Home town same town blues / Same old walls closing in" and point an accusing finger at the "man in a tie," who will "bum your dime before he'll break a twenty dollar bill" ("Graveyard Shift"). "Madmen in suits" populate the bleak urban blues of "Factory Belt," and the ironically titled "Life Worth Livin'" is dedicated to the "broken spirited man," the victim of a political system where "this trickledown theory / Has left all these pockets empty" ("Postcard"). Three of these songs are built on the foundations of pile-driver guitar and propulsive rhythms that, musically, bear some resemblance to contemporaneous college rock bands and, connotatively, bring to mind the merciless punch and grind of heavy machinery. Farrar's clenched and indignant vocal gives voice to all those "disengaged, severed and forsaken" by an unforgiving economic system ("Fall Down Easy"), a world blighted by "the sound of people making money, /And money getting away" ("Whiskey Bottle").

On the release of the *March* album, some critics and audiences voiced a degree of skepticism at the prospect of "two young Belleville residents giving voice to murder ballads, union-style songs and tales of old moonshiners."[69] The assumption was that the wide gap between these musicians' life experiences and the content of the songs they chose to play implied a lack of authenticity. Such criticism misses the point by a country mile. The justification is in the profound connection between the circumstances that gave rise to the songs on *March* and the post-Reagan urban blues that informed Farrar's lyrics on the first two albums: songs of factory belts, graveyard shifts, and dead-end towns where Farrar, half-accusingly and half-sympathetic, asks the man drinking next to him, "What has life, fifty years in this town, ever done for you, / Except to earn your nameplate on a barstool?" ("Looking for a Way Out"). Farrar paints a brown- and gray-toned landscape of "slash and burn cities" where, "If God still reads the headlines / Front page: 'hope is missing'" ("Punch Drunk"). Lined up opposite the victims are the men in suits, who have now become simultaneously more shadowy, metaphorical, and political: "those with words of power forever on their breath" ("True to Life"). "Still Be Around," ostensibly a love song, provides a neatly turned phrase summarizing how hegemony works.

They're paid to move it off the shelves,
And into our minds,
Till you can't tell the truth
When it's right in front of your eyes.

During "Criminals," Farrar viciously paraphrases George Bush Sr.'s talk of a "kindlier [*sic*], gentler nation" in his 1988 inaugural speech: "They want us kindlier and gentler / At their feet." The song's rhythm, with the lyrics left hanging for a moment after each triplet ("kindlier . . . and gentler . . . at their feet"), operates as a punch line, emphasizing the line's bitterness and sardonic wit.

With *Trace* continuing *Anodyne*'s drift toward a more obscure lyrical tone, the social critique becomes more meditative and metaphorical. As well as the lyrics from "Live Free" cited earlier, the caustic "Route" depicts a landscape where the "city bleeds all over itself"; the acceptance of permanent nature and transient human life sung about in "Live Free" is replaced by the bleak, repetitive despair that "We're all living proof that nothing lasts." While *Straightaways* seemed to be made up largely of more personal material, the album's closing song returned with a growing poetic sensibility to the theme of apparent progress and real, heartbreaking loss: "Way Down Watson" weaves a reflective, nostalgic lyric around finger-picked acoustic guitar and mournful harmonica, a lament for the loss of a specific landmark, the Coral Court Motel in St. Louis, torn down to make way for another strip mall. Farrar's regretful, buzzing baritone muses on the loss of the building ("Another treasure found / Another tumbling down"), a comment, as Mike Heidorn notes, on "what's been lost, our lost ways, and what used to be."[70] However, arrestingly, the grief at the destruction of something aged and beautiful is matched by an empathic engagement with the wrecking ball operator himself: "Twenty years pulling the lever / These windows shield the cold / From the weather of my soul."

On *Okemah and the Melody of Riot*, Farrar largely abandoned his tendency to obfuscate lyrics and sharpened the political edge. Even before the first note is played, *Okemah*'s political intent is signaled by the sleeve illustration, the guitar raised in a red fist, the title scrawled across it in an obvious evocation of one of the album's key reference points, Woody Guthrie (whose own guitar bore the inscription "This machine kills fascists" and who hailed from Okemah, Oklahoma). In some ways, *Okemah* represented a return to Uncle Tupelo's finger-pointing style but with a more mature political conscience and some more specific targets in sight: "Jet Pilot" was readily legible as a satirical swipe at George Bush Jr., and "Endless War" was equally transparent. The environmental concerns darkening the likes of "Ten Second News" (*Trace*) and "Cahokian" (*Terroir Blues*) bled into "Bandages and Scars" and "Ipecac," which, after a series of relatively obscure meditations on modern living, launches a direct assault on corporate business and capitalism in a scathing final verse.

Great buildings of majesty
Made by the rat race whore.
Backed by the graves of the laborer's toil.
Backed by the graves of the laborer's toil.

The ideas of "underground . . . reaction" and "rebellion" Farrar sings about on *Okemah*'s "6 String Belief" have become a prominent motivating force in his recent songs in recent years. The third track on *The Search,* "Underground Dream," kicks off with a melancholy pun—"Had a thought that consumer goods were bad / Like a rat can never beat the wheel"—while insisting in the determinedly repetitive chorus, amid a litany of thinly veiled attacks on the U.S. administration, "They can't take away / This underground dream." In "Beacon Soul," he asks, scornfully, "Who the hell is Dow Jones anyway / Society's bones on a cafeteria tray," and the rather too literal "Automatic Society" lambastes a throwaway era of "Planned obsolescence manufactured senseless" and sneers, "Catch back heart attack you want fries with that / It's automatic." Against the dominant ideology and political status quo, Farrar pitches the world of the underground dream: "Faith to the forgotten places / Where the real world / Contra ideas thrive" ("L Train"). The album's closing number refuses to countenance defeat or despair no matter how high the odds are stacked: "The best is within not with who or where you've been . . . Can only get better from here / Don't have any fear" ("Phosphate Skin").

> "Find a way out of these blues"
>
> —"DENT COUNTY"

In a genre that valorizes the authentic in such a wide variety of forms, Farrar's roots often seem to stretch farther and deeper. In the same way in which a generation of alt.country artists acknowledged their indebtedness to their own immediate influences, as well as the music of a previous generation, so Farrar's solo and recent Son Volt releases, in their own ways, find space for similar acts of homage, acknowledging tradition even while seeking out new forms of musical expression. *Sebastopol*'s most unambiguous nod to the past is the extraordinary roll call of Saint Louis blues singers in "Outside the Door" (a musical family tree fully explored by Michael Pemberton),[71] a song that might force us to read somewhat skeptically Farrar's attempt to shrug off the label "music historian."[72] The album *Death Songs for the Living,* meanwhile, offers a collection of traditional tunes, drawing on the songs of the Stanley Brothers and Woody Guthrie, among others, but often updating the lyrics to draw attention to the persistence of the past in an equally troubled present.

Perhaps most poignantly, much of Farrar's last solo album, *Terroir Blues*—which is also by far his most personal collection of songs—can be understood as an homage to a private past inasmuch as some of its key songs are offered in tribute to his father, Jim "Pops" Farrar, who died in 2002 and whose presence hovers around the haunting compositions "Hard Is the Fall" and "Dent County" in particular.[73] Pops Farrar, although he spent many years traveling as a merchant mariner, seems to have had his own very strong sense of rural roots, having grown up in the Depression-era Ozarks, the son of musical parents. In later life, he became a familiar character in Saint Louis, well known for his song collection; Chris King describes him as "a songster . . . [one who] remembers a little, misconstrues some and makes up the rest."[74] In "Hard Is the Fall I," Farrar's voice is swathed in ghostly echo (the result of three different takes of the song tracked over each other) as he recalls Pops Farrar's meeting with Hank Williams: "Shaking the hand of the rambling man from Montgomery / The music evangelist, the never-ending quest." Consciously or not, Farrar's act of commemoration offers another link in the chain of musical tradition, back through his own father to the father of country music himself.

In an interview conducted shortly after Pops died, Farrar commented on how their lives seemed to have become "intertwined" in his father's final years and how Pops took a new lease on life after being diagnosed with cancer, performing and recording an album: "I felt like he was living the same life I did when I was a teenager."[75] In "Dent County," Farrar movingly acknowledges the debt he owes his father musically, emotionally, and spiritually. And in that state of meditation and painful, thankful reminiscence, Farrar finds a place for himself, too.

Beat bars and the maritime,
Postwar peace and paid your dues.
Now the burden is passed on:
Find a way out of these blues.

For Jay Farrar, the continuing renegotiation of his relation to tradition, the incorporation of the past into a vital musical present, another "never-ending quest," goes on.

NOTES

1. There are four Uncle Tupelo albums, 1988–94; three Son Volt albums, 1994–2000; and, in a new Son Volt configuration, two more, 2004–present.

2. These include two albums, a soundtrack, a collaboration, and an extended (EP) released between 2000 and 2006.

3. Capitalism's "abstracted economic drives, its fundamental priorities in social relations, its criteria of growth and of profit and loss, have over several centuries altered our country and created our kinds of city. In its final forms of imperialism it has altered our world." Raymond Williams, *The Country and the City* (London: Chatto and Windus, 1973), 302.

4. Gerald W. Creed and Barbara Ching, "Recognizing Rusticity: Identity and the Power of Place," in *Knowing Your Place: Rural Identity and Cultural Hierarchy,* ed. Barbara Ching and Gerald W. Creed (New York: Routledge, 1997), 2–3.

5. Williams, *The Country and the City,* 1.

6. "Methamphetamine" is from Son Volt's *The Search* (2007).

7. Keir Keightley, "Reconsidering Rock," in *The Cambridge Companion to Rock and Pop,* ed. Simon Frith, Will Straw, and John Street (Cambridge: Cambridge University Press, 2001),127–28.

8. The albums were *Trans* (1983), *Everybody's Rockin'* (1983), and *Old Ways* (1985).

9. The tension between major and independent is familiar in all genres of alternative popular music and is epitomized by the tortured figure of Kurt Cobain, whose commitment to the alternative (the scorching noise of Nirvana's *Bleach,* released on Sub Pop in 1989) came under scrutiny when the band hit pay dirt with the release of *Nevermind* on the major label DGC in September 1991. Cobain was caught in the anomaly of an unusual cultural moment, as the alternative washed suddenly and unexpectedly into the mainstream and "Smells Like Teen Spirit" took over the radio and music television. Some still attribute Cobain's suicide in 1994 to his inability to come to terms with the magnitude of his fame and the accompanying pressures on his professional and personal life.

10. Jonathan Cohen, "Wilco: In the Comfort Zone," http://www.billboard.com/bbcom/feature/article_display.jsp?vnu_content_id=1003571465 (accessed June 29, 2007).

11. Jane Ganahl, "Jay Farrar: Rising Son," *Harp,* July–August 2005, http://harpmagazine.com/articles/detail.cfm?article_id=3195 (accessed July 12, 2007).

12. Ibid.

13. James Mann, "Jay Farrar: Rock and Roll's Greta Garbo," *Ink19.com,* November 1998, http://www.ink19.com/issues_F/98_11/ink_spots/son_volt_nf.html (accessed August 20, 2002).

14. Dylan Gaughan, "Interview with Jay Farrar," http://members.tripod.com/swizzlestickzine/features/jayfarrar.html (accessed August 20, 2002).

15. Roy Kasten, "The *Terroir*ist," *Riverfront Times,* June 18, 2003, http://www.jayfarrar.net/press/riverfronttimes061803.htm (accessed June 25, 2004).

16. The change came about when a longer established record label, ACT Music, expressed concerns about potential confusion between their names.

17. J. D. Rush, "Profile: Jay Farrar," *Unbarred,* November 2003, http://www.jayfarrar.net/press/unbarred1103.htm (accessed June 25, 2004).

18. Paul Salfen, interview with Jay Farrar, *Dallas Music Guide,* 2002, http://www.dallasmusicguide.com/interviews/JayFarrar2.htm (accessed June 25, 2004).

19. Julie Borovik, interview with Jay Farrar, Nadamucho.com, http://www.jayfarrarnet/press/nadamucho072103.htm (accessed June 25, 2004).

20. The live recording dates from September 14, 2003; the album was released the following year.

21. Ganahl, "Jay Farrar."

22. Jason Fine, "Heart of the Country," *Option* 53 (November–December 1993): 87.

23. Keightley, "Reconsidering Rock," 137.

24. Indeed, the liner notes for the CD reissue of *March* reveal that three of the cover songs on the album were sourced from a 1974 release of a 1965 collection of field recordings, *High Atmosphere.*

25. The tape loop used in "Blind Hope" (on *Wide Swing Tremolo*) is an anomaly in Son Volt Mark I's recording career. It was not created with digital techniques but, instead, was manually cut and looped by engineer and mixer David Barbe.

26. Adam Jackson, "Life after Tupelo: Jay Farrar and His New Band, Son Volt," *Music Monitor,* 1995, http://www.penduluminc.com/MM/articles/sonvolt.html (accessed June 25, 2004).

27. Mallay Charters, "Night Vision: Son Volt," *Guitarworld,* December 1995, http://www.guitarworld.com/artistindex/9512.sonvolt.html (accessed June 22, 2004).

28. See Aaron A. Fox, "'Ain't It Funny How Time Slips Away?' Talk, Trash, and Technology in a Texas 'Redneck' Bar," in *Knowing Your Place: Rural Identity and Cultural Hierarchy,* ed. Barbara Ching and Gerald W. Creed, 105–30 (New York and London: Routledge, 1997).

29. "Son Volt," Artist Direct Showcase, http://imusic.artistdirect.com/showcase/modern/sonvolt.html (accessed August 20, 2002).

30. Farrar built on this strategy with the so-called Space Junk, which segued a number of tracks on his 2003 solo release *Terroir Blues* and the instrumental interludes on his collaboration with Anders Parker, *Death Songs for the Living* (2006).

31. Keightley, "Reconsidering Rock," 137.

32. Angie Carlson, "Don't Fence Me In," interview with Jay Farrar, October 3, 2001, http://www.indyweek.com/durham/2001-10-03/music.html (accessed July 5, 2004).

33. Anders Smith Lindall, "Jay Farrar: Blues Traveler," *Harp,* June/July 2003, accessed on-line at http://harpmagazine.com/articles/detail.cfm?article_id=1202 May 1, 2008.

34. Kasten, "The *Terroir*ist."

35. Brian Baker, "Jay Farrar Resurrects Son Volt and Woody Guthrie," *Country Standard Time,* July 2005, http://www.countrystandardtime.com/sonvolt4FEATURE.html (accessed August 17, 2005).

36. Richard Gintowt, "Low Voltage: Jay Farrar's Son Volt Phones It In," June 14, 2005, *Lawrence.com,* http://www.lawrence.com/news/2005/jun/14/wakarusa2005_sonvolt/ (accessed August 19, 2005).

37. See Joli Jensen, *The Nashville Sound: Authenticity, Commercialization, and Country Music* (Nashville: Country Music Foundation and Vanderbilt University Press, 1998).

38. See the essay by Aaron Smithers in this collection.

39. A number of songs ("Looking for a Way Out," "Watch Me Fall") were recorded in alternate versions with "fast" versions of both of these included as bonus tracks on the CD reissue of the album (2003).

40. Peter Blackstock, "Being There, Done That," *No Depression* 5 (September–October 1996): http://www.nodepression.net/archive/nd05/features/wilco.html (accessed July 5, 2004).

41. Greg Kot, *Wilco: Learning How to Die* (New York: Broadway, 2004), 43.

42. Fine, "Heart of the Country," 89.

43. The Primatives' name was apparently taken from a garage rock song by a 1960s band called the Groupies (Kot, *Wilco,* 18).

44. Chris King, "Favorite Uncle," *Riverfront Times,* June 5–11, 1991, reproduced at http://www.factorybelt.net/articles/blue_tux.htm (accessed June 24, 2004).

45. The parenthetical years indicate approximate dates when the song was featured in the set list.

46. Steve Pick, "Uncle Tupelo, No Longer Primitive," *Saint Louis Post-Dispatch,* January 28, 1988, http://www.factorybelt.net/articles/post_2–88.htm (accessed June 24, 2004).

47. Kot, *Wilco: Learning How to Die,* 64–65.

48. Farrar is quoted in Gina Vivinetto, "Son Volt Makes Alt-country Cool," *Saint Petersburg Times,* February 9, 1999, http://www.sptimes.com/News/20999/Entertainment/Son_Volt_makes_alt_co.html (accessed July 8, 2004).

49. I am indebted to Joli Jensen for this suggestion.

50. David Goodman, *Modern Twang: An Alternative Country Music Guide and Directory* (Nashville: Dowling, 1999), 309.

51. Farrar mentioned in a 2003 interview (Rush, "Profile") that "I Walk the Line" was one of the first riffs he learned to play on the guitar.

52. Daniel Durchholz, interview, *Request,* November 1993, http://www.gumbopages.com/music/uncle-tupelo/text/are_you_ready.html (accessed June 24, 2004).

53. S. Renee Dechert, interview with Mike Heidorn, review of "Uncle Tupelo 89/93: Anthology," April 22, 2002 *PopMatters.com,* http://www.popmatters.com/music/reviews/u/uncletupelo-8993.shtml (accessed June 28, 2002).

54. See, for example, Ronnie Dannelley, "Interview with Jay Farrar of Son Volt," *Pop Culture Press* 42 (1997), http://earcandy_mag.tripod.com/blasonv.htm (accessed August 20, 2002); Dana Cerick, interview with Jay Farrar, *Uno Mas*, 1995, http://www.unomas.com/features/sonvolt1.html (accessed June 24, 2004); and Charters, "Night Vision."

55. BBC News, "Farrar Abandons 'Alt Country'," January 22, 2004, http://www.news.bbc.co.uk/1/hi/entertainment/music/3420055.stm (accessed January 28, 2004).

56. See Peter Doggett, *Are You Ready for the Country: Elvis, Dylan, Parsons, and the Roots of Country Rock* (London: Penguin, 2000).

57. John Schact, "Uncle Tupelo," *Swizzle-Stick.com*, April 2, 2002, http://members.tripod.com/swizzlestickzine/features/uncletupelo.html (accessed August 20, 2002).

58. Annie O'Brien, "Playback: The Underlying Overtones of Jay Farrar," October 2002, http://www.jayfarrar.net/press/playback1002.htm (accessed June 25, 2004).

59. Dannelley, "Interview with Jay Farrar of Son Volt."

60. The song is on the Byrds' *Ballad of Easy Rider* (1969).

61. Rob Hughes, "Jay Farrar: A Record That Changed My Life—the Byrds, *Fifth Dimension* (1966)," *Uncut*, January 26, 2004, http://www.jayfarrar.net/press/uncut0104.htm (accessed June 25, 2004).

62. Richard Byrne, "Here Comes the Son." *Riverfront Times*, September 20–26, 1995, reprinted at http://www.gumbopages.com/music/son-volt/text/trace-rev-rft.html (accessed June 25, 2004).

63. Song introduction at a radio session recorded at Cat's Paw Studios, Atlanta, March 4, 1996. Doug Sahm also made a guest vocal appearance on *Anodyne*, helping out on "Give Back the Key to My Heart."

64. Jackson, "Life after Tupelo."

65. Jane Ganahl, "Profile: Jay Farrar," *San Francisco Chronicle*, February 20, 2004, http://www.jayfarrar.net/press/sfchronicle022004.htm (accessed June 25, 2004).

66. Peter Blackstock, "Dim Lights, Small Cities: Son Volt," *No Depression* 1 (fall 1995), http://www.nodepression.net/archive/nd01/features/sonvolt.html (accessed August 27, 2002).

67. Jackson, "Life after Tupelo." *Entertainment Weekly* summed up a short review of *Trace* with the remark, "Call it hillbilly alchemy: Son Volt turns heartland rust into gold." Josef Woodward, "Music Capsule Review: *Trace*," *Entertainment Weekly*, November 10, 1995, http://www.ew.com/ew/article/0,,299474,00.html (accessed June 29, 2007).

68. Goodman, *Modern Twang*, 309.

69. See Kot, *Wilco*, 65. The same fate awaited Gillian Welch, the middle-class Hollywood urbanite, on the release of her folk-, bluegrass-, and gospel-steeped debut *Revival* (1996), which was dismissed by many as "fake" for similar reasons.

70. Anders Smith-Lindall, "Son Volt, Farrar to Whirl into Detroit," *Michigan*

Daily, September 26, 1997, http://www.pub.umich.edu/daily/1997/sep/09–26–97/arts/arts2.html (accessed July 13, 2007).

71. Michael Pemberton, "Jay Farrar, 'Outside the Door', and St. Louis Blues," http://www.gumbopages.com/music/son-volt/text/outside.html (accessed June 25, 2004).

72. Carlson, "Don't Fence Me In."

73. Jay Farrar notes that he based his version of "Hard Times," on the *Death Songs* album, on what he learned of the original Stephen Foster song from his father. "Notes on *Death Songs for the Living*," http://www.jayfarrar.net/discs/index-gobiron.htm (accessed July 13, 2007).

74. Chris King, liner notes to Pops Farrar's *Memory Music*, 2006, http://www.hoobellatoo.org/folksdetail.cfm?FPID=8 (accessed July 14, 2007).

75. Ganahl, "Profile."

PAMELA FOX AND BARBARA CHING

Conclusion: New Alternatives?—Top 40 "Outlaws" Gretchen Wilson, Miranda Lambert, and the Dixie Chicks

Ironically, Nashville, aiming for a broader demographic, sometimes gets the jump on alt.country in discovering and promoting alternative country music. As noted in our volume's introductory essay, alt.country's songwriters often denigrate mainstream country's largely female audience, and their fans follow suit with their own misogynistic "rants": on "The Other Side of Country: The Twin Cities' Only Alt-Country Hillbilly Rant Blog," for example, Jack Sparks describes the songs played on Minneapolis' Top 40 country music station as "tampon commercials disguised as Martina McBride songs."[1] Yet women are undoubtedly emerging as the new emblems of country authenticity. We thus look to Gretchen Wilson, current multiplatinum artist, newcomer Miranda Lambert, and the all-woman group the Dixie Chicks as a closing set of contrasts not only to underscore the gender dynamics at work in definitions of alt.country but also to examine the continued negotiation over cultural capital involved in the assessment and evaluation of music genres. These artists illustrate and complicate the professed tastes of alt.country fans and gatekeepers, raising noteworthy questions about what constitutes authentic country music *and* alternative cultural politics in the twenty-first century.

Gretchen Wilson has the sound, look, and genuine class credentials of an exemplary alt.country performer, yet she has soared to fame as a mainstream, rather than alternative, country artist. Her first and signature hit, "Redneck Woman" (2004), unabashedly celebrated her white trash roots with a hard-partying attitude more akin to Hank Williams Jr. or Tanya Tucker than any contemporary female country singer (both made cameo appearances in the song's video). As Wilson recalls of her initial dismal efforts to win a Nashville recording contract, "I didn't have the right look. My hair was dated. I didn't have the beauty-queen bone structure of many of the female stars currently topping the charts. I was a little too old, a little too heavy, a little too hard-edged."[2] Subsequent singles, like "When I Think about Cheatin'," sounded much more at home at the Opry (referenced in the video) than in a Country Music Television studio. So why has alt.country journalism and radio shown little interest in her music, tacitly placing her in the musical camp dismissed for artistic banality,[3] even as she has achieved some hip credibility by ranking ahead of über-alt.troubadour Steve Earle in the 2004 *Village Voice*'s Pazz and Jop poll?[4] After all, as a representative of "real country" life, Wilson can be seen as reaching back to those meanings and values that were created in actual societies and situations in the past and still seem to have significance because they represent areas of human experience, aspiration, and achievement that the dominant culture neglects, undervalues, opposes, represses, or cannot even recognize.[5] Isn't this what alt.country professes to offer its audiences, the very thing that it accuses Nashville of ignoring? In this instance, which institution is guilty of "repression" or nonrecognition?

For us, Gretchen Wilson finally reveals what is problematic about both mainstream and alternative claims to authenticity and country "tradition." As the "politically uncorrect" survival of a *complex* past —not a frozen relic but a vocal, dynamic, messy image—Wilson has the potential to resist incorporation into mainstream country's reverential visions of an earlier era, and she has already avoided fetishization as an "oppositional" icon by the alt.country tastemakers.[6] While both alternative and mainstream country often conflate country music tradition with a nostalgic vision of rough-hewn, rural Americana, neither risks tracing the effects of such conflation into the present moment in the way that Wilson does. She may appear to some to be trading on her white trash identity; in her subsequent efforts, *All Jacked Up* (2006) and the recently released *One of the Boys* (2007), her songs' class sensibilities don't develop much beyond the themes articulated in "Redneck Woman." However, even these variants suggest that Wilson can succeed at offering an "alternative" that falls outside of alt.country as it currently defines itself. Moreover, this redneck woman cannot be squared with the bland ambition that supposedly characterizes Nashville, nor does she apologize for the riches she has gained by marketing her ragged past. In fact, she sees herself simply as one of a long line of hard-working and independent women—"the strongest, most dependable, most reliable people in my life."[7]

Foiling the mythologies of both alternative and mainstream country, Wilson can be marshaled to represent what Raymond Williams called the "actively residual" mode of tradition.[8] In this case, Wilson's life story activates country music's more colorful, less "sanitized" past while her success demonstrates its continuing "live," active presence. In the enormous rush of publicity surrounding Wilson since she first emerged on the scene, her biography became essential to her success, distilled to a few key signifiers: bartender at fifteen in a trailer-park town; single mother of a young daughter; brassy, no-nonsense gal who'll "whup" any "home wrecker" messin' with her man (and down Jack Daniels with the best of them).[9] Her 2004 debut album, *Here for the Party,* followed the formula of her now out of fashion predecessors, including songs about drinking ("When It Rains," "Here for the Party"), marital woes ("The Bed"), cars ("Chariot," which also manages to be a hybrid rap-gospel tune), and her own life story ("Redneck Woman," "Pocahontas"). Other Top 40 country albums might simulate such a structure in alternating upbeat songs with ballads or alternating fun, clever lyrics with sentimental ones, but both their musical arrangements and class-inflected language—would Faith Hill ever use the term *home wrecker* when singing of infidelity?—have a distinctly middle-class sensibility. Think, for example, of the way "Mississippi Girl" (2005), Hill's self-portrait, contrasts with "Redneck Woman": Hill underscores good motherhood by claiming that she "still likes wearing my old ball cap / ride my kids around piggy back," while Wilson depicts herself in a more defiant posture, "stand[ing] barefooted in my own front yard with a baby on my hip." Wilson's an "outlaw woman" cut from Loretta Lynn's homespun cloth yet also on the road with the boys in a distinctly new way:[10] her collaboration with the MuzikMafia, headed by maverick duo Big and Rich (of "Save a Horse, Ride a Cowboy" fame), significantly puts her on an equal footing with its other, all male members—if anything, she is the breakout star of the pack.[11]

Miranda Lambert, a twenty-three-year-old Texan with an attitude, if not the personal history, to rival Wilson's, currently seems destined to follow her explosive path to Nashville stardom, already touting one platinum album, *Kerosene;* debuting her new release, *Crazy Ex-Girlfriend,* at number one on the Nielsen Country Chart (both on Wilson's label, Sony); and winning the 2007 Academy of Country Music's Top New Female Vocalist award. Unlike Wilson, however, she is also poised to emerge as alt.country's newest darling: in spring 2007 she landed a *No Depression* cover story—trumpeted as "Country's New Alternative"—as well as a laudatory *New York Times* piece, which similarly branded her "an alt.country singer operating covertly in the mainstream."[12] Has the borderline itself shifted in alt.discourse or is Lambert a more palatable "cover girl" for its discriminating fan base? It may be a bit of both. As mentioned earlier, alt.country's premier journal recently engaged in a formal flourish of reinvention, transmuting both the *alt* and the *country* in its tagline into the much more ambitious "American" music. As with any act of naming, this one had a political (and polemical) effect,[13] allowing *No Depression* to simultaneously preserve and erase the line dividing alternative from mainstream country and to claim the "center" for what had previously been the "margin." The change also displays the omnivorous tastes of cultural capitalists and reflects the long-standing name of the music's primary industry organization, the Americana Music Association. But in the issue showcasing Lambert, editor Grant Alden also appears to be acknowledging that the mainstream itself is changing, opting, on occasion, for what he considers authentic artistry.

> Twelve years ago . . . we [he and Peter Blackstock] envisioned *No Depression,* in part, as a kind of argument against what Music Row was then selling. As an argument for good music which deserved an audience. Our early marketing literature very pointedly noted that we were about country music, not about Garth Brooks and Shania Twain. . . . But . . . that battle is largely over and fundamentally won. For the moment. Just listen . . . to country radio. Sure, there's plenty of schlock; there always has been. But there's also real life there: fine songs, good singers, plenty of heart. Country music—mainstream country music—deserves once again to be taken seriously.[14]

Such an admission of victory solidifies alt.country's position as arbiter of taste. Indeed, Alden admits that Lambert's appearance on the cover was a strategic decision with intertwined "commercial" and conversion aims, noting, "We hope that by luring fans of Miranda Lambert into our pages, . . . we might also introduce them to Uncle Earl and Elizabeth Cook and the Avett Brothers [more obscure alt.performers]." But in the final analysis, he insists,

"She's on this cover because she made a very good record," and Barry Mazor's cover story portrays Lambert as a gifted and essentially *alternative* country artist who serves as a bellwether for the "new expansiveness" in Nashville's music industry. He compares her to Dierks Bentley, whose music, representing a new coalescence between these two modes of country, fills a "gap that once seemed such a chasm." This last clause, echoing Alden's prefatory piece, exemplifies a turning point in alt.rhetoric, envisioning a "real expansion of the possibilities for mainstream country music in this surprising decade." Mazor acknowledges that Lambert's *Crazy Ex-Girlfriend* is crafted to appeal to mainstream country radio but also points to the roster of songs written by noteworthy alt.country artists such as Gillian Welch. Although it is Lambert in this interview who raises the names of MuzikMafia members Big and Rich and Gretchen Wilson—notable strangers to the *No Depression* archive—as precursors of this latest trend in Top 40 country, Mazor seems sincere about his blinkered conclusion: "[T]hese are all tendencies that would have been found only in alternative country in the 1990s."[15]

Still, it's not surprising that Lambert, rather than Wilson, has won this exclusive position in the alt.country arena. She can claim the Texas roots so coveted by fans, which translate into both "authentic" musical influences (Pat Green, Jack Ingram) and authentic biography (gun-packing, smart-mouthed, small-town girl), without becoming too déclassé: she has two loving, supportive parents (her father himself an aspiring country singer-songwriter) and, with her selection of songs from Gillian Welch et al., better aesthetic tastes, seeking to stay initially in the "backwater." In fact, she admitted to Mazor that her first hit, "Kerosene," was "unconsciously" plagiarized from Steve Earle's "I Feel Alright": "I guess I'd listened to it so much that I just kind of had it in there." (They finally shared cowriting credits on the song.)[16] And, in spite of remarkably similar CD cover designs, Lambert's blonde glamour contrasts strongly with Wilson's trampy look (figs. 8 and 9). Additionally, Lambert seems anxious to establish that her wild persona is, to some extent, a performance: "I don't want people to always put me in the category, 'She's mean; she's fiery! Don't mess with her!' Anyway, songs, to me, are stories."[17] Contrast this statement to Wilson's attitude, as she continues to boast that she is an "open book" in her music.[18] Lambert's arty ambiguity seems better suited to the tongue-in-cheek approach to authenticity demonstrated by many alt.fans, enabling that ironized distance necessary to preserve their connoisseurship. It remains to be seen whether the hard-core

Fig. 8. Cover of Miranda Lambert's *Kerosene* (Sony, 2005).

Fig. 9. Cover of Gretchen Wilson's *One of the Boys* (Sony, 2007).

alt.country community will fully embrace Lambert as she also seems to unapologetically court a mainstream audience by expressing fear of "cool" tastemakers (in the *New York Times*, no less): "When people I thought were really cool started telling me 'I like your record,' I was like, 'Oh gosh, oh gosh. I'm not going to be popular' . . . and I want to be mainstream."[19] At least for his part, Mazor offers an optimistic prediction: Lambert "seems to have a workable, emulation-worthy handle on how the once-warring sides in the country—alt-country divide have come together in 2007, and how it's possible to make the most of both alleged worlds."[20]

But alt.country tradition has already established a morbid reverence for the reckless way Hank Williams, to borrow a line from Waylon Jennings, "done it," and the commercially ambitious Lambert doesn't want to travel that lost highway. In this respect, she is like the Dixie Chicks. Their early hit song about escaping this fate, "Long Time Gone" (2002), describes how a country boy left the farm to make it big in Nashville, got tired of sleeping in his car and singing on the street, then went home and married a girl named Delia. He and Delia listen to the radio, although they don't much like what they hear: "they sound tired but they don't sound Haggard / They've got money but they don't have Cash." The song was written by alt.country songwriter Darrell Scott, who recorded it with alt.country artist Tim O'Brien in 2000 and whose latest claim to fame is his 2007 Song of the Year award from the Americana Music Association for "Hank Williams' Ghost." In Scott's repertoire, "Long Time Gone" is another alt.country attack on Nashville. The lyrics work the familiar alt.country trope about the marketplace's depressing logic in which Nashville sacrifices authentic country music for profit—taking the money but rejecting the magisterial [Johnny] Cash and thus sounding "tired" as it forfeits Merle Haggard's old-fashioned artistry. The way the Dixie Chicks play and sing "Long Time Gone" maintains the male point of view[21] yet makes the song sound like a celebration, as if the departure of the old guard has made room for them, and, in fact, their version reached the number two spot on the country charts and crossed over to number seven on the pop charts.

Ultimately, the Dixie Chicks gleefully abandoned mainstream country after it sent them packing in 2003 for expressing opposition to George W. Bush and the Iraq War.[22] Their latest album, *Taking the Long Way*, celebrates this departure, relishing their new artistic "independence" and venting anger at their red-state former fans, particularly in the song "Not Ready to Make Nice." "The Long Way Around" refashions "Long Time Gone," examining mainstream country's perfidy from their latest, explicitly autobiographical, vantage point: this time, the song's narrator has achieved Nashville stardom, "on top of the world," but feels that she has had to sacrifice her authentic "self"—one of alt.country's touchstones. After voicing her liberal political opinions, *that* world comes "crashing down," spurring a satisfying if lonely return to her maverick identity. She resolves to follow her own path by "takin' the long way around" to professional success. In this scenario, she also sets herself apart from the Nashville wannabe of "Long Time Gone," who was lured back home to the rural route by his old flame waiting "out on her daddy's farm." In "The Long Way Around," she proudly announces that she "could never follow" her high school friends who married and settled down—she boasts that she's "a long time gone" from that mainstream lifestyle.

Unlike Delia's prodigal lover, then, in the newer song the thinly veiled persona of lead singer Natalie Maines rejects both the conservative values of the Dixie Chicks' earlier fan base and the "sellout" values of Top 40 country celebrity. And the musical community envisioned in this later song to which she's taking the "long way around" constitutes the hip "club" of alt.country itself. In *Time* magazine's cover story of May 29, 2006, the Dixie Chicks echo some of the latter's elitist sentiments as they say "good riddance" to commercial country. Martie Maguire confesses, "I'd rather have a smaller following of really cool people who get it . . . than people that have us in their five-disc changer with Reba McEntire and Toby Keith. We don't want those kinds of fans. They limit what you can do."[23] The artistic choices that built the album—well documented in Barbara Kopple and Cecelia Peck's 2006 documentary, *Shut Up & Sing*—further demonstrate this aspiration. *Taking the Long Way* was produced by Rick Rubin, the man who resurrected Johnny Cash's career and featured the alt.country eminence Gary Louris (of the Jayhawks) as a principal songwriting partner with the three women.

At the same time, this new release is being reviewed primarily as a pop record for adults, the least authentically "country-sounding" record of their career. As Josh Tyrangiel notes in *Time*, "The Dixie Chicks talk about *Long Way* as the end of their commercial salad days but they're shrewd enough to know that only suckers choose between art and commerce. 'I'm not ready to fly coach,' jokes Maguire."[24] The 2006 Grammy Awards (bestowed on February 11, 2007) announced the group's accession to the pop mainstream as they won both Record of the Year and Song of the Year for "Not Ready to Make Nice" and Album of the Year for *Taking the Long Way*. Their evolving story thus epitomizes alt.country's contradictions and exposes its ironies to the specter of hypocrisy. Still, if alt.country creates a progressive form of tradition and provides an authentic alternative to country music's most extreme cultural and political pandering, we want to hear it.

NOTES

1. http://blogs.citypages.com/jsparks/2007/10/top_100_country.php (accessed December 29, 2007).

2. Gretchen Wilson with Allen Rucker, *Redneck Woman: Stories from My Life* (New York: Grand Central, 2006), 1.

3. Aaron A. Fox makes a similar observation about alternative fans' scorn for Shania Twain, a working-class woman and Native American who hit the big time, in his "'Alternative' to What? 'O Brother,' September 11th, and the Politics of Country Music," in *There's A Star-Spangled Banner Waving Somewhere: Country Music Goes to War*, ed. Charles K. Wolfe and James E. Akenson, 164–91 (Lexington: University of Kentucky Press, 2005), 186.

4. We thank Jon Smith for drawing this poll to our attention.

5. Raymond Williams, *Marxism and Literature* (New York: Oxford University Press, 1977), 124.

6. "Politically Uncorrect" is one of the singles from Wilson's 2006 CD *All Jacked Up*.

7. Wilson, *Redneck Woman*, 22. She elaborates on this gendered heritage: "I can't really explain it, but when I was growing up in rural Illinois, a lot of men were troubled, irresponsible, or in their own male world. They were often more the problem than the solution. I'm no man-hater—far from it—but from a very early age I learned that if you ever expected a man to step in and make your life run more smoothly, you could be setting yourself up for a big heartache. In my experience, not only does a woman not need a man to 'complete' herself, she can often get much further along in life without one, or at least certain ones" (22–23).

8. Williams opposes the "actively residual" to the idealisms of inert visions of tradition (*Marxism and Literature*, 122). Pierre Bourdieu also argues for an active form of "subversion oriented toward conservation or restoration" of past forms of class solidarity in *Acts of Resistance: Against the Tyranny of the Market*, trans. Richard Nice (New York: New Press, 1999), 104.

9. See brief biographical sketches on the Country Music Television Web site and Wilson's official Web site (gretchenwilson.com). The venerable CBS news program *60 Minutes* also profiled Wilson on December 16, 2004, focusing specifically on her life story. See the transcript "Richer Life for 'Redneck Woman'" at http://www.cbsnews.com/stories/2004/12/16/60minutes/main661556 (accessed December 29, 2007).

10. Wilson and Hank Williams Jr. performed Williams' song, "Outlaw Women," on Country Music Television's program *CMT Outlaws*. She herself points to "Loretta, Tammy, Dolly" as the few prior country female artists who have been equally "rough-edged" and allowed to "inhabit that persona publicly as well as privately." Gretchen Wilson Web site, "About Gretchen," http://www.gretchenwilson.com (accessed May 23, 2007).

11. The MuzikMafia bills itself as a "Nashville-based artists' collaborative that promotes greatness in all genres of music and performance"; in addition to John Rich, Big Kenny, and Gretchen Wilson, this "alliance" includes performers Jon Nicholson, "Hick-Hop" rapper Cowboy Troy, Mista D, and dwarf emcee Two-Foot Fred Gill. Rachel Kice, a "painter of fine music" who "performs" her art onstage, is the only other female member of the group. The Mafia's motto is "music without prejudice" (www.MuzikMafia.com). To further compound the irony of this collaboration, it's worth noting that John Rich and Adam Shoenfeld wrote Faith Hill's "Mississippi Girl."

12. See Jon Caramanica, "Mess with This Texan, You'll Pay in a Song," *New York Times*, April 29, 2007, 2.27.

13. See Diane Pecknold's essay in this volume for an extended discussion of the issues and historical context of the naming issue.

14. Grant Alden, "Hello Stranger," *No Depression* 69 (May–June 2007): 2.

15. Barry Mazor, "Nashville Lonestar," *No Depression* 69 (May–June 2007): 59.

16. Ibid., 61.

17. Ibid., 61–62.

18. http://www.gretchenwilson.com/index.php?page=about (accessed December 29, 2007).

19. Caramanica, "Mess with This Texan," 2.27.

20. Mazor, "Nashville Lonestar," 63.

21. It's interesting to consider the Dixie Chicks' version of this song as a sort of riposte to Johnny Cash's 1994 version of "Delia's Gone," his celebrated cover of the Blind Willie McTell murder ballad, and the first cut on his first *American Recordings* album. Cash hyperbolically portrays the misogyny of Delia's murder and revels in the self-pity of the murderer condemned to life in prison, but in "Long Time Gone," as sung by the Dixie Chicks, life with Delia is lived happily ever after—even if it is a life outside of country music stardom.

22. For a thorough discussion of this incident, see Chris Willman, *Rednecks and Bluenecks: The Politics of Country Music* (New York: New Press, 2005), 21–54.

23. Josh Tyrangiel, "In the Line of Fire," *Time,* May 29, 2006, 65.

24. Ibid.

COMPILED BY KELLY BURCHFIELD AND BARBARA CHING

Alt.Country Chronology

1908 Olive Dame Campbell recognizes Child ballads in an Appalachian singer's repertoire

1909 International Workers of the World (IWW) publishes its *Little Red Songbook*, featuring songs of Joe Hill

1917 Campbell brings her collection to the attention of noted British collector Cecil Sharp

1918 Cecil Sharp collects a version of "Man of Constant Sorrow"

1927 In the Bristol Sessions, Ralph Peer records the Carter Family and Jimmie Rodgers

1928 Jimmie Rodgers records "California Blues (Blue Yodel No. 45)"
Carter Family records "Keep on the Sunny Side" and "Wildwood Flower"

1936 Carter Family records "No Depression (in Heaven)"

1937 Dorothy Scarborough publishes her *Song Catcher in the Southern Mountains*

1946–47 First popular recordings of bluegrass bands the Stanley Brothers and the Blue Sky Boys

1946 Gram Parsons born Ingram Cecil Connor III

1954 Release of Elvis Presley's first record, "That's Alright Mama" / "Blue Moon of Kentucky"

1959 The Stanley Brothers record and perform "Man of Constant Sorrow" at the first Newport Folk Festival

1961 First birth year of Generation X according to Neil Howe and William Strauss

1962 Release of Bob Dylan's first album, *Bob Dylan*, which includes his version of "Man of Constant Sorrow"

1967 Bob Dylan records *John Wesley Harding* in Nashville

1968 Release of Gram Parsons and the International Submarine Band's *Safe at Home*
The Byrds record *Sweetheart of the Rodeo* in Nashville

1969 Release of the Flying Burrito Brothers' *The Gilded Palace of Sin*
Release of the Byrds' *Ballad of Easy Rider*
Release of Bob Dylan's *Nashville Skyline,* which includes "Girl from the North Country," a duet with Johnny Cash

1970 Rounder Records founded in Cambridge, Massachusetts, by Ken Irwin, Marion Leighton Levy, and Bill Nowlin
Neko Case born in Alexandria, Virginia; family moves almost immediately thereafter
Release of the Byrds' *Untitled*
Release of Flying Burrito Brothers' second and final studio album with Gram Parsons, *Burrito Deluxe*

1972 Release of Nitty Gritty Dirt Band's first *Will the Circle Be Unbroken* collaboration
Gram Parsons records his first solo album, *GP,* with Emmylou Harris

1973 Gram Parsons records his second and last solo album, *Grievous Angel,* with Emmylou Harris
Death of Gram Parsons in Joshua Tree, California

1974 Justin Treviño born in Brownsville, Texas

1975 Sex Pistols formed in London
Release of Emmylou Harris' first solo album on a major label, *Pieces of the Sky*
David Mansfield (music director of *Songcatcher*) and T-Bone Burnett (music director of *O Brother, Where Art Thou?*) play in Bob Dylan's Rolling Thunder Revue (through 1976)

1976 David Mansfield, T-Bone Burnett, and Steven Soles form the Alpha Band (through 1979)

1978 Death of Maybelle Carter

1981 Last birth year of Generation X according to Neil Howe and William Strauss
Launch of Music Television (MTV)

1982 Release of Jason and the Scorchers' *Reckless Country Soul*
Release of Elvis Costello's *Almost Blue,* an album of country music covers, including two songs cowritten by Gram Parsons

1983 Compact disc format introduced to the U.S. market

1984–87 The Primatives perform live; Jay Farrar, Jeff Tweedy, and Mike Heidorn's first band also includes Farrar's brother Wade on vocals

1984 Emergence of a London-based scene described in 1985 by New Musical Express as "country-billy, cow-punk (call it what you will)"

1985 Release of the Mekons' *Fear and Whiskey*

1987 The first South by Southwest Music Conference and Festival is held in Austin, Texas

The Primatives is renamed Uncle Tupelo, becomes a three-piece band, and self-releases three tapes between 1987 and 1989

Release of the Cowboy Junkies' *The Trinity Session*

1988 Release of Steve Earle's *Copperhead Road*

1989 Release of the Nitty Gritty Dirt Band's *Will the Circle Be Unbroken*, vol. 2

Release of Nirvana's *Bleach* on the independent label SubPop

Bad Livers is formed in Austin, Texas

Zero Skills, Inc. records *Tractor Down*

1990 Release of Uncle Tupelo's *No Depression*

Introduction of MP3 format

1991 Douglas Coupland, alumnus of the Emily Carr Institute of Art and Design (Vancouver, British Columbia), publishes *Generation X: Tales for an Accelerated Culture*

Nirvana's "Smells Like Teen Spirit" single brings grunge sounds to the mainstream

Release of Uncle Tupelo's sophomore album *Still Feel Gone*

Release of Bad Livers' cassette *Dust on the Bible* and the 45 rpm record "Lust for Life" / "Stumpy's Comeupance"

Garth Brooks' *Ropin' the Wind* generates advance orders of four million copies

1992 William J. Clinton elected president

Release of Nirvana's *Nevermind*

Release of Uncle Tupelo's *March 16–20, 1992*, produced by REM guitarist Peter Buck

Bad Livers records *Delusions of Banjer* with producer Paul Leary of the Butthole Surfers for release on the Quarterstick label; the band also releases *The Golden Years* EP on limited edition gold vinyl, featuring covers of "Lust for Life" by Iggy Pop, "Jailbait" by Motorhead, and "Ring of Fire" by Johnny Cash

1993 Release of Uncle Tupelo's final album, *Anodyne*

Release of Nirvana's *In Utero*

1994 Bloodshot records founded in Chicago

Release of Bloodshot records' *For a Life of Sin* compilation

Johnny Cash releases the first *American Recordings* album in collaboration with Rick Rubin; "Delia's Gone" is the first and most celebrated cut

Uncle Tupelo plays its final show on May 1 at Mississippi Nights, Saint Louis, Missouri

Jay Farrar records demos and forms Son Volt, and Jeff Tweedy forms Wilco; both bands are signed to Warner Brothers

Bad Livers records *Horses in the Mines* for Quarterstick and re-releases *Dust on the Bible* on CD

1995 *No Depression* begins publication

Release of Wilco's *AM*; release of Son Volt's *Trace*

Split Lip Rayfield is formed in Wichita, Kansas

First Gavin Americana chart is published

Postcard2 mailing list is initiated

1996 William J. Clinton elected to second presidential term

Telecommunications Act of 1996 allows individual broadcasting corporations to own an unlimited number of stations in a single radio market

Release of Whiskeytown's *Faithless Street*

Release of Maow's only album, *The Unforgiving Sounds of Maow*

Gillian Welch records *Revival*

Release of Son Volt's *Straightaways*; release of Wilco's double album *Being There*

Meat Purveyors is formed in Austin, Texas

Release of Zero Skills, Inc.'s *Drunker 'n Hell* on cassette and CD-R

Bad Livers contributes a version of "Wild Bill Jones" to a CD to benefit the legendary Chicago rock club the Lounge Ax; fiddler and accordionist Ralph White leaves the touring band, and mandolin player Bob Grant steps in

1997 Release of Neko Case's first album, *The Virginian*

Freakwater records *Springtime*

Bad Livers records *Hogs on the Highway*, its first for the mostly acoustic and traditional label Sugar Hill of North Carolina

Danny Barnes moves from Austin to Port Townsend, Washington

Mark Rubin supervises the soundtrack for Rick Linklater's *The Newton Boys;* Danny Barnes composes music for the film and the Seattle Symphony

Twangfest is founded

1998 Release of Son Volt's *Wide Swing Tremolo*

Bad Livers records its second record on Sugar Hill, *Industry and Thrift*, and self-releases *The Ridgetop Sessions*, recorded straight to Digital Audio Tape at the home of Mark Rubin; included are tunes by Sun Ra, Don Stover, and Thelonious Monk

Meat Purveyors and Split Lip Rayfield both release debut records, *Sweet in the Pants* and *Split Lip Rayfield*, on Chicago's Bloodshot records

Release of Justin Treviño's first album, *Texas Honky Tonk*

1999 Americana Music Association is founded
Shawn Fanning and Sean Parker found the Napster file-sharing service
Label consolidations leave five companies in control of 80 percent of the world's music market
Freakwater records *End Time*
The members of Son Volt Mark I play their final show together at Mississippi Nights, Saint Louis, Missouri, on November 11
Release of Wilco's *Summer Teeth*
Meat Purveyors and Split Lip Rayfield release second records for Bloodshot, *More Songs about Buildings and Cows* and *In the Mud;* Meat Purveyors breaks up
Release of *Return of the Grievous Angel,* a compilation of Gram Parsons songs performed by alt.country, rock, and pop artists

2000 George W. Bush elected president
Release of Corn Sisters' *The Other Women,* recorded in 1998
Naomi Klein's *No Logo* published
Release of Neko Case's *Furnace Room Lullaby*
Release of Bad Livers' final album on Sugar Hill, *Blood and Mood;* the band breaks up
Neil Howe and William Strauss publish *Millennials Rising: The Next Great Generation*
Theatrical release of *O Brother, Where art Thou?* (dir. Coen Brothers) and *Songcatcher* (dir. Maggie Greenwald)
Gavin ceases publication of Americana chart
First full meeting of the Americana Music Association
Tim O'Brien records "Long Time Gone," written by Darrell Scott

2001 Al-Qaeda attack on the World Trade Center
The Dixie Chicks' "Long Time Gone" peaks on the country charts at number 8
Gillian Welch records *Time (the Revelator)*
Release of *Sebastopol,* "a project by Jay Farrar," on the independent label Artemis Records
Release of Zero Skills, Inc.'s *Christmassacre*
Release of Justin Treviño's *Travelin' Singin' Man*
Apple Computer launches the iPod
Soundtrack from *O Brother, Where Art Thou?* wins Grammy Award for Album of the Year

2002 Release of Neko Case's *Blacklisted*
Release of LCD Soundsystem's (James Murphy's) single "Losing My Edge"
Meat Purveyors reunite and record *All Relationships Are Doomed to Fail*

After being let go by Warner/Reprise, Wilco releases *Yankee Hotel Foxtrot* on Nonesuch
Dixie Chicks records its version of "Long Time Gone"
2003 Release of Justin Treviño's *The Scene of the Crying*
Dixie Chicks falls from mainstream country grace after lead singer Natalie Maines criticizes George W. Bush during a concert in London
Gillian Welch records *Soul Journey*
Release of Jay Farrar's soundtrack CD, *The Slaughter Rule,* in March and his second solo album, *Terroir Blues*
2004 George W. Bush elected to second term as president
Release of Neko Case's live album, *The Tigers Have Spoken*
Release of live album *Stone, Steel and Bright Lights,* featuring Jay Farrar and Canyon
Release of Wilco's *A Ghost Is Born*
Release of the documentary film *Gram Parsons: Fallen Angel*
Release of the feature film *Grand Theft Parsons*
Release of Justin Treviño's *Too Many Heartaches*
Release of Gretchen Wilson's first hit, "Redneck Woman," from her debut album *Here for the Party*
2005 Release of Son Volt Mark II's *Okemah and the Melody of Riot*
Release of Son Volt Mark I's best-of collection, *A Retrospective, 1995–2000*
Release of Zero Skills, Inc.'s *Cornstalked Her, Tractor Down,* and *Andy Kilter* on Pecan Crazy Records
Release of Justin Treviño's *More Loud Music and Strong Wine*
Release of Miranda Lambert's debut album, *Kerosene*
2006 Release of Neko Case's *Fox Confessor Brings the Flood*
Jay Farrar and Anders Parker collaborate on *Death Songs for the Living,* released under the name Gob Iron
Meat Purveyors break up again
Jesse Fox Mayshark asks, "Whatever happened to alt-country?"
Release of Justin Treviño's *Before You Say Amen*
Release of Gretchen Wilson's *All Jacked Up*
Release of Barbara Kopple and Cecelia Peck's documentary film *Dixie Chicks: Shut Up & Sing*
Release of Dixie Chicks' *Taking the Long Way,* which wins Record of the Year, as well as Song of the Year for the single "Not Ready to Make Nice," at the 2006 Grammy Awards
2007 Release of Son Volt's *The Search*
Release of Wilco's *Sky Blue Sky*

Kirk Rundstrom, guitarist and songwriter for Split Lip Rayfield, dies at age thirty-seven in February
Release of Gretchen Wilson's *One of the Boys*
Release of Miranda Lambert's *Crazy Ex-Girlfriend;* Lambert is featured on cover of *No Depression,* billed as "Country's New Alternative"
2008 *No Depression* ceases print publication but maintains its website

Works Cited

Aaker, David. *Building Strong Brands.* New York: Free Press, 1996.

Alden, Grant. "Deconstruction Blues." *No Depression* 8 (March–April 1997). http://www.nodepression.net/issues/nd08/badlivers.html (accessed July 5, 2007).

Alden, Grant. "A Few Words about Philosophy." http://www.nodepression.net/adfaq.html (accessed July 30, 2004).

Alden, Grant. "Hello Stranger." *No Depression* 45 (May–June 2003).

Alden, Grant. "Hello Stranger." *No Depression* 69 (May–June 2007).

Alden, Grant. Liner Notes to *No Depression: What It Sounds Like.* Vol. 1. Dualtone Records 1153, 2004.

Alden, Grant. *No Depression: An Introduction to Alternative Country Music, Whatever That Is.* Nashville: Dowling, 1998.

Alden, Grant, and Peter Blackstock. Liner notes to *The Best of Alt.Country: Exposed Roots.* K-tel Records 6428–2, 1999.

Alden Grant, and Peter Blackstock, eds., *The Best of No Depression: Writing about American Music.* Austin: University of Texas Press, 2005.

Alexander, Constance. Review of *Generation X. Louisville Courier-Journal.* April 3, 1993. http://www.geocities.com/SoHo/Gallery/5560/genx15.html (accessed July 30, 2004).

Alterman, Loraine. "Parsons Knows . . ." *Melody Maker,* April 7, 1973.

Americana Music Association. "F.A.Q.: What Is Americana Music?" http://www.americanamusic.org/php/index.php?content=faq (accessed December 2006).

"Appalachian Music." http://lcweb2.loc.gov/cocoon/ihas/html/dollyparton/country-appalachian.html#ret3 (accessed February 2, 2007).

Armstrong, Rod. "Catching a Groove with Director Maggie Greenwald." http://www.reel.com/reel.asp?node=features/interviews/greenwald (accessed February 3, 2007).

"Arrivals/Departures." *The Face,* September 2003, 47–48.

Austin Americana Music Guide. Review of Justin Treviño, *Travelin' Singin' Man.* http://home.austin.rr.com/austinamericana/reviews/review-justin.html (accessed December 2006).

Azerrad, Michael. *Our Band Could Be Your Life: Scenes from the American Indie Underground, 1981–1991.* Boston: Little, Brown, 2001.

Bailey, Steve. "Faithful or Foolish: The Emergence of the 'Ironic Cover Album' and Rock Culture." *Popular Music and Society* 26, no. 2 (2003): 141–59.

Baker, Brian. "Jay Farrar Resurrects Son Volt and Woody Guthrie." *Country Standard Time,* July 2005. http://www.countrystandardtime.com/sonvolt4FEA TURE.html (accessed August 17, 2005).

Bakhtin, M. M. "Discourse in the Novel." In *The Dialogic Imagination,* 301–55. Austin: University of Texas Press, 1981.

Barker, Hugh, and Yuval Taylor. *Faking It: The Quest for Authenticity in Popular Music.* New York: Norton, 2007.

Baudrillard, Jean. *Simulations.* Trans. Paul Foss, Paul Patton, and Philip Beitchman. New York: Semiotext(e), 1983.

BBC News. "Farrar Abandons 'Alt Country'." January 22, 2004. http://www.news.bbc.co.uk/1/hi/entertainment/music/3420055.stm (accessed January 28, 2004).

Beaudoin, Jeff. "Without Compromise: Split Lip Rayfield Ain't Over Yet." *Wichita City Paper,* December 7, 2006. http://www.wichitacitypaper.com/articles/article.23.shtml (accessed July 5, 2007).

Beets, Greg. "Phases and Stages: Zero Skills, Inc." *Austin Chronicle,* December 12, 2001. http://www.austinchronicle.com/gyrobase/Issue/review?oid=oid:84085 (accessed July 5, 2007).

Bendix, Regina. *In Search of Authenticity: The Formation of Folklore Studies.* Madison: University of Wisconsin Press, 1997.

Bennett, Stephen Earl, and Stephen C. Craig with Eric W. Rademacher. "Generations and Change: Some Initial Observations." In *After the Boom: The Politics of Generation X,* ed. Stephen C. Craig and Stephen Earl Bennett, 1–19. New York: Rowman and Littlefield, 1997.

Bernstein, Joel. "Gillian Welch: The Real Retro Artist." *Country Standard Time,* July–August 1998. http://countryst2/gillianwelchFEATURE.html (accessed July 28, 1998).

Blackstock, Peter. "Being There, Done That." *No Depression* 5 (September–October 1996). http://www.nodepression.net/archive/nd05/features/wilco.html (accessed July 5, 2004).

Blackstock, Peter. "Destiny Rides Again." *No Depression* 26 (March–April 2000).

Blackstock, Peter. "Dim Lights, Small Cities: Son Volt." *No Depression* 1 (fall 1995).

http://www.nodepression.net/archive/nd01/features/sonvolt.html (accessed August 27, 2002).

Blackstock, Peter. "Falling Down, Standing Up." *No Depression* 10 (July–August 1997). http://www.nodepression.net/issues/nd10/whiskeytown.html (accessed June 10, 2007).

Blackstock, Peter. "Personal Parsonage: *Return of the Grievous Angel—A Tribute to Gram Parsons.*" *No Depression* 22 (July–August 1999). http://www.nodepres sion.net/archive/nd22/depts/waxed.html (accessed July 2004).

Bloodshot Records. "The Meat Purveyors." http://www.bloodshotrecords.com/artists/themeatpurveyors/ (accessed July 5, 2007).

Boehlert, Eric. "Radio's Big Bully: A Complete Guide to *Salon*'s Reporting on Clear Channel." *Salon.com.* http://www.salon.com/ent/clear_channel/index.html (accessed July 3, 2007).

Booth, Stanley. "Records: *The Gilded Palace of Sin.*" *Rolling Stone,* May 15, 1969.

Borovik, Julie. Interview with Jay Farrar. Nadamucho.com. http://www.jayfarrar net/press/nadamuchoo72103.htm (accessed June 25, 2004).

Bourdieu, Pierre. *Acts of Resistance: Against the Tyranny of the Market.* Trans. Richard Nice. New York: New Press, 1999.

Bourdieu, Pierre. *Distinction: A Social Critique of the Judgement of Taste.* Trans. Richard Nice. Cambridge: Harvard University Press, 1984.

Boyd, Andrew. *Life's Little Deconstruction Book: Self-Help for the Post-Hip.* New York: Norton, 1998.

Brackett, David. *Interpreting Popular Music.* New York: Cambridge University Press, 1995.

Bufwack, Mary A., and Robert K. Oermann. *Finding Her Voice: Women in Country Music, 1800–2000.* Nashville: Country Music Foundation Press and Vanderbilt University Press, 2003.

Bufwack, Mary, and Robert Oermann. "Meeting the Millennium: Female Country Triumphs." In *Finding Her Voice: Women in Country Music, 1800–2000,* 473–507. Nashville: Vanderbilt University Press, 2003.

Burns, Lori, and Mélisse Lafrance, eds. *Disruptive Divas: Feminism, Identity, and Pop Music.* New York: Routledge, 2002.

Byrd, Kim. "Chilton County: Where Peaches Are Tops!" Unpublished graduate seminar paper, University of Montevallo, 2006.

Byrne, Richard. "Here Comes the Son." *Riverfront Times,* September 20–26, 1995. http://www.gumbopages.com/music/son-volt/text/trace-rev-rft.html (accessed June 25, 2004).

Caligiuri, Jim. "The Americana Chart, Alternative Country, and Austin: The Great Roots-Rock Scare of '96." *Austin Chronicle,* December 27, 1996.

http://www .austinchronicle.com/issues/vol16/issue17/music.altcountry.html (accessed September 16, 2005).

Caligiuri, Jim. "Where Idealism Is Still Alive: The First Annual Americana Music Association Meeting." *Austin Chronicle,* November 24, 2000. http://www .austinchronicle.com/issues/vol16/issue17/music.altcountry.html (accessed July 3, 2007).

Cantwell, Robert. *Bluegrass Breakdown: The Making of the Old Southern Sound.* Urbana: University of Illinois Press, 1984.

Caramanica, Jon. "Mess with This Texan, You'll Pay in a Song." *New York Times,* April 29, 2007, B27.

Carlin, Richard. *Country Music: A Biographical Dictionary.* New York: Routledge, 2003.

Carlson, Angie. "Don't Fence Me In." Interview with Jay Farrar, October 3, 2001. http://www.indyweek.com/durham/2001-10-03/music.html (accessed July 5, 2004).

Cartwright, Christine. "'Barbara Allen': Love and Death in an Anglo-American Narrative Folksong." In *Narrative Folksong: New Directions,* ed. Carol L. Edwards and Kathleen Manley, 240–65. Boulder: Westview, 1985.

Case, Neko. Interview with Gavino Trabasos. *Mote,* August 1999. http://www .moregoatthangoose.com/interviews/neko.htm (accessed July 30, 2004).

Case, Neko. "Neko's Ladies." http://www.nekocase.com/ladies.html (accessed July 30, 2004).

Cash, Johnny, with Patrick Carr. *Cash: The Autobiography.* New York: Harper, 1997.

Cerick, Dana. Interview with Jay Farrar. *Uno Mas,* 1995. http://www.unomas.com/features/sonvolt1.html (accessed June 24, 2004).

Chamberlain, Dave. "Phat Lip." Split Lip Rayfield fan site. http://www.geocities.com/ splitliprayfieldfanclub/ (accessed July 5, 2007).

Chamberlain, Dave. "So, You Wanna Start a Record Label?" *Newcity Chicago,* April 11, 2002. http://www.newcitychicago.com/chicago/1620.html (accessed September 16, 2005).

Charters, Mallay. "Night Vision: Son Volt." *Guitarworld,* December 1995. http://www.guitarworld.com/artistindex/9512.sonvolt.html (accessed June 22, 2004).

Child, Francis J. *The English and Scottish Popular Ballads.* 5 vols. Boston and New York: Houghton, Mifflin, 1883–98.

Ching, Barbara. "Acting Naturally: Cultural Distinction and Critiques of Pure Country." *Arizona Quarterly* 49 (1993): 107–25.

Ching, Barbara. "Country Music." In *The Blackwell Companion to the Literature and Culture of the American South,* ed. Richard Gray and Owen Robinson, 203–20. Oxford: Blackwell, 2004.

Ching, Barbara. "Going Back to the Old Mainstream: *No Depression,* Robbie Fulks, and Alt.Country's Muddied Waters." In *A Boy Named Sue: Gender and Country Music,* ed. Kristine M. McCusker and Diane Pecknold, 178–95. Jackson: University Press of Mississippi, 2004.

Ching, Barbara. "Happily Ever After in the Marketplace: The Ballads of the Southern Mountains and the Escape from Old Europe." In *Transatlantic Exchanges: The American South in Europe, Europe in the American South,* ed. Richard Gray and Waldemar Zacharasiewicz, 519–32.Vienna: Verlag der Osterreichischen Akademie der Wissenschaften, 2007.

Ching, Barbara. *Wrong's What I Do Best: Hard Country Music and Contemporary Culture.* New York: Oxford University Press, 2001.

Christgau, Robert. "Diffusion Rools." *Village Voice,* June 16, 2003. http://www.vil lagevoice.com/music/0325,christgau,44871,22.html (accessed July 30, 2004).

Clifford, James. *The Predicament of Culture.* Cambridge: Harvard University Press, 1988.

Cline, Cheryl. *Country Grrl.* http://www.steamiron.com/cgrrl/cgrrl-ed1.html (accessed January 3, 2008).

Coen, Ethan, and Joel Coen. Liner notes to *O Brother, Where Art Thou?* Mercury Records 088 170 069–2, 2000.

Coen, Ethan, and Joel Coen. *O Brother, Where Art Thou?* London: Faber and Faber, 2000. Screenplay.

Cohen, Jonathan. "Wilco: in the Comfort Zone." http://www.billboard.com/bbcom/feature/article_display.jsp?vnu_content_id=100357145 (accessed June 29, 2007).

Coltman, Robert. "Sweethearts of the Hills: Women in Early Country Music." *John Edwards Memorial Foundation Quarterly* (winter 1978): 161–80.

Connor, Mike. "Roots Seller: How Former Santa Cruz Songstress Gillian Welch Beat the Odds to Become an Americana Sensation." http://www.metroactive.com/ cruz/welch-0226.html (accessed September 9, 2003).

Corcoran, Michael. "Meat Purveyors Serve Up Slices of Bluegrass Heaven." *Austin 360,* July 29, 2004. http://www.austin360.com/search/content/music/xl/04-july/music_07–29–04.html (accessed July 5, 2007).

Cornelison, Jimmy. "Gram Parsons' Music Continues to Live On." *Music City News,* August 1983.

"Country Love Song." Interview with Neko Case. *Playboy.* http://www.playboy.com/sex/features/indierock (accessed July 30, 2004).

Country Standard Time. "CD Review: Justin Treviño." http://www.countrystandardtime.com/CDjustintrevino.html (accessed July 2007).

"The Country and Western Portfolio." *Vanity Fair,* November 2006, 291.

Coupland, Douglas. *Generation X: Tales for an Accelerated Culture.* New York: St. Martin's, 1991.

Coupland, Douglas. "Picking Brains." *Wired,* April 1997. http://hotwired.wired.com/hardwired/wiredstyle/97/04/pickingbrains.html (accessed July 30, 2004).

Craig, Stephen C., and Stephen Earl Bennett, eds. *After the Boom: The Politics of Generation X.* New York: Rowman and Littlefield, 1997.

Cravens, Jayne. "Connecting Humans: Twang in Cyberspace—How One Music-Related Online Community Blurs the Line between 'Real' and 'Virtual'." 2000. http://www.coyotecommunications.com/culture/twang.html (accessed January 3, 2008).

Creed, Gerald W., and Barbara Ching. "Recognizing Rusticity: Identity and the Power of Place." In *Knowing Your Place: Rural Identity and Cultural Hierarchy,* ed. Barbara Ching and Gerald W. Creed, 1–38. New York: Routledge, 1996.

Dannelley, Ronnie. "Interview with Jay Farrar of Son Volt." *Pop Culture Press* 42 (1997). http://earcandy_mag.tripod.com/blasonv.htm (accessed August 20, 2002).

Dechert, S. Renee. Interview with Mike Heidorn, review of "Uncle Tupelo 89/93: Anthology." April 22, 2002. *PopMatters.com.* http://www.popmatters.com/music/reviews/u/uncletupelo-8993.shtml (accessed June 28, 2002).

Dechert, S. Renee. "'Oh, What a Life a Mess Can Be': Uncle Tupelo, Bakhtin, and the Dialogue of Alternative Country Music." In *Country Music Annual,* ed. Charles K. Wolfe and James E. Akenson, 70–91. Lexington: University of Kentucky Press, 2001.

Dechert, S. Renee, and George H. Lewis. "The Drive-By Truckers and the Redneck Underground: A Subcultural Analysis." In *Country Music Annual, 2002,* ed. Charles Wolfe and James Akenson, 130–50. Lexington: University of Kentucky Press, 2002.

deMause, Neil. "Louisville Lip: An Interview with Catherine Irwin." *Here.* http://www.heremagazine.com.html (accessed August 12, 2003).

Dettmar, Kevin, and William Richey, eds. *Reading Rock and Roll: Authenticity, Appropriation, Aesthetics.* New York: Columbia University Press, 1999.

Dodds, M. S. "Insurgency Plan," *Illinois Entertainer* 30, no. 7 (May 2004).

Doggett, Peter. *Are You Ready for the Country: Elvis, Dylan, Parsons and the Roots of Country Rock.* New York: Penguin, 2000.

Dombal, Ryan. "Interview: Neko Case," *Pitchfork Media,* April 10, 2006. http://www.pitchforkmedia.com/article/feature/31252-interview-neko-case (accessed October 31, 2007).

Dombal, Ryan. "Neko Case: *Fox Confessor Brings the Flood,*" *Pitchfork Media,*

March 6, 2006. http://www.pitchforkmedia.com/article/record_review/16041-fox-confessor-brings-the-flood (accessed October 31, 2007).

Duck, Leigh Anne. *The Nation's Region: Southern Modernism, Segregation, and U.S. Nationalism.* Athens: University of Georgia Press, 2006.

Durchholz, Daniel. "Are You Ready for the Country?" *Request,* November 1993. http://www.gumbopages.com/music/uncle-tupelo/text/are_you_ready.html (accessed June 24, 2004).

Dutton, Monte. *True to the Roots: Americana Music Revealed.* Lincoln: University of Nebraska Press, 2006.

Ehler, Jay. "Gram Parsons Sweeps Out the Ashes." *Crawdaddy,* July 1973, 70–74.

Einarson, John. *Desperadoes: The Roots of Country Rock.* New York: Cooper's Square, 2001.

Ellison, Curtis W. *Country Music Culture: From Hard Times to Heaven.* Jackson: University Press of Mississippi, 1995.

Farber, Jim. "A Fresh Country Fusion, Americana, Has Legs," *San Diego Union-Tribune,* April 15, 2001, F7.

Feinstein, Howard. "Singing Story." Interview with Maggie Greenwald. *Indiewire,* June 14, 2001. http://www.indiewire.com/people/int_Greenwald_Magg_010614 .html (accessed July 30, 2006).

Filene, Benjamin. *Romancing the Folk: Public Memory and American Roots Music.* Chapel Hill: University of North Carolina Press, 2000.

Fine, Jason. "Heart of the Country." *Option* 53 (November–December 1993): 87.

Fong-Torres, Ben. *Hickory Wind: The Life and Times of Gram Parsons.* New York: Pocket Books, 1991.

Forman, Murray. *The 'Hood Comes First: Race, Space, and Place in Rap and Hip-Hop.* Middletown, CT: Wesleyan University Press, 2002.

Forman, Murray, and Mark Anthony Neal, eds. *That's the Joint! The Hip-Hop Studies Reader.* New York: Routledge, 2004.

Fox, Aaron A. "'Ain't It Funny How Time Slips Away?' Talk, Trash, and Technology in a Texas 'Redneck' Bar." In *Knowing Your Place: Rural Identity and Cultural Hierarchy,* ed. Barbara Ching and Gerald W. Creed, 105–30. New York: Routledge, 1996.

Fox, Aaron A. "'Alternative' to What? 'O Brother,' September 11th, and the Politics of Country Music." In *There's A Star-Spangled Banner Waving Somewhere: Country Music Goes to War,* ed. Charles K. Wolfe and James E. Akenson, 164–91. Lexington: University of Kentucky Press, 2005.

Fox, Aaron A. "Honky-Tonk Music." In *Encyclopedia of Popular Musics of the World,* ed. J. Shepherd et al. London: Continuum, forthcoming.

Fox, Aaron A. "The Jukebox of History: Narratives of Loss and Desire in the Discourse of Country Music." *Popular Music* 11, no. 1 (1992): 53–72.

Fox, Aaron A. *Real Country: Music and Language in Working-Class Culture.* Durham: Duke University Press, 2004.

Fox, Aaron A. "White Trash Alchemies of the Abject Sublime: Country as Bad Music." In *Bad Music: The Music We Love to Hate,* ed. Christopher Washburn and Maiken Derno, 39–61. New York: Routledge, 2004.

Fox, Pamela. *Natural Acts: Gender, Race, and Rusticity in Country Music.* Ann Arbor: University of Michigan Press, forthcoming.

Fox, Pamela. "Recycled 'Trash': Gender and Authenticity in Country Music Autobiography." *American Quarterly* 50, no. 2 (June 1998): 234–66.

Frank, Thomas. *The Conquest of Cool: Business Culture, Counterculture, and the Rise of Hip Consumerism.* Chicago: University of Chicago Press, 1997.

Frank, Thomas, and Matt Weiland, eds. *Commodify Your Dissent: Salvos from the Baffler.* New York: Norton, 1997.

Frere-Jones, Sasha. "Red-Hot Pop." *New Yorker,* October 4, 2004, 108.

Friskics-Warren, Bill. "Freakwater: Fundamental Things." *Puncture* 45 (1999). http://www.freakwater.net/readingroom.html (8/12/03) (accessed August 12, 2003).

Friskics-Warren, Bill. "Gillian Welch: Orphan Girl of the Hollywood Hills Finds a High Lonesome Musical Home in the Heart of the Appalachians." *No Depression* 1 (summer 1996).

Frith, Simon. *Performing Rites: On the Value of Popular Music.* Cambridge: Harvard University Press, 1996.

Frith, Simon, and Andrew Goodwin, eds. *On Record: Rock, Pop, and the Written Word.* New York: Routledge, 2000.

Frye, Northrop. *Anatomy of Criticism.* Princeton: Princeton University Press, 1957.

Gallo, Phil. "Music Biz Mows the Grassroots." *Variety,* February 16–22, 1998, 1.

Ganahl, Jane. "Jay Farrar: Rising Son." *Harp,* July–August 2005. http://harpmagazine.com/articles/detail.cfm?article_id=3195 (accessed July 12, 2007).

Ganahl, Jane. "Profile: Jay Farrar." *San Francisco Chronicle,* February 20, 2004. http://www.jayfarrar.net/press/sfchronicleo22004.htm (accessed June 25, 2004).

Garofalo, Reebee. *Rockin' Out: Popular Music in the U.S.A.* 2nd ed. Upper Saddle River, NJ: Prentice Hall, 2002.

Gaughan, Dylan. "Interview with Jay Farrar." http://members.tripod.com/swizzle stickzine/features/jayfarrar.html (accessed August 20, 2002).

George-Warren, Holly. Liner notes to *Hot Burritos: The Flying Burrito Brothers Anthology, 1969–1972.* A&M, 2000.

George-Warren, Holly. "A Long Lost Soul for a Long Time." *No Depression* 22 (July–August 1999). http://www.nodepression.net/archive/nd22/features/parsons.html (accessed 2004).

Gillian Welch Web site. "Biography." http://www.geffen.com/almo/gillian/revival.html (accessed April 14, 1997).

Gillian Welch Web site. "Revival." http://www.geffen.com/almo/gillian/revival.html (accessed April 14, 1997).

Gilroy, Paul. "Sounds Authentic: Black Music, Ethnicity, and the Challenge of a 'Changing' Same." *Black Music Research Journal* 11, no. 2 (autumn 1991): 111–36.

Gintowt, Richard. "Low Voltage: Jay Farrar's Son Volt Phones It In." June 14, 2005. *Lawrence.com.* http://www.lawrence.com/news/2005/jun/14/wakarusa2005_sonvolt/ (accessed August 19, 2005).

Goodman, David. *Modern Twang: An Alternative Country Music Guide and Directory.* Nashville: Dowling, 1999.

Graham, George. *The Graham Weekly Album Review,* no. 1251. http://www.georgegraham.com/reviews/welch3.html (accessed September 24, 2003).

Gray, Christopher. "Driving and Cranking." *Austin Chronicle,* August 2, 1999. http://weeklywire.com/ww/08-02-99/austin_music_feature1.html (accessed July 5, 2007).

Green, Douglas B. *Singing in the Saddle: The History of the Singing Cowboy.* Nashville: Country Music Foundation Press and Vanderbilt University Press, 2002.

Gretchen Wilson Web site, "About Gretchen," http://www.gretchenwilson.com (accessed May 23, 2007).

Griffin, Sid. *Gram Parsons: A Musical Biography.* Pasadena: Sierra Records and Books, 1985.

Grimshaw, Ted. "Redneck Religion and Shitkickin' Saviours? Gram Parsons, Theology, and Country Music." *Popular Music* 21, no. 1 (2002): 93–106.

Grossberg, Lawrence. *We Gotta Get Out of This Place: Pop, Conservatism, and Postmodern Culture.* New York: Routledge, 1992.

Haiken, Melanie. "Gillian Welch: The Orphan Girl Opens Up." *Paste* 5. July 23, 2003 http://www.pastemagazine.com/action/article?article_id=208 (accessed September 9, 2003).

Handler, Richard. "Authenticity." *Anthropology Today* 2, no. 1 (February 1986): 2–4.

Harrington, Richard. "Gillian Welch's Rural Delivery." *Washington Post,* May 5, 1997, D10.

Harris, Steve. *Texas Troubadours: Texas Singer Songwriters.* Austin: University of Texas Press, 2007.

Harris, Trudier. "Genre." *Journal of American Folklore* 108, no. 430 (autumn 1995): 509–27. Special Issue: *Common Ground: Keywords for the Study of Expressive Culture.*

Havighurst, Craig. "Carrying the Torch for Twang." *Nashville Tennessean,* November 16, 2000, 1E.

Hebdige, Dick. *Subculture: The Meaning of Style.* New York: Methuen, 1979.

Hernandez, Raoul. "Complete Freedom." *Austin Chronicle,* November 5, 1999. http://www.austinchronicle.com/gyrobase/Issue/story?oid=oid:74552 (accessed July 5, 2007).

Hill, Trent. "Why Isn't Country Music Youth Culture?" In *Rock over the Edge: Transformations in Popular Music Culture,* ed. Roger Beebe, Denise Fulbrook, and Ben Saunders, 161–90. Durham: Duke University Press, 2002.

Hinton, Brian. *South by Southwest: A Road Map to Alternative Country.* London: Sanctuary, 2003.

Hoekstra, Dave. "Chicago: America's Music City That Works." Press page, the Hideout, http://www.hideoutchicago.com/press/musicCityThatWorks.html (accessed February 4, 2004).

Howe, Neil, and William Strauss. *Millennials and the Pop Culture.* New York: LifeCourse Associates, 2006.

Howe, Neil, and William Strauss. *Millennials Rising: The Next Great Generation.* New York: Vintage, 2000.

Howe, Neil, and William Strauss. *13th Gen: Abort, Retry, Ignore, Fail.* New York: Vintage, 1993.

Hughes, Rob. "Jay Farrar: A Record That Changed My Life: The Byrds—*Fifth Dimension* (1966)." *Uncut,* January 26, 2004. http://www.jayfarrar.net/press/uncut0104.htm (accessed June 25, 2004).

Hulbert, Ann. "Look Who's Parenting." *New York Times,* July 4, 2004. http://www.nytimes.com/2004/07/04/magazine/04WWLN.html (accessed July 13, 2004).

Hutcheon, Linda. *Irony's Edge: The Theory and Politics of Irony.* London: Routledge, 1994.

Ivey, Bill. "The Bottom Line: Business Practices That Shaped Country Music." In *Country: The Music and the Musicians,* ed. Paul Kingsbury and Alan Axelrod, 407–51. New York: Abbeville, 1988.

Jackson, Adam. "Life after Tupelo: Jay Farrar and His New Band, Son Volt." *Music Monitor,* 1995. http://www.penduluminc.com/MM/articles/sonvolt.html (accessed June 25, 2004).

Jacoby, Russell. *The End of Utopia: Politics and Culture in an Age of Apathy.* New York: Basic Books, 2000.

Jameson, Fredric. "On Cultural Studies." *Social Text* 34 (1993): 17–52.

Jameson, Fredric. *The Political Unconscious: Narrative as a Socially Symbolic Act.* Ithaca: Cornell University Press, 1982.

Jensen, Joli. *The Nashville Sound: Authenticity, Commercialization, and the*

Nashville Sound. Nashville: Country Music Foundation and Vanderbilt University Press, 1998.

Jensen, Joli. "Taking Country Music Seriously: Coverage of the 1990s Boom." In *Pop Music and the Press,* ed. Steve Jones, 183–201. Philadelphia: Temple University Press, 2002.

Jones, Allan. "Country Parsons." *Melody Maker,* July 27, 1974.

Kasten, Roy. "The *Terroirist.*" *Riverfront Times,* June 18, 2003. http://www.jayfarrar.net/press/riverfronttimes061803.htm (accessed June 25, 2004).

Keightley, Keir. "Reconsidering Rock." In *The Cambridge Companion to Rock and Pop,* ed. Simon Frith, Will Straw, and John Street, 109–42. Cambridge: Cambridge University Press, 2001.

Kendrick, Monica. "Reel Live Women: A Video Essay." *Journal of Country Music* 21, no. 3 (2000): 32–37.

Kielty, Tom. "Lost Highway Hopes Independence is Route to Success," *Boston Globe,* July 7, 2001. http://www.boston.com/dailyglobe2/188/living/Lost Highway hopes independence is route to success+.shtml (accessed 8/13/03).

Kienzle, Rick. Liner notes to *Heroes of Country Music, Vol. 5: Legends of Country Rock.* Rhino R2 72444, 1996.

Kienzle, Rick. *Southwest Shuffle: Pioneers of Honky Tonk, Western Swing, and Country Jazz.* New York: Routledge, 2003.

King, Chris. "Favorite Uncle." *Riverfront Times,* June 5–11, 1991. http://www.factorybelt.net/articles/blue_tux.htm (accessed June 24, 2004).

King, Chris. Liner notes to Pops Farrar's *Memory Music,* 2006. http://www.hoobella too.org/folksdetail.cfm?FPID=8 (accessed July 14, 2007).

Klein, Naomi. *No Logo.* 1st rev. ed. New York: Picador, 2002.

Kot, Greg. *Wilco: Learning How to Die.* New York: Broadway, 2004.

Kruse, Holly. *Site and Sound: Understanding Independent Music Scenes.* New York: Peter Lang, 2003.

Kruse, Holly. "Subcultural Identity in Alternative Music Culture." *Popular Music* 12, no. 1 (1993): 33–41.

La Chapelle, Peter. *Proud to Be an Okie: Cultural Politics, Country Music, and Migration to Southern California.* Berkeley: University of California Press, 2007.

Lange, Jeffrey J. *Smile When You Call Me a Hillbilly: Country Music's Struggle for Respectability, 1939–1954.* Athens: University of Georgia Press, 2004.

Langer, Andy. "Mark Rubin: Against the Grain." *Austin Chronicle,* November 5, 1999. http://www.austinchronicle.com/gyrobase/Issue/story?oid=oid:74553 (accessed July 5, 2007).

Langford, Jon. *Nashville Radio: Art, Words, and Music.* Portland, OR: Verse Chorus Press, 2006.

Lanham, Robert. *The Hipster Handbook.* New York: Anchor, 2003.

Lawson, Richard. "The Great Divide: Nashville Music Industry Separating into the Rich and Poor." *Nashville Tennessean,* February 13, 2000, 1E.

LeClear, Rachel. "Can't Stand Losing Him: Kirk Rundstrom Loses His Battle with Cancer at 38." Lawrence.com, February 27, 2007. http://www.lawrence.com/news/2007/feb/22/kirkrundstrom/ (accessed July 5, 2007).

Lee, Steve S., and Richard A. Peterson. "Internet-Based Virtual Music Scenes." In *Music Scenes: Local, Translocal, and Virtual,* ed. Andy Bennett and Richard A. Peterson, 187–204. Nashville: Vanderbilt University Press, 2004.

Leland, John. *Hip: The History.* New York: Ecco, 2004.

Levy, Marian Leighton. Interview with Barbara Ching, August 6, 2007, Rounder Records Warehouse, Burlington, Massachusetts.

Lewis, John. "Universal Soldiers: Freakwater's Themes for Life." *Option,* 1996. http://www.freakwater.net/readingroom.html (accessed August 12, 2003).

Lindall, Anders Smith. "Jay Farrar: Blues Traveler," *Harp.* June/July 2003. http://harpmagazine.com/articles/detail.cfm?article_id=1202.

Lipsitz, George. *Dangerous Crossroads: Popular Music, Postmodernism, and the Poetics of Place.* London: Verso, 1994.

Liu, Alan. *The Laws of Cool: Knowledge Work and the Culture of Information.* Chicago: University of Chicago Press, 2004.

Livingston, Tamara. "Music Revivals: Toward a General Theory." *Ethnomusicology* 43, no. 1 (winter 1999): 66–85.

Lott, Eric. *Love and Theft: Blackface Minstrelsy and the American Working Class.* New York: Oxford University Press, 1995.

MacIntosh, Dan. "Freakwater Doesn't Keep It on the Sunnyside of Life." *Country Standard Time.* (March–April 1998). http://www1.usa1.com/~cst.freakwater CONCERT.html (accessed April 21, 1998).

Malone, Bill C. *Country Music, U.S.A.* 2nd ed. Austin: University of Texas Press, 1985.

"Man of Constant Sorrow." http://www.bobdylanroots.com/sorrow.html (accessed January 3, 2008).

Mann, James. "Jay Farrar: Rock and Roll's Greta Garbo." *Ink19.com,* November 1998. http://www.ink19.com/issues_F/98_11/ink_spots/son_volt_nf.html (accessed August 20, 2002).

Marcuse, Herbert. *One Dimensional Man: Studies in the Ideology of Advanced Industrial Society.* Boston: Beacon, 1968.

Marsh, Dave. "Barbara Allen." In *The Rose and the Briar: Death, Love, and Liberty in the American Ballad,* ed. Sean Wilentz and Greil Marcus, 9–17. New York: Norton, 2005.

Martin, Richard A. "King of the Road." *Seattle Weekly,* September 2, 1999, 59.

Mayshark, Jesse Fox. "Recalling the Twang That Was Alt-Country." *New York Times,* July 16, 2006, B26.

Mazor, Barry. "Nashville Lonestar." *No Depression* 69 (May–June 2007): 56–63.

Mazor, Barry. "Where the Twang Finally Met: How New York's Short-Lived Country Craze Spawned the Stars of Americana." *Journal of Country Music* 24, no. 1 (2006): 34–39.

McCusker, Kristine M., and Diane Pecknold, eds. *A Boy Named Sue: Gender and Country Music.* Jackson: University Press of Mississippi, 2004.

McLeod, Kembrew. "Authenticity within Hip-Hop and Other Cultures Threatened with Assimilation." *Journal of Communication* 49, no. 4 (December 1999): 134–50.

McRobbie, Angela. "Second-Hand Dresses and the Role of the Ragmarket." In *Zoot Suits and Second-Hand Dresses,* ed. Angela McRobbie. London: Macmillan, 1989. Reprinted in *The Subcultures Reader,* ed. Ken Gelder and Sarah Thornton, 191–99. New York: Routledge, 1997.

McRobbie, Angela, and Jenny Garber. "Girls and Subcultures." In *Resistance through Rituals,* ed. Stuart Hall and Tony Jefferson. London: Routledge, 1973. Reprinted in *The Subcultures Reader,* ed. Ken Gelder and Sarah Thornton, 112–20. New York: Routledge, 1997.

Meyer, David N. *Twenty Thousand Roads: The Ballad of Gram Parsons and His Cosmic American Music.* New York: Villard, 2007.

Middleton, Richard, ed. *Reading Pop: Approaches to Textual Analysis in Popular Music.* Oxford: Oxford University Press, 2000.

Middleton, Richard, ed. "Rock Singing." In *The Cambridge Companion to Singing,* ed. John Potter, 28–41. Cambridge: Cambridge University Press, 2000.

Molinaro, John. "Urbane Cowboys: Alt Country in the '90s." Master's thesis, Department of English, University of Virginia, 1998. http://www.lib.virginia.edu/etd/theses/rtsSci/English/1998/Molinaro/front.html (accessed July 5, 2007).

Morris, Mitchell. *The Persistence of Sentiment: Essays on Display and Feeling in '70s Pop.* Berkeley: University of California Press, forthcoming.

Morris, Mitchell. "The Voice of Karen Carpenter." In *The Persistence of Sentiment: Essays on Display and Feeling in '70s Pop* (Berkeley: University of California Press, forthcoming).

Murray, James. "Freakwater at VZD's in Oklahoma City, March 18, 1999." *100 Year War.* http://www.freakwater.net/readingroom.html (accessed August 12, 2003).

Naujeck, Jeanne A. "Nashville Is at the Root of Americana's Growth." *Nashville Tennessean,* September 19, 2003, E1.

Neal, Mark Anthony. *What the Music Said: Black Popular Music and Black Public Culture.* New York: Routledge, 1999.

Negus, Keith. *Music Genres and Corporate Cultures.* New York: Routledge, 1999.

"Notes on *Death Songs for the Living*." http://www.jayfarrar.net/discs/index-gob iron.htm (accessed July 13, 2007).

O'Brien, Annie. "Playback: The Underlying Overtones of Jay Farrar," October 2002. http://www.jayfarrar.net/press/playback1002.htm (accessed June 25, 2004).

Oermann, Robert K. "Mother, Sister, Sweetheart, Pal: Women in Old Time Country Music." *Southern Quarterly* 22, no. 3 (spring 1984): 125–34.

Olson, Ted. "Country Music at the Millennium: Three Recent Studies of a Remarkably Resilient Musical Genre." *American Music* 18, no. 2 (summer 2000): 222–28.

Olson, Ted. "Hippie Hootenanny: Gram Parsons and the Not-Quite-Nashville Cats." *Journal of Country Music* 20, no. 3 (1999): 26–36.

Oppenheimer, Jean. "Elusive Tunes." *American Cinematographer,* December 2000, 77–78.

Orshoski, Wes. "Labels Strive to Make Most of Americana Tag." *Billboard,* June 30, 2001, 1.

Ortner, Sherry. *Anthropology and Social Theory.* Durham: Duke University Press, 2006.

Ortner, Sherry. "Generation X: Anthropology in a Media-Saturated World." *Cultural Anthropology* 13 (August 1998): 414–40.

Osgerby, Bill. "Chewing Out a Rhythm on My Bubble-Gum: The Teenage Aesthetic and Genealogies of American Punk." In *Punk Rock: So What?* ed. Roger Sabin,154–69. New York: Routledge, 1999.

Parsons, Polly, and Jessica Hundley. *Grievous Angel: An Intimate Biography of Gram Parsons.* New York: Thunder's Mouth Press, 2005.

Pecknold, Diane. *The Selling Sound: The Rise of the Country Music Industry.* Durham: Duke University Press, 2007.

Pemberton, Michael. "Jay Farrar, 'Outside the Door', and St. Louis Blues." http://www.gumbopages.com/music/son-volt/text/outside.html (accessed June 25, 2004).

Perry, Imani. *Prophets of the Hood: Politics and Poetics in Hip Hop.* Durham: Duke University Press, 2004.

Peterson, Richard A. *Creating Country Music: Fabricating Authenticity.* Chicago: University of Chicago Press, 1997.

Peterson, Richard, and Bruce A. Beal. "Discographic Essay: Alternative Country—Origins, Music, Worldview, Fans, and Taste in Genre Formation." *Popular Music and Society* 25, nos. 1–2 (2001): 233–49.

Peterson, Richard, and Roger M. Kern. "Changing Highbrow Taste: From Snob to Omnivore." *American Sociological Review* 61, no. 5 (1996): 900–907.

Phipps, Keith. "Neko Case's *Fox Confessor Brings the Flood,*" *Onion A/V Club,* March 7, 2006. http://www.avclub.com/content/node/46067 (accessed October 31, 2007).

Pick, Steve. "Uncle Tupelo, No Longer Primitive." *Post-Dispatch* (Saint Louis), January 28, 1988. http://www.factorybelt.net/articles/post_2–88.htm (accessed June 24, 2004).

Polhemus, Ted. *Style Surfing: What to Wear in the 3rd Millennium.* New York: Thames and Hudson, 1996.

Potter, John. *Vocal Authority: Singing Style and Ideology.* Cambridge: Cambridge University Press, 1998.

Pough, Gwendolyn D. *Check It While I Wreck It: Black Womanhood, Hip Hop Culture, and the Public Sphere.* Boston: Northeastern University Press, 2004.

Poynor, Rick. *No More Rules: Graphic Design and Postmodernism.* New Haven: Yale University Press, 2003.

Price, Deborah Evans, and Phyllis Stark. "Country Music Leaders Predict Trends for the New Year." *Billboard,* January 13, 2001.

Pugh, Ronnie. "Country Music Is Here to Stay?" *Journal of Country Music* 19, no. 1 (1997): 32–38.

Purdy, Jedediah. *For Common Things: Irony, Trust, and Commitment in America Today.* New York: Vintage, 2000.

Reid, Jan. *The Improbable Rise of Redneck Rock.* 2nd. ed. Austin: University of Texas Press, 2004.

Rischar, Richard. "A Vision of Love: An Etiquette of Vocal Ornamentation in African-American Popular Ballads of the Early 1990s." *American Music* 22, no. 3 (2004): 407–43.

Rose, Tricia. *Black Noise: Rap Music and Black Culture in Contemporary America.* Hanover, NH: Wesleyan University Press, 1994.

Ross, Andrew, and Tricia Rose, eds. *Microphone Fiends: Youth Music and Youth Culture.* New York: Routledge, 1994.

Rubin, Mark. "Biography." http://badlivers.com/bio.html (accessed July 5, 2007).

Rush, J. D. "Profile: Jay Farrar." *Unbarred,* November 2003. http://www.jayfarrar .net/press/unbarred1103.htm (accessed June 25, 2004).

Salfen, Paul. Interview with Jay Farrar. *Dallas Music Guide,* 2002. http://www.dallas musicguide.com/interviews/JayFarrar2.htm (accessed June 25, 2004).

Sanneh, Kalefa. "In the Desert, a Festival of Country and Its Kin." *New York Times,* May 8, 2007, E1.

Scarborough, Dorothy. *A Song Catcher in the Southern Mountains: American Folk Songs of British Ancestry.* New York: Columbia University Press, 1937.

Schact, John. "Uncle Tupelo." *Swizzle-Stick.com,* April 2, 2002. http://members.tri pod.com/swizzlestickzine/features/uncletupelo.html (accessed August 20, 2002).

Schocket, Eric. "Undercover Explorations of the 'Other Half'; or, the Writer as Class Transvestite." *Representations* 64 (fall 1998): 109–33.

Schor, Juliet. *The Overspent American: Upscaling, Downshifting, and the New Consumer.* New York: Basic Books, 1998.

Scoppa, Bud. *The Byrds.* New York: Scholastic Book Services, 1971.

Scoppa, Bud. Liner notes to *Return of the Grievous Angel: A Tribute to Gram Parsons.* Almo Sounds AMSD–80024, 1999.

Scoppa, Bud. "Records: *GP.*" *Rolling Stone,* March 1, 1973, 69.

Scott, Jessie. Interview with Barbara Ching, November 2, 2005, XM Studios, Washington, DC.

Shank, Barry."Daniel Johnston and the Fetishization of Sincerity." In *Dissonant Identities: The Rock 'n' Roll Scene in Austin, Texas,* 153–59. Hanover, NH: Wesleyan University Press, 1994.

Shank, Barry. *Dissonant Identities: The Rock 'n' Roll Scene in Austin, Texas.* Hanover, NH: Wesleyan University Press, 1994.

Sims, Judith. "Ex-Byrd Gram Solos: He's No Longer in a Hurry." *Rolling Stone,* March 1, 1973, 14.

Smith, Rob. "Founders Upbeat over No Depression's Growth." *Puget Sound Business Journal,* July 24, 2000. http://www.bizjournals.com/seattle/stories/2000/07/24/focus2.html (accessed December 16, 2003).

Smith-Lindall, Anders. "Son Volt, Farrar to Whirl into Detroit." *Michigan Daily,* September 26, 1997. http://www.pub.umich.edu/daily/1997/sep/09-26-97/arts/arts2.html (accessed July 13, 2007).

Smith-Nonini, Sandy. "Federally Sponsored Mexican Migrants in the Transnational South." In *The American South in a Global World,* ed. James L. Peacock, Harry L. Watson, and Carrie R. Matthews, 59–79. Chapel Hill: University of North Carolina Press, 2005.

"Son Volt," Artist Direct Showcase. http://imusic.artistdirect.com/showcase/modern/sonvolt.html (accessed August 20, 2002).

Sontag, Susan. "Notes on Camp." In *Against Interpretation.* New York: Farrar, Straus and Giroux, 1966, 275–92.

Taylor, Timothy D. *Beyond Exoticism: Western Music and the World.* Durham: Duke University Press, 2007.

Stegall, Tim. "The Return of the Bad Livers: Phantom Power and Spiritual Benefits." *Austin Chronicle* (February 13, 1997). http://www.auschron.com/issues/vol16/is sue24/music.badlivers.html (accessed July 5, 2007).

Stewart, Allison. "Spring Forward, Fall Back: Freakwater Does the Two-Step around Fame and Fortune." *No Depression* 13 (January–February 1998).

Straw, Will. "Cultural Scenes." *Loisir et société/Society and Leisure* 27, no. 2 (1997): 411–22.

Straw, Will. "Systems of Articulation, Logics of Change: Communities and Scenes in Popular Music." In *The Subcultures Reader,* ed. Ken Gelder and Sarah Thornton, 494–505. London: Routledge, 2004.

Striffler, Steve. "We're All Mexicans Here: Poultry Processing, Latino Migration, and the Transformation of Class in the South." In *The American South in a*

Global World, ed. James L. Peacock, Harry L. Watson, and Carrie R. Matthews, 152–65. Chapel Hill: University of North Carolina Press, 2005.

Thee Whiskey Rebel [Phil Irwin]. "Country Western Music: 'The Next Level' beyond Punk Rock." *Traitor Baitor* (n.d.), 8. http://home.conectiv.net/~whiskyreb/coun try.html (accessed March 10, 2003).

Thomas, Jean. Liner notes to *American Folk Song Festival: Jean Thomas, the Traipsin' Woman.* Smithsonian Folkways Records FW02358, 1960.

Thornton, Sarah. *Club Cultures: Music, Media, and Subcultural Capital.* Hanover, NH: Wesleyan University Press, 1996.

Townsend, Bob. "Americana Rising: Rock-Country beyond Its Roots." *Atlanta Journal-Constitution,* November 2, 2003, M1.

"Traipsin Woman." *Time,* June 18, 1934. http://www.time.com/time/magazine/article/0,9171,747518,00.html (accessed December 28, 2007).

Travasos, Gabino. "Neko Case." Interview. *Mote,* August 1999. http://www.moregoatthangoose.com/interviews/neko.htm (accessed July 30, 2004).

Trilling, Lionel. *Sincerity and Authenticity.* Cambridge: Harvard University Press, 1972.

Tyrangiel, Josh. "In the Line of Fire." *Time,* May 29, 2006, 65.

Vale, V. *Swing! The New Retro Renaissance.* San Francisco: V/Search, 1998.

Vivinetto, Gina. "Son Volt Makes Alt-Country Cool." *Saint Petersburg Times,* February 9, 1999. http://www.sptimes.com/News/20999/Entertainment/Son_Volt_ makes_alt_co.html (accessed July 8, 2004).

Waggoner, Eric."Profile: Radio Cure." *Seattle Weekly,* April 1–8, 2003. http://www .seattleweekly.com/features/0314/music-waggoner.php (accessed June 12, 2004).

Walker, Jason. *God's Own Singer: A Life of Gram Parsons.* London: Helter Skelter, 2002.

Walker, Rob. "The Marketing of No Marketing." *New York Times Magazine,* June 22, 2003, 42–45.

Walser, Robert. "Out of Notes: Signification, Interpretation, and the Problem of Miles Davis." *Musical Quarterly* 77, no. 2 (summer 1993): 343–65.

Weinzierl, Rupert, and David Muggleton. "What Is 'Post-subcultural Studies' Anyway?" In *The Post-Subcultures Reader,* ed. David Muggleton and Rupert Weinzierl, 3–23. New York: Berg, 2003.

Weisberger, Jon. "Foggy Mountain New Grass Breakdown." *No Depression* 23 (September–October 1999).

Wener, Ben. "Americana, What Art Thou?" *Orange County Register,* July 29, 2001, http://www.ocregister.com/ocregister/archives.

Whisnant, David E. *All That Is Native and Fine: The Politics of Culture in an American Region.* Chapel Hill: University of North Carolina Press, 1983.

Wickes, Sammie Ann. "A Belated Salute to the 'Old Way' of 'Snaking' the Voice on Its (ca.) 345th Birthday." *Popular Music* 8, no. 1 (1989): 59–96.

Williams, Raymond. *The Country and the City.* New York: Oxford University Press, 1975.

Williams, Raymond. *Keywords: A Vocabulary of Culture and Society.* New York: Oxford University Press, 1985.

Williams, Raymond. *Marxism and Literature.* New York: Oxford University Press, 1977.

Willman, Chris. *Rednecks and Bluenecks: The Politics of Country Music.* New York: New Press, 2005.

Wilson, Gretchen, with Allen Rucker. *Redneck Woman: Stories from My Life.* New York: Grand Central, 2006.

Wodskou, Chris. "The End of *No Depression.*" *Exclaim!* June 1, 1999. http://www.exclaim.ca/articles/multiarticlesub.aspx?csid1=1&csid2=779&‹d1=747 (accessed July 5, 2007).

Wolfe, Charles K., and Ted Olson. *The Bristol Sessions: Writings about the Big Bang of Country Music.* Jefferson, NC: McFarland, 2005.

Woodward, Josef. "Music Capsule Review: *Trace.*" *Entertainment Weekly,* November 10, 1995. http://www.ew.com/ew/article/0,,299474,00.html (accessed June 29, 2007).

Yates, Don. "Justin Treviño: Texas Honky Tonk." Record review. *No Depression* 16 (July–August, 1998). http://www.nodepression.net/issues/nd16/waxed.html (accessed January 3, 2008).

Zanes, R. J. Warren. "A Fan's Notes: Identification, Desire, and the Haunted Sound Barrier." In *Rock over the Edge: Transformations in Popular Music Culture,* ed. Roger Beebe, Denise Fulbrook, and Ben Saunders, 291–310. Durham: Duke University Press, 2002.

Zero Skills, Inc. *The Austin Chronicle Musicians Register,* 2002. http://www.austinchronicle.com/gyrobase/MusiciansRegister/BandProfile?oid=oid:48488/4 (accessed July 5, 2007).

Zimmerman, Keith, and Kent Zimmerman. *Sing My Way Home: The Voices of the New American Roots Rock.* San Francisco: Backbeat, 2004.

Zwonitzer, Mark, and Charles Hirshberg. *Will You Miss Me When I'm Gone? The Carter Family and Their Legacy in American Music.* New York: Simon and Schuster, 2002.

DISCOGRAPHY

Avett Brothers. *Emotionalism.* Ramseur Records, 2007.

Bad Livers. *Blood and Mood.* Sugar Hill, 2000.

Bad Livers. *Delusions of Banjer.* Quarterstick, 1992.
Bad Livers. *Dust on the Bible.* Quarterstick, 1994.
Bad Livers. *Hogs on the Highway.* Sugar Hill, 1997.
Bad Livers. *Horses in the Mines.* Quarter Stick, 1994.
Bad Livers. *Industry and Thrift.* Sugar Hill, 1998.
Bare, Bobby, Jr. *Young Criminals' Starvation League.* Bloodshot, 2002.
Big Mouth Blues: A Conversation with Gram Parsons. Sierra, 2002.
Borges, Sarah. *Diamonds in the Dark.* Sugar Hill, 2007.
Byrds. *The Notorious Byrd Brothers.* Columbia, 1968.
Byrds. *Sweetheart of the Rodeo.* Columbia, 1968.
Byrds. *Turn! Turn! Turn!* Columbia, 1965.
Case, Neko. *Blacklisted.* Bloodshot, 2002.
Case, Neko. *Fox Confessor Brings the Flood.* Anti, 2006.
Case, Neko. *Furnace Room Lullaby.* Bloodshot, 2000.
Case, Neko. *The Tigers Have Spoken.* Anti, 2004.
Case, Neko. *The Virginian.* Bloodshot, 1997.
Cash, Johnny. *American Recordings.* American/Sony, 1994.
Coal Porters. *The Gram Parsons Tribute Concert.* Prima, 1998.
Corn Sisters. *The Other Women.* Mint Records, 2000.
Dixie Chicks. *Home.* Sony, 2002.
Dixie Chicks. *Taking the Long Way.* Columbia, 2006.
Dylan, Bob. *John Wesley Harding.* Columbia, 1967.
Dylan, Bob. *Nashville Skyline.* Columbia, 1969.
Earle, Steve. *Copperhead Road.* MCA, 1988.
Farrar, Jay. *Sebastopol.* Artemis, 2001.
Farrar, Jay. *Terroir Blues.* Transmit, 2003.
Flying Burrito Brothers. *Burrito Deluxe.* A&M, 1969.
Flying Burrito Brothers, *Gilded Palace of Sin.* A&M, 1969.
Freakwater. *End Time.* Thrilljockey, 1999.
Freakwater. *Springtime.* Thrilljockey, 1997.
Fulks, Robbie. *Revenge.* Yep Roc, 2007.
Fulks, Robbie. *South Mouth.* Bloodshot, 1993.
Gob Iron. *Death Songs for the Living.* Sony, 2006.
Harris, Emmylou. *Elite Hotel.* Reprise, 1975.
Harris, Emmylou. *Luxury Liner.* Reprise, 1977.
Harris, Emmylou. *Pieces of the Sky.* Reprise, 1975.
International Submarine Band. *Safe at Home.* LP LHI/ABC, 1968.
Jason and the Scorchers. *Still Standing.* Mammoth, 1986.
Jeff and Janet. *Jesus Built a Ship to Sing a Song To.* Kokopop, 1993.
Jennings, Shooter. *Put the O Back in Country.* Universal South, 2005.

Lambert, Miranda. *Crazy Ex-Girlfriend.* Columbia, 2007.
Lambert, Miranda. *Kerosene.* Columbia, 2005.
Maow. *The Unforgiving Sounds of Maow.* Mint Records, 1996.
Marchman, Houston. *Leaving Dallas.* Texas Music Group, 1999.
Meat Purveyors. *Sweet in the Pants.* Bloodshot, 1998.
Myles, Heater. *Sweet Talk and Good Lies.* Rounder, 2002.
New Pornographers. *Electric Version.* Matador, 2003.
New Pornographers. *Mass Romantic.* Matador, 2000.
New Pornographers. *Twin Cinema.* Matador, 2005.
Parsons, Gram. *Another Side of This Life: The Lost Recordings of Gram Parsons, 1965–1966.* Sundazed, 2000.
Parsons, Gram. *The Early Years, 1963–1965.* LP. Sundazed, 1983.
Parsons, Gram. *GP.* Reprise, 1972.
Parsons, Gram. *Grievous Angel.* Reprise, 1973.
Son Volt. *Okemah and the Melody of Riot.* Sony, 2005.
Son Volt. *The Search.* Transmit Sound/Legacy, 2007.
Son Volt. *Sraightaways.* Warner Brothers, 1997.
Son Volt. *Trace.* Warner Brothers, 1995.
Son Volt. *Wide Swing Tremolo.* Warner Brothers, 1998.
Southern Culture on the Skids. *Countrypolitan Favorites.* Yep Roc, 2007.
Split Lip Rayfield. *In the Mud.* Bloodshot, 1999.
Treviño, Justin. *Loud Music and Strong Wine.* Neon Nightmare, 2000.
Treviño, Justin. *The Scene of the Crying.* Texas Music Group, 2003.
Treviño, Justin. *Texas Honky Tonk.* Neon Nightmare, 1998.
Treviño, Justin. *Travelin' Singin' Man.* Texas Music Group, 2001.
Uncle Tupelo. *Anodyne.* Sire/Warner, 1993.
Uncle Tupelo. *March 16–20, 1992.* Rockville, 1992.
Uncle Tupelo. *No Depression.* Rockville, 1990.
Uncle Tupelo. *Still Feel Gone.* Rockville, 1991.
Various artists. *Anchored in Love: A Tribute to June Carter Cash.* Dualtone, 2007.
Various artists. *Conmemorativo: A Tribute to Gram Parsons.* Rhino, 1993.
Various artists. *Dressed in Black: A Tribute to Johnny Cash.* Dualtone, 2002.
Various artists. *Exposed Roots: The Best of Alt.Country.* K-Tel, 1998.
Various artists. *Heroes of Country Music, Vol. 5: Legends of Country Rock.* Rhino, 1996.
Various artists. *Insurgent Country, Vol. 1: For a Life of Sin.* Bloodshot, 1994.
Various artists. *Keep on the Sunny Side: A Tribute to the Carter Family.* Amoeba, 1991.
Various artists. *O Brother, Where Art Thou?* Mercury 088 170 069–2, 2000.
Various artists. *Points West: New Horizons in Country Music.* Hightone, 1990.

Various artists. *Return of the Grievous Angel: A Tribute to Gram Parsons.* Almo Sounds, 1999.
Various artists. *Timeless: A Hank Williams Tribute.* Lost Highway, 2001.
Various artists. *A Town South of Bakersfield,* vols. 1–3. Restless Records, 1988–92.
Various artists. *Tulare Dust: A Songwriters' Tribute To Merle Haggard.* Hightone, 1994.
Watson, Dale. *Cheatin' Heart Attack.* Hightone, 1995.
Wayne, Dallas. *Big Thinkin'.* Hightone Germany, 2000.
Welch, Gillian. *Revival.* Almo, 1996.
Welch, Gillian. *Time (the Revelator).* Acony, 2001.
Whiskeytown. *Faithless Street.* Mood Food, 1996.
Wilco. *A Ghost is Born.* Nonesuch, 2004.
Wilco. *Being There.* Reprise, 1996.
Wilco. *Sky Blue Sky.* Nonesuch, 2007.
Wilco. *Summer Teeth.* Reprise, 1999.
Wilco. *Yankee Hotel Foxtrot.* Nonesuch, 2002.
Wilson, Gretchen. *All Jacked Up.* Epic, 2005.
Wilson, Gretchen. *Here for the Party.* Epic, 2004.
Wilson, Gretchen. *One of the Boys.* Columbia, 2007.
Zero Skills, Inc. *Cornstalked Her.* Pecan Crazy, 2005.
Zero Skills, Inc. *Drunker 'n Hell.* CD Baby, 2005.

FILMS

The Devil and Daniel Johnston. Dir. Jeff Feuerzeig. Sony, 2005.
Down from the Mountain. Dir. Nick Doob, Chris Hegedus, and D. A. Pennebaker. Lions Gate, 2001.
Gram Parsons: Fallen Angel. Dir. Gandulf Hennig. Rhino, 2004.
Grand Theft Parsons. Dir. David Caffrey. Redbus Film Distribution/Swipe Films, 2003.
O Brother, Where Art Thou? Dir. Joel Coen and Ethan Coen. Universal Pictures, 2000.
Return to Sin City: A Tribute to Gram Parsons. Dir. Mark Lucas. Image Entertainment, 2005.
Songcatcher. Dir. Maggie Greenwald. Lions Gate, 2000.

About the Contributors

Kelly Burchfield is a graduate student in the Textual Studies concentration in English at the University of Memphis. She is interested in minority literature and history, particularly African American and Native American, and is currently looking at the ways these two cultures intersect in some literature of the twentieth century.

Barbara Ching is Associate Professor of English at the University of Memphis. She is the author of *Wrong's What I Do Best: Hard Country Music and Contemporary Culture* (Oxford University Press, 2001) and several articles on popular music, including film soundtracks and southern rock. With the ethnographer Gerald Creed, she introduced and edited *Knowing Your Place: Rural Identity and Cultural Hierarchy* (Routledge, 1996).

Aaron A. Fox is Associate Professor of Music and Director of the Center for Ethnomusicology at Columbia University. The author of *Real Country: Music and Language in a Working-Class Culture* (Duke University Press, 2004), he is also a guitarist and singer who has played with many bands in Texas. He has hosted country music radio programs on several stations in New York City and continues to guest host shows on a regular basis.

Pamela Fox is Associate Professor of English and Director of the Women's and Gender Studies Program at Georgetown University. The author of *Class Fictions: Shame and Resistance in the British Working-Class Novel, 1890–1945* (Duke University Press, 1994), she is a feminist literary and cultural studies scholar who focuses on working-class writing and culture. Currently, she is completing a book entitled *Natural Acts: Gender, Race, and Rusticity in Country Music,* to be published by the University of Michigan Press.

Olivia Carter Mather holds a doctorate in musicology from the University of California, Los Angeles. Her dissertation focused on place in country rock of the

1960s and 1970s. Besides rock and country, her interests include bluegrass, folk revivalism, music and spirituality, and Hildegard von Bingen.

Diane Pecknold is a Postdoctoral Fellow for the Commonwealth Center for the Humanities and Society at the University of Louisville, where she teaches in the Department of Women's and Gender Studies and the Humanities Program. Her chief research area is the country music industry during the 1950s and 1960s and the cultural implications of commercial discourse. She also explores how gender has shaped male and female experiences in the industry's development and is currently at work on an exploration of African American engagements with country music. She is the author of *The Selling Sound: The Rise of the Country Music Industry* (Duke University Press, 2007) and was coeditor with Kristine M. McCusker of *A Boy Named Sue: Gender and Country Music* (University Press of Mississippi, 2004).

Stevie Simkin is Senior Lecturer in Drama in the Faculty of Arts at the University of Winchester, United Kingdom. His publications include *A Preface to Marlowe* (Longman, 2000), *Analysing Texts: Christopher Marlowe* (Palgrave, 2001), *Revenge Tragedy: A New Casebook* (Palgrave, 2001), and *Early Modern Tragedy and the Cinema of Violence* (Palgrave, 2006). He is currently finishing a study of Sam Peckinpah's *Straw Dogs* for a series of books on controversial films that he will be editing for Wallflower Press.

Jon Smith is Associate Professor of English at Simon Fraser University. As a scholar, he is interested in examining the American South from the global, cultural studies, and postcolonial perspectives. He coedited the book series The New Southern Studies for the University of Georgia Press and also coedited the essay collection *Look Away! The U.S. South in New World Studies* (Duke University Press, 2004). From March through August 2005, he was a Fulbright Scholar at the Institut für Anglistik und Amerikanistik at Universität Dortmund in Dortmund, Germany.

Aaron Smithers is a graduate student in the Curriculum in Folklore at the University of North Carolina. He is interested in media production and the representation of folklife and all forms of music, foodways, and urban and suburban culture. He has also worked as chief audio engineer for the Austin Music Network and on numerous short films.

Index

Text design by Paula Newcomb

Typesetting by Delmastype, Ann Arbor, Michigan

Text font: New Caledonia

Caledonia was designed by William A. Dwiggins in 1939 and originally appeared under the name Cornelia with the Mergenthaler typesetting machine factory in Berlin. Dwiggins conceived of this typeface as a reworking of the Scotch Roman which was designed for Mergenthaler Linotype in New York. The neotransitional Caledonia has serene, vertical forms, unflexed serifs, and a transitional style italic. Linotype reworked the typeface in 1982 and released it as New Caledonia.

—*courtesy* linotype.com